PRAISE FOR *ORGANIZATIONAL CHANGE EXPLAINED*

"This is a treasure trove of advice from a deeply credible expert group. A collection of stories each with immaculate technical pedigree and referencing - this is a book to read in bite sized chunks, or all at once, and then revisited time and again as a source of wisdom for dealing with practical challenges at work. I look forward to dipping into this resource again and again."
Alastair Ramage, transformational change specialist and formerly Director Transformation, The British Council

"I expect professionals seeking good change management practice will find *Organizational Change Explained* to be a welcome and valuable resource. The themes of the book are ones that I see leading organizations consider for change and transformation. It provides meaningful insights, drawing on current academic research and relevant change experiences across public, private and not-for-profit sectors."
Dr Andrew Schuster FAPM FIC FIOD, academic specializing in the projectification of change, Director Programme Assurance, PwC, and co-author, *Management of Risk: Guidance for practitioners*

"The contributors d have done a great service for the change management community in sharing these practical cases which, taken together with the insightful and contemporary thought pieces, offer members of the global change community a rich harvest of learning."
Richard Smith, leadership and change consultant and editor, *The Effective Change Manager's Handbook*

"Presents a wide range of lively and current perspectives about organizational transformation and change, and how this territory is changing. Those responsible for business change within organizations, who are keen to develop their thinking and glean insights from change practitioners, will find rich pickings here!"
Esther Cameron, co-author, *Making Sense of Change Management*

Organizational Change Explained

Organizational Change Explained

Case studies on transformational change in organizations

Sarah Coleman and Bob Thomas

First published in Great Britain and the United States in 2017 by Kogan Page Limited

2nd Floor, 45 Gee Street	c/o Martin P Hill Consulting	4737/23 Ansari Road
London	122 W 27th Street	Daryaganj
EC1V 3RS	New York, NY 10001	New Delhi 110002
United Kingdom	USA	India

© Sarah Coleman and Bob Thomas 2017

ISBN   978 0 7494 7547 5
E-ISBN   978 0 7494 7548 2

British Library Cataloguing-in-Publication Data

A CIP record for this book is available from the British Library.

Library of Congress Control Number
2017001497

Typeset by Integra Software Services, Pondicherry
Print production managed by Jellyfish
Printed and bound in Great Britain by Ashford Colour Press Ltd.

CONTENTS

05   The brain and adaptive change 104
Paul Brown and Kate Lanz

06   Working with resistance to change 124
Rod Willis, Anthony Burrows and Sarah Coleman

07   Creating the resilient organization 136
Tianne Croshaw

11　Operational readiness for change 199
Rod Willis, John McLelland, Kevin Parry and Sarah Coleman

12　Managing change in Asia and the West: different windows, different views 213
Kevin Parry

13　Developing change capacity and capability in organizations 228
Robert Cole and Sarah Coleman

14　Risk and organizational change 246
Ruth Murray-Webster

PART 2 The future of organizational change –
opinion pieces from future thinkers 299

ABOUT THE EDITORS

Sarah Coleman helps organizations deliver better outcomes and value. She is an experienced programme director working in an interim and consultancy capacity with boards and senior leadership teams. She has worked extensively with multinationals, corporates and medium-sized enterprises across public and private sector organizations to plan, implement and assure major change programmes in the UK and internationally.

Her early career was spent in software and telecoms and, as technology is an acknowledged driver of change, she developed her passion for improving capability within organizations for successful change: the right change, landing well. She draws on over 25 years' practical experience of leading and supporting multi-million-pound strategic projects, programmes and transformation, including technology implementation, outsourcing, procurement and culture change. She is valued for her ability to challenge positively and constructively, her ability to provide clarity and focus, and for her excellent communication skills.

Sarah is a Fellow of, and former non-executive director for, the Association for Project Management and a Chartered Fellow of the Chartered Management Institute. She holds an MBA from Cranfield School of Management, is Visiting Fellow at Lincoln University and Cranfield University, and is sought after to speak at business schools in the UK and abroad, and at events and conferences. She is a published author (*Project Leadership*, Gower, 2015; 'Dealing with power and politics' for *Business Analysis and Leadership* edited by Pullen and Archer, Kogan Page, 2013) and regularly contributes to professional journals on all things project, programme and change. Sarah is a Director at Business Evolution Ltd and can be contacted at sarah.coleman@businessevolution.co.

Bob Thomas is an experienced business change programme, portfolio, PMO and assurance manager with over 25 years' operational experience delivering and assuring major change programmes across leading public and private sector organizations. He has implemented green field corporate PMIS systems into Railtrack, DVLA licensing systems into Toyota and Suzuki, provided delivery assurance on the NHS's £1 billion CRS system and programme-managed numerous multi-million-pound business transformational programmes for Innovate UK, the Medical Research Council and Kent County Council. Recently, for the Post Office, he worked on its £125 million Crown Transformation Programme, which rolled out a new operating business model across 300 Crown Post Office branches nation-wide as part of its £1.3 billion modernization strategy. Bob has been an active Member of the Association for Project Management (APM) for over 25 years. He is a past chairman of the APM's People & Team Working SIG, past committee member of the Programme Management SIG and a founder member of the APM's Enabling Change SIG where he pioneered UK Industry Change Practitioner Groups involving organizations such as the NHS, British Council, Heathrow Airport, Reuters and the Bank of America. He has published numerous articles on aspects of project manage-ment and contributed to the fifth and sixth editions of the APM Body of Knowledge. Bob holds MAPM, MoP, MSP, Prince and MoR qualifications and has worked as a Professional Industrial Mentor at Aston University. He is a Director of RDT IT Services Ltd and works helping organizations to plan, implement or assure major transformational change across their business.

Bob can be contacted at bobt8973@gmail.com

ABOUT THE CONTRIBUTORS

Kelly Angus is Deputy Director of Human Resources at Northumbria Healthcare NHS Foundation Trust. She has worked closely alongside co-authors Paul Taylor and Karen Dumain on several important Do OD projects. Kelly is a Fellow of the Chartered Institute of Personnel and Development (CIPD), has an MBA, MA in HR Management and Development and is currently studying for an Executive Coaching and Mentoring Qualification. Kelly has over 20 years' experience within the NHS in Human Resources, OD and General Management roles at a senior level. She has recently become an inaugural graduate of the Nye Bevan Programme being Awarded the NHS Leadership award in Executive Healthcare Leadership.

Heather Bewers' experience ranges from several years in publishing to different roles in her 24 years at KPMG – audit, corporate finance and M&A, dotcom advisory, CRM implementation and innovation. Her last 15 years focused on internal change projects, all with deep behavioural and cultural implications. Most recently she was the founder of KPMG's Future Institute, offering foresight internally and to clients to provoke debate about change and disruption.

Heather stills works with KPMG, involved with their C-Suite Leadership programme which offers senior leaders the opportunity to continue that debate. Through Change Is An Opportunity she works with senior leadership teams to help organizations move from a risk mindset to seeing opportunity in the VUCA world. Contact Heather at ciao.heather@btinternet.com.

Ira Blake's expertise in change management has been developed through working with clients in pharmaceuticals, travel, local and central government, transport, not-for-profit, retail, media, retail banking and professional services sectors for over 15 years. She advises a portfolio of clients on complex, strategic and transformational change, focusing on building change leadership and change management capability in organizations.

Ira is an experienced consultant, mentor, speaker and writer on change management. A Global Assessor for the Change Management Institute's ACMM (Accredited Change Manager – Master) and one of the first to achieve ACMM in the UK, Ira was Co-Lead for CMI UK from 2012 to

2015. Ira is a Director at Uncommon Expertise Ltd and can be contacted at ira.blake@uncommonexpertise.co.uk.

Paul Brown is Faculty Professor, Organizational Neuroscience, Monarch Business School Switzerland; International Chairman of the Vietnam Consulting Group, Saigon; International Director of SIRTailors, Saigon; and Senior Adviser, the Vietnam Veterans of America Foundation, Hanoi.

A clinical and organizational psychologist and executive coach, he is creating a General Theory of the Individual and the Organization based upon mapping how energy flows or gets blocked in the pursuit of profit or other outcomes within the organizational system. He has recently co-authored *Neuropsychology for Coaches: Understanding the basics* (2012, McGraw-Hill/Open University Press); *River Dragon* (a novel, 2014); *Neuroscience for Leadership: Harnessing the brain gain advantage* (2015, Palgrave Macmillan); and *The Fear-Free Organization* (2015, Kogan Page).

Anthony Burrows is passionate about employee engagement, communication and helping businesses get better at the people side of change. He has worked in financial services for nearly 20 years and has helped a number of businesses turn around their fortunes through delivering record-breaking increases in employee engagement. He has built a reputation for transforming communications and engagement teams from tactical operators to strategic enablers and has won several awards in recognition of this.

Anthony is co-founder and a Managing Partner of Intelligent Emotion, a new and dynamic engagement, change and internal communication consultancy. 'Intelligent Emotion' reflects his belief that when used intelligently, emotion in business can unlock innovation and pride, and create competitive advantage.

David Caddle started his career as an engineering apprentice, before moving into blue-chip organizations in the aerospace, special-purpose machinery and telecommunication industries. During his career, David held positions in Production, Project and Quality engineering roles before moving into Quality and Programme Management. He has several years' consulting experience throughout the supply chain in change management, leading to significant enhanced quality, cost and delivery performance. David is an experienced engineer with a post-graduate qualification in manufacturing systems, and is also a member of The Chartered Quality Institute.

Robert Cole is an experienced, methodical and sensitive change management mentor, consultant and trainer. His clients have included financial, commercial, central and local government and charities, across many business sectors. He is involved in the development of professional qualification structures for change managers to recognize their growing competence. He also runs a company offering vocational change qualifications for those seeking to demonstrate their competence, both individuals and organizations.

Robert has moved through research project management, business management to change management, becoming involved in a dotcom start-up along the way. He has developed competence models and assessment tools for both innovation and change.

Tianne Croshaw has nearly 30 years' experience in the personal and business development field. She is a Mental and Emotional Resilience Coach and Trainer. She is also a Clinical Master Hypnotherapist and Stress Management Consultant as well as an NLP and EFT Practitioner.

Over the years Tianne has worked with organizations including Virgin Trains, an international pharmaceutical company, Her Majesty's Prison Service, Penna of London, Ted Baker, Superdry, Severnside Housing, Weaver Vale Housing, the Railway Children and Cheshire East Council as well as a number of primary and secondary schools.

Tianne is the co-creator of 'The Resilience Programme', which took an organization with 8 per cent stress and anxiety absenteeism to 0 per cent absence during the three years the programme ran. She can be contacted at: www.sustainableengagementpartnership.com.

Karen Dumain is the National Programme Lead for Organizational Development for the NHS Leadership Academy. Karen co-leads Do OD: Putting Theory into Practice – the expert resource on OD for the NHS. Karen shaped her practice working in the private and third sector before joining the NHS. Karen has a first degree in Behavioural Sciences and a master's in Leadership & Organization of Public Services, and is a CIPD Fellow as well as having the NTL applied behavioral sciences OD certificate.

The golden thread in all her work is the passion to enable and challenge people and organizations to be the best they can be, bringing a curiosity and belief in developing potential wherever people and teams might be within organizations and across systems.

Adi Gaskell is currently the Managing Director of the Horizons Tracker, an innovation consultancy based in London that helps organizations to respond to the change that's occurring in their industry. He has exceptional links with academia, government and companies both large and small to help you understand what is happening in your industry, and the knowledge of innovation and change management to know how best to respond to those changes.

He is also a thought leader in the field and has published a number of whitepapers on innovation, and also pens regular columns for Forbes and the Huffington Post. During this time, he has also judged a number of innovation competitions, including the NHS Innovation Challenge and the Katerva Innovation Challenge.

Peter Glynne is a management consultant with PwC specializing in leading complex change. He has over 20 years' experience across a range of sectors. Peter was formerly Head of Change and Programme Management for Westminster City Council and previously at Deloitte. He holds a master's degree in Project Management and is a qualified Chartered Secretary. Peter has authored many publications on project, programme and change management.

Peter is a Fellow of the Association for Project Management (APM), a member of the Audit and Assurance Committee and a member of the Specific Interest Group (SIG) Steering group since 2009. He is a member of the Portfolio Management SIG Committee and was also chair of the Benefits SIG for five years. In addition, Peter is chair of a leading UK charity.

Kevin Holmes is currently Senior Director for GSK's Accelerating Delivery and Performance (ADP) initiative and has been in that role since 2010. He has spearheaded the expansion of ADP from GSK's UK headquarters to its R&D facilities in the UK and Philadelphia and to its Vaccines division in Brussels, and is currently leading the deployment across Asia from Singapore.

Kevin has nearly 40 years' experience in the use of performance coaching, process improvement and management systems to lead enterprise transformation and re-engineering programmes for global MNC clients. His work has profoundly impacted tens of thousands of people, delivered many hundreds of millions of pounds in financial benefits and dramatically changed the way that client organizations change. He can be reached at kevinholmes@firebrandassociates.com.

Viren Lall is a business transformation and international executive education expert. His corporate experience includes delivery of transformation benefits of £410 million for telecoms, services and IT organizations. His business transformation hothouses were voted the best in BT's corporate memory. As the MD of ChangeSchool he is responsible for developing organizational capability in the UK, GCC and India. He has worked with UBS, Lloyds, Vodafone, Al

Rashid Group (Bahrain), SMEF (Oman), Landmark Group (UAE), AIESEC, Barclays, Graphisoft (Japan) and Satven (India). He also teaches the core MBA course at the Indian School of Business and executive education for London Business School. Viren has an Executive MBA with distinction from London Business School and can be reached at viren@changeschool.org.

Kate Lanz specializes in working with senior executives and teams, including the board. Kate's successful corporate career was notably as an International General Manager with Diageo. Kate holds degrees in languages, marketing and psychology and an MBA. She is a qualified coaching supervisor and is completing a doctorate in applied neuroscience.

Kate's clients include AXA, Accenture, Disney, Diageo, EY, GSK, Lloyds Bank and Morgan Stanley, among others. She is coaching faculty at INSEAD where she works globally.

A founder member of the Worldwide Association of Business Coaches, Kate is also accredited with the Association of Professional Executive Coaches and Supervisors. Kate has published numerous coaching articles and book chapters on supervision and team coaching. Kate has two teenage sons and recently dared to take up horse riding again!

Stephanie McGregor is an infrastructure specialist with 20+ years spanning public and private sectors, including energy, education, health, the arts, car sharing and urban planning. Known for delivering in complex regulatory and financing environments, Stephanie's diverse pedigree provides a rich perspective on navigating change challenges and making projects happen.

As the Director, Offshore Transmission, with UK energy regulator Ofgem, Stephanie played a leading role in creating the UK offshore electricity transmission market. She structured and executed a world-leading regulated asset competition, taking £1.1 billion in projects to market, attracting £4 billion of funding and saving UK consumers over £400 million. This model now covers over £2.2 billion in assets and has influenced future energy market models.

Stephanie holds urban planning, business administration and sustainable development qualifications.

John McLelland has recently retired from a major aerospace company where he was Head of Product Introduction. He began his career as an engineering graduate in product development in 1979, and after various business and programme management roles he attained his MBA at Glasgow Business School in 1990. Since then he has led the programme management of several major new product developments for his company, from concept through to entry into service, ensuring readiness in both internal and external supply chains. This experience established him as the company's expert in the field and he spent the final two years of his career leading improvements to the process itself. John currently resides with his wife Louise in Derby and can be contacted via LinkedIn.

Jacqueline Mitchell has 30 years' experience of people management; in later years as a board-level HR&OD Director. She has a deep understanding of an unusually broad range of people management issues, and an insightful and intuitive understanding of what it takes to lead an organization successfully; crucially, not just by talking about it, but by doing it.

Jacqueline now consults to UK businesses on people management and engagement practices through her business GrantaHR. She has a particular interest in helping businesses to improve employee engagement, as well as exploring her personal interest in team dynamics and causes of conflict.

Jacqueline has been a Chartered Fellow of the Chartered Institute of Personnel and Development since 2000 and can be contacted at jmitchell@ grantahr.com.

Ruth Murray-Webster is Director, Change Portfolio for Associated British Ports Ltd and an Honorary Fellow of APM. Ruth has 30 years of experience in a series of roles across most sectors, supporting the delivery of change objectives. These include Director of the Risk in the Boardroom practice for KPMG LLP in the UK and 10 years as a Director of Lucidus Consulting Ltd.

Along this journey, Ruth researched organizational change from the perspective of the recipients of change for an Executive Doctorate at Cranfield School of Management. She has also taken a keen interest in risk management along the way, co-authoring four books on the people aspects of risk management with collaborators David Hillson and Penny Pullan.

Kevin Parry is a highly experienced Programme Director now working in healthcare transformation. He is a specialist in operational readiness with experience in the UK, Ireland, Mainland Europe and Asia. Kevin has advised international companies at board level on change management and in this capacity he planned and advised on operational readiness for a leading global airline prior to his current role.

Kevin is a Fellow of the Association for Project Management (APM) and has written articles on change for *Project Magazine* as well as speaking at APM events. He has more than 20 years of leading international and multicultural teams delivering major change. Kevin is a visiting lecturer at the University of Manchester and holds post-graduate Diplomas in Management and Company Direction.

John Pelton joined CH2M in 2011 and has since worked on HS2 and Crossrail. A civil engineering graduate of Imperial College, London, he has travelled around the world tackling a variety of challenges, increasingly focusing on the human dimension. John spent 29 years serving as a Royal Engineer officer. Towards the end of his Army career he undertook an Open University MBA and began to investigate different ways of managing change. After looking at how significant efficiencies could be achieved constructing HS2, he moved on to Crossrail to lead the pioneering Crossrail innovation programme. John relaxes by fishing and running mountain marathons, and enjoys challenging accepted practices whenever he has the opportunity.

Gillian Perry has been a leader in the field of change management for over 15 years. She is currently a Director of Change on a major change programme. She advises on change management strategy and is the Change Management Institute UK Co-Chair. She has worked across a number of industry sectors, and has significant experience in the utilities industry, most recently for National Grid. During that time, she has led and advised major change programmes across the international business.

She has a diverse skill set with a significant number of years working within human resources, information technology, finance and corporate centre functions, working in everything from change management and employee engagement through to corporate strategy.

Hilary Scarlett is an international speaker, consultant and author. Her work has spanned Europe, the United States and Asia and concentrates on the development of people-focused change programmes and employee engagement. Hilary works with leadership teams in the private and public sectors to help them build resilience and introduce change efficiently and effectively. She has won various global awards for her work in employee engagement and change management.

Hilary regularly writes and speaks on neuroscience and employee engagement. Her book *Neuroscience for Organizational Change: An evidence-based, practical guide to managing change* was published by Kogan Page in 2016 and has been widely praised.

Hilary is the Founder and Director at Scarlett & Grey: www.scarlettand-grey.com. Contact Hilary via info@scarlettandgrey.com.

Kate Stuart-Cox is a founding partner of the UK-based professional services firm Perspectiv, which works to increase the quantity and quality of creative problem solvers. She has experience working with clients in the United States, Asia and Europe across a wide range of businesses and functions. Kate is also a visiting lecturer at Cass Business School and part of the Centre for Creativity in Professional Practice, which carries out research and delivers both knowledge transfer programmes and the Masters in Creativity, Innovation and Leadership. Contact Kate at kate@perspectiv.co.uk; www.perspectiv.co.uk.

Paul Taylor created Do OD, the expert organizational development resource for the NHS. Paul works with the system to enable OD practitioners to connect, share, learn and grow. Paul is a member of CIPD, with a degree in Psychology and a Masters in HR Leadership, and is currently working on his Doctorate in Organizational Development. Paul joined the NHS in 2003 after a range of successful roles in local government and in the private and voluntary sectors. Paul's career encompasses organizational development, human resources, learning and development, and strategic workforce development roles. Paul's work is driven by a desire to help people unleash their full potential.

Andy Wilkins is a senior honorary visiting fellow at Cass Business School and part of the Centre for Creativity in Professional Practice, which carries out research and delivers both knowledge transfer programmes and the Masters in Creativity, Innovation and Leadership. He is also a founding partner of the UK-based professional services firm Perspectiv, which works to increase the quantity and quality of creative problem solvers. He has experience across a wide range of businesses, functions and needs across the world. E-mail: andy@perspectiv.co.uk. Twitter: @AndrewNWilkins.

Rod Willis FRSA FCMI MSc MBA is an APECS Accredited Executive Coach and a Talent & Leadership Development Partner. He is a Fellow of the International Talent Advisory Board (ITAB), a Legal Education & Training Group recommended provider, an Associate & Accredited Coach and Facilitator of 'The Management Shift' programme and a Facilitator for Windsor Leadership. In 2016, he brought a Peer-Coaching process to the UK called CoachingOurselves – A Henry Mintzberg Program. He is a CoachingOurselves Certified Facilitator, and Assentire Ltd became a listed Partner of CoachingOurselves providing Certified Facilitator training within the UK for HR, L&D, OD & Coaching Professionals. He also specializes in exploring agility in Groups & Teams, optimising Group & Team Performance. E-mail: rod.willis@assentire.net. Twitter: @RodWillisGTC.

FOREWORD

The variety of challenges that face organizations are exciting, stimulating and at times fraught with danger. The demanding pace for change brings a particular complexity and pressure to the organizational leader driving hard to achieve required results. Often the most testing challenge that presents itself is organizational transformation and change: promising careers have been stalled or even halted when transformation has not been successful. The rate of change is now relentless and this challenge is regularly exposing those businesses unable to successfully evolve and respond to what is happening in the market, with increasing competition, with their supply chain and customer expectations. Organizational flexibility and agility, the ability to change fast and appropriately to the situation, is increasingly seen as the holy grail. Successful organizations now appear to be those able to grow through the development of new styles, new behaviours and new sets of practices.

My own experience has been gained from business leadership roles within the divisions of a blue chip organization, with an increasing transformational element. In recent years, transformation leadership and coaching other leaders through change has been a core part of my responsibilities with my present role leading Rolls-Royce's Civil Aerospace Transformation. Through these experiences I have learnt many lessons, many of which are reflected in *Organizational Change Explained*. This timely book has a broad appeal to organizations across industry sectors, regardless of size or maturity, and to all those individuals involved in change and transformation from Senior Leadership Teams to Operations.

There are many excellent articles, books and research available on how to lead and manage change, and on the mechanistic and procedural aspects of change. There are also numerous businesses preoccupied with selling their advice, proprietary methodology or approach to change and transformation. Whilst these are all of course important and useful, there is something further that I consider to be of specific relevance: the power of learning from the insights, shared experience and success of others. *Organizational Change Explained* provides just that. It is different because it consolidates vital lessons learnt from those who have experienced it for themselves, and because it addresses the realities of change and transformation. It explains change themes through the eyes of leading practitioners who have helped organizations change; who are candid about the difficulties they have faced and what they needed to do and mobilize to overcome them. The ideas and insights are based upon real situations, of particular benefit to all those who undertake or are involved in change within organizations. While Part 1 presents leading practitioner insights across 12 change themes gained from 18 industries, Part 2 challenges the reader to better understand how change might influence industry sectors and organizations for the future.

Organizational Change Explained will strike a chord with all those involved with organizational change and transformation, whether seasoned and experienced or new and aspiring. The benefit of such experience is invaluable, making *Organizational Change Explained* something you can read and reference throughout your career.

Rob Campling
Head of Strategic Programmes
Civil Aerospace Group
Rolls-Royce plc

Introduction

SARAH COLEMAN AND BOB THOMAS

Turn and face the strange.
DAVID BOWIE, 'CHANGES'

Change happens. Context matters. Business-as-usual is no longer an option. Disruption across geography and industry sectors is forcing organizations to re-examine what they considered to be the established rules of engagement, producing a 'new rhythm' of business life. Organizations simply cannot afford to be blindsided and to 'act with yesterday's logic' (Peter Drucker attributed). Whether because of new innovation, technology, independent review recommendations, working practices or breaking into new markets, these all represent change initiatives that have similar issues and challenges for organizations across industry sectors and across geographies.

Clichéd though it is, organizational change has become the new constant, and those organizations which do not keep up with current trends will find it progressively difficult to thrive, if not survive. In fact, it is clear that embracing change is now the only sensible option for organizations to take if they wish to keep up with what is increasingly a VUCA (volatile, uncertain, changeable and ambiguous) world.

Over the past 15 years, we've noticed that conversation about organizational change has evolved from the very basic level (for example, an occasional discrete, local change programme) through to a more mature level (for example, where an organization is managing a portfolio of multiple and often overlapping change initiatives). And now, increasingly, the change conversation is evolving further and, as it does so, it is becoming more obvious that 'change' is a generic term covering a whole spectrum of activities, key performance indicators and success factors. As organizations drive to change their culture, strategic focus and underlying processes, so 'developmental' (for example, process improvements) and 'transitional' (for example, reorganizations or mergers) change is being challenged by more radical 'transformational' change. Transformational change is unpredictable, iterative, experimental and often involves high risk.

Such change typically reinvents organizations or creates new business models, usually focusing on a portfolio of initiatives, which are either interdependent or intersecting. In the UK, HS2, Crossrail and the Thames Tideway Tunnel are all examples of such transformational change where new business entities have emerged demanding changed mindsets and behaviours.

What makes *Organizational Change Explained* different? A quick internet search will show that organizational change is a field rich in information. Much of the literature consists of academic-based books aimed at the business studies and MBA market, or reflective change books aimed at the individual. There is much less literature providing real, industry and organizational-based case studies which can be used by organizations, business leaders, change practitioners and students alike to help inform their thinking about how they might approach and deliver change. *Organizational Change Explained* helps to redress that balance.

The chapters and opinion pieces in *Organizational Change Explained* have been written by a range of authors, each providing practical content and insight through examples and case studies. The book describes change at the organizational level and, necessarily by extension, its impact at the individual level. It is real world based, as well as introducing new thought. We invited 28 inspiring, experienced and reflective change practitioners to write about their experiences and insights from their own work with organizational change. Together, these authors have provided a wide range of case studies each focused on particular change themes, and on particular industry sectors. In all, *Organizational Change Explained* covers 12 change themes and 18 industry sectors. Having worked across many different industry sectors ourselves, we recognize that learning from one sector can be used and refined for another sector; knowledge sharing can help us all improve the way we support organizations to work their way through change. We hope the collective perspectives and experiences, thoughts and insights provided in the chapters and opinion pieces help the reader to explore and model solutions to their own organizational change challenges.

Business life trends

When we think of businesses (that is, commercial, industrial or professional organizations), we tend to think of the big names and the global brands: Virgin, Coca-Cola, GlaxoSmithKline, BAE Systems, Barclays, Rolls Royce, Vodafone. However, in the UK the majority of businesses are small and medium-sized enterprises (SMEs) by virtue of number of personnel and turnover.

Daepp *et al* (2015) examined more than 25,000 publicly traded North American companies, from 1950 to 2009, focusing on longevity and 'mortality' rate. Based on their analysis, the longevity of an enterprise is independent of a company's age, and the typical half-life of a publicly traded company is about a decade, regardless of business sector.

Hannah (2009) identifies the 1920s and 1960s as crucial periods for the formation of the UK's modern corporate system, suggesting that they also supported the trend improvement (by historical if not international standards) in Britain's growth performance. He calculates that the average 'half-life' of big companies – that is, the time taken to die by half of the firms in the world's top 100 by market capitalization in any given year – was 75 years during the 20th century.

In the UK, we now see that SMEs account for 99.9 per cent of the business population. At the start of 2015 there were an estimated 5.4 million UK private sector businesses: SMEs now account for three-fifths of the employment and almost half of turnover in the UK private sector at 15.6 million (60 per cent) and £1.8 trillion (47 per cent) respectively (Department for Business, Innovation and Skills, 2015).

Where are the organizations that last and thrive? There are over 5,000 companies older than 200 years across 41 countries (Jae-kyoung, 2008; Baer, 2014) spanning industry sectors. Examples are:

- Hoshi, a Japanese inn founded in 718 and a 46th-generation family business;
- the Weihenstephan Brewery in Freising, Germany established in 1040;
- the gun maker Beretta, started in 1526 in Gardone, Italy;
- Cambridge University Press in Cambridge, England, founded in 1534 – the world's oldest publishing house;
- Bushmills in County Antrim, Northern Ireland, founded in 1608, the world's oldest whiskey distillery;
- Zildjian, founded in 1623 in Istanbul, Turkey before the percussion company moved to the United States;
- the Tysmenytsia Fur Company, established in 1638 and one of the oldest and most traditional industries in Ukraine.

O'Hara (2004) looked at Kongo Gumi, founded by a Korean in Osaka, Japan over 40 generations ago in 578. The builder of Buddhist temples, Shinto shrines and castles and now also offices, apartment buildings and private houses was the world's oldest continuously ongoing independent company, operating for over 1,400 years. The once family-owned construction company went into liquidation in January 2006; its assets were subsequently purchased and it became a wholly owned subsidiary of the Takamatsu Corporation.

In an age where new enterprises are established at an astonishing rate and where many collapse within the first five years, there is something intriguing about businesses which have persisted for 200, 700 and over 1,000 years. Long-lived businesses are highly unusual given that they have to survive economic, social and political changes, competitors and new entrants and that the majority are subject to merger, acquisition, bankruptcy or break-up.

So are these businesses just lucky survivors, or is this a reflection of their productivity, innovation and resourcefulness, and their ability to adapt and respond successfully to changing market conditions and other forces?

Organization challenges

Dobbs *et al* (2015) describe four fundamental disruptive forces (urbanization, technology, an ageing population and greater global connections through trade, people, finance and data) which are driving dramatic change, and which are happening 10 times faster and at 300 times the scale, or roughly 3,000 times the impact, compared with the Industrial Revolution. The reality now is that organizations cannot afford to trust that what got them where they are today will continue to serve them best in the future. Beinhocker (2007) writes that although markets are highly dynamic, the 'brutal truth' is that the majority of organizations are not; moreover, that typically organizations have very little capacity and capability to evolve and adapt in response to events as diverse as technology (witness Polaroid filing for bankruptcy protection in 2001) and *black swan* events (random, unexpected and difficult to predict) (Taleb, 2008).

It is this inability to adapt quickly that is exposing many organizations at this time, whether this is a result of them not seeing new trends, wilfully ignoring what is happening or not being sufficiently agile to pivot. Organizations now more than ever desperately need to show that they can rapidly adapt appropriately and be flexible to new situations. Some of the future economic business predictions underpin this and make for difficult reading, citing a future of unsettled and highly changeable environments of which the UK's exit from the European Union – Brexit – is only one example.

Why do some organizations change more successfully than others? How do they successfully meet the challenges typically thrown up by change? Much organizational change still seems to be linear and top down in its thinking. How can we move this thinking to making change part of the established and sustained organizational culture – one that decreases risk, resistance and stress on individuals and the enterprise?

Greiner (1972, 1998) developed an organizational growth model describing six phases that organizations go through as they grow over time. The model covers all industry sectors from construction and manufacturing to professional service firms, and highlights that organizational growth calls for change. Organizations pass through different phases and each of these calls for a different approach: each growth phase is made up of a period of relatively stable 'evolutionary' growth, followed by a 'crisis', 'transition' or 'revolution' when major organizational change is needed if the company is to continue. Greiner originally proposed his model in 1972 with five phases of growth, adding a sixth in 1998 (see Figure 0.1).

The model recognizes that management style, processes and behaviours that were appropriate for a smaller size and earlier time aren't appropriate for the next phase, and that these come under scrutiny, particularly during periods of crisis. It is during these periods of crisis that businesses that are unable or unwilling to abandon past practices and deliver the necessary organizational changes are likely to fold or level off in their growth rates, possibly falling victim to merger, acquisition, asset stripping or bankruptcy. So, the critical task for management during each crisis period is to find a new style, new behaviours and sets of organizational practices that will become the basis for successfully managing the next period of growth. The implication is that each set of new practices eventually becomes redundant as the organization enters the next crisis; the irony is, therefore, that managers see the solution they developed for one phase become a major problem in the future.

Regardless of criticism and continuing debate about the validity of Greiner's model, it remains a favourite model to start a conversation with an organization about where it considers itself to be along its journey, where it would like to be and how it needs to plan to achieve that vision.

Figure 0.1 Six phases of organizational growth

Time →

Business Size →

Phase 6: Growth through alliances - growth continues through merger, outsourcing, networks and other solutions involving other organizations.

.... *Internal growth crisis: develop partnerships with complementary organizations* ....

Phase 5: Growth through collaboration - strong interpersonal collaboration and cross-functional team-working emphasized to try to overcome formal systems and process red tape. Innovation and problem-solving focuses on matrix teams grouping and re-grouping.

.... *Red-tape crisis: introduce new culture and structure* ....

Phase 4: Growth through coordination – top down introduction of formal systems to achieve greater coordination. Decentralized units merged (eg product groups into investment centres). Formal planning procedures established. Centralization of technical functions.

.... *Control crisis: increased centralization and co-ordination processes* ....

Phase 3: Growth through delegation – decentralized organizational structure. Delegation supports increased motivation (authority and incentives) to penetrate larger markets, respond faster to customers, and develop new products. HQ senior team further removed from the day to day.

.... *Autonomy crisis: delegation, trust and decision-making required* ....

Phase 2: Growth through direction - more formal methods of process and communication (eg information systems, work flow systems, word standards). Begin to separate managment activities into discreet activities (eg marketing and production).

.... *Leadership crisis: professional managment required* ....

Phase 1: Growth through creativity – emphasis on products/services and market expansion. Entrepreneurial culture. Internal communication frequent and informat. Highly sensitive to the market. Modest salaries and promise of ownership benefits.

SOURCE Adapted from Greiner (1972, 1998)

Since change now rarely means a move from one steady state to another, how are we going to change the way we undertake organizational change in the future? As we continue to move away from the very traditional linear, top-down change processes and lean more towards flexibility and agile thinking within organizations, how will this affect our views towards applying the very traditional and established change management methods and approaches presented by Lewin (1947), Kotter (1996) and others? One of the threads within *Organizational Change Explained* is that we need to think again about how organizations change in order to accommodate the future. In effect, we need to change the way we change; but what will this mean for the organization and what will it mean for the individual?

Future business models

There are now organizations leading their fields, and designing and exploring disruptive technologies, which actively seek value creation and competitive advantage that they can exploit and benefit from. Haeckel (1992) contrasted these organizations and labelled them as either 'make and sell' (where certainty is assumed in terms of both customer expectation and market conditions) or 'sense and respond' (where uncertainty is the norm). The reader will identify a coherent thread running throughout this book, which is this idea of creating a change culture to support change that is continual and 'always on'; in other words, a constantly moving change environment.

Amazon, a survivor from the dotcom boom, is now moving towards printing on demand, so potentially taking control away from publishing houses. We see newcomers exploiting the internet to create portals to link consumers with a range of products and services (GoCompare, Hungry House, Airbnb, Funding Circle). Although we are familiar with contracting, zero hours and temporary work, Uber has introduced the concept of the 'gig economy' where their business model is dependent on paying individuals on a per-job basis and treating them as suppliers and independent contractors, rather than employees with compensation packages, benefits and the legal protection this implies. As at December 2016, two drivers challenged Uber in the UK courts and won the right to be treated as employees. It is expected that Uber will appeal against the ruling.

What's interesting about all these examples is that each disrupted the more traditional rules of business, often pioneering change through adopting new ways of doing things: how they reach their customers; how they deliver the product or service; their relationship with their employees, independent contractors and suppliers. How can long-established organizations such as large corporates and multinationals learn from these 'new kids on the block', their entrepreneurialism and their ability to rapidly recognize and embrace the opportunities around the Internet of Things and social media?

Technology is only one of a range of drivers for organizational change. In 2004, the Clementi Report published its recommendations following an independent review of the regulation of legal services in England and Wales. These recommendations continue to impact the legal sector, with the arrival of new entrants, increased use of competitive tenders and the use of panel suppliers, and more competition, particularly as a result of Alternative Business Structures (Legal Services Act 2007). The report facilitated the market liberalization that some considered was long overdue in legal services. The result has been increased price competition, a shift in the balance of power to clients and new business structures through which lawyers can operate by permitting ownership and investment by individuals who have not qualified as lawyers, and allowing legal businesses access to external capital (Mayson, 2014).

The future and organizations

Organizations of the future will need to consider and focus on a range of factors when embracing future change. In 2014, the Chartered Management Institute (CMI) noted that:

- Technology is transforming how organizations function. By 2020, each person will have six different devices that will be connected to the internet.
- Managers will need to be able to lead teams consisting of workers who work flexibly, independently and in a broad range of geographical locations.
- Managers will have tools for analysing staff e-mails and social media accounts in order to gauge staff engagement and manage performance.
- Organizations will need to adapt to increasing diversity and the likelihood that the proportion of Baltic, Asian and other ethnic minorities in the UK population will rise to 20 per cent by 2051.

How will this affect how organizations structure themselves and function? To answer this, we should consider factors such as:

- *Recognizing uncertainty and ambiguity* will be part of the future. Now is the time for organizations to be thinking about developing and increasing their in-house change capability, not just at senior levels but diffused across levels and functions as a core competence, and not just as a discretionary 'nice to have'.

- *Applying new organizational structures and practices* all caused by and, in turn, supporting a new leadership and management consciousness (Laloux, 2014; Robertson, 2015; Hlupic, 2014). These also have implications for the future of recruitment, working practices, teams, collaboration, remote working, and working across multiple geographies and time-zones in organizations.

- *Identifying the real differences in different generations' attitude to work*, working and career mobility, and recognizing what this means for organizations, communities and individuals.

- *Creating a flexible change environment* that can rapidly be embedded into an organization's culture along with a new way of working to help it to adapt more rapidly to opportunities and threats.

- *Ensuring people are supported* and helping them work more effortlessly with change through effective communication, engagement and involvement, and by building their resilience in times of ambiguity and unrest. CMI (2014) estimated that 60–65 per cent of the total worth of limited companies across the globe consists of intangible assets such as the skills and relationships of their people. Therefore, intelligent organizations make certain their people are supported.

Who this book is written for

The editors have spent their careers working with and in organizations of all sizes and across industry sectors, in the UK and abroad. We've worked with high-growth businesses and 'gazelles', with start-ups and long-established businesses, with family businesses and public limited companies, with public services organizations and with multinationals of tens of thousands of employees spread across different geographies. We've seen organizations plan and undertake change initiatives with varying degrees of success. These organizations continue to recognize the need to change and cannot afford to fail; they are desperate to ensure that new change is successful and that change becomes an integral part of what the organization does.

Organizational Change Explained has therefore been written for a variety of readers. It is aimed at:

- full-time and part-time in-house and external professional and experienced change agents who lead and support the shaping, scoping, design, delivery and embedding of organizational change;
- junior and aspiring change agents who wish to understand more about this field, and about their particular issues and challenges;
- 'accidental' change agents who, by virtue of their business acumen and organizational experience, have been given the responsibility to lead and manage change even though they have no direct experience or training in this field.

Organizational Change Explained is also aimed at those whose job titles do not mention the word 'change' at all. This might include professionals in human resources (HR) and organizational design (OD) as well as business owners, leadership teams and Boards who are responsible for the decisions, governance of and ultimately the success of organizational change. Finally, it has been written for students of change management courses to help illustrate real-life, practical examples in order to help them develop their awareness and understanding of organizational change.

The common theme across these different groups is that they are involved in changing what organizations do or provide, and how they function. They exist across public services, the private sector and the not-for-profit sector.

How this book is structured

Organizational Change Explained contains contributions from a wide variety of authors each with their own set of experiences and specialisms, and each with their own approach to their chapter or opinion piece. Together, they cover:

- a range of industry sectors (for example, healthcare, manufacturing, not for profit, telecoms, energy and utilities, pharmaceuticals, construction, manufacturing, food, marketing, leisure and travel, energy, logistics, local and central government, transport, financial services and electronics);
- a range of change themes (for example, leadership, resilience, communication and engagement, resistance, innovation, culture, capacity and capability, sustainability, change approaches, risk, implementation, operational readiness).

This provides the reader with a rich set of views and perspectives, insights and learnings about organizational change now and for the future.

Organizational Change Explained is divided into two parts:

- Part 1 uses case studies and vignettes across different industry sectors to look at how change is practically shaped, scoped, designed, delivered and embedded at the organizational level.
- Part 2 uses shorter opinion pieces to look at the future to better understand how change might influence industry sectors and organizations in the future, and the way organizations might change to accommodate this future.

Part 1 – The reality of organizational change – practitioner case studies and insights

Part 1 focuses on the practical experience of and insights about change in industry sectors, organizations and at the individual level through case studies and vignettes. The summary below shows the change themes that each chapter addresses and how each chapter relates to other chapters, their themes and the industry sectors they cover.

Chapter 1 – Why change?

'Changing culture through conversation: organizational development in the NHS' authored by Kelly Angus, Karen Dumain and Paul Taylor This chapter focuses on culture change within the UK's National Health Service (NHS). It discusses why the NHS OD community has

Table 0.1

Industry Sector(s) Featured	Healthcare
Key change themes covered	This chapter also strongly relates to the following change chapters and opinion pieces
<ul><li>Culture change</li><li>OD theory and practice</li><li>Digital interventions</li><li>Capability</li></ul>	3 – Shaping and design *(pharmaceuticals)* 10 – Change implementation *(telecoms)* 11 – Change readiness *(construction, ICT, electronics manufacturing)* 13 – Change: organizational capacity and capability *(engineering, local government, central government, telecoms)* 15 – Change: sustainability *(food, marketing, engineering consultancy)* 22 – The future and healthcare *(healthcare)*

prioritized culture change and how it developed and built a digital OD intervention to support the work. It also illustrates a successful culture change initiative through an NHS Trust case study and concludes with reflections, top tips and a note on the importance of building capability in NHS change practice.

Chapter 2 – Vision

'Sparking change: a world of change in electricity transmission' authored by Stephanie McGregor This chapter describes the recent changes in the UK's electricity transmission market in response to the rapid growth in offshore wind development. The response saw a new disruptive market model being created and led by the regulator, Ofgem, and the UK government. Known as the OFTO regime, the chapter describes the nature of the change and how it was disruptive, determines those key change drivers and enablers, and concludes with impacts and lessons for other disruptive industries.

Table 0.2

Industry Sector(s) Featured	Energy
Key change themes covered	This chapter also strongly relates to the following change chapters and opinion pieces
• Role of active policy development in market change	9 – Change communication and engagement *(leisure and travel)* 10 – Change implementation *(telecoms)*
	13 – Change: organizational capacity and capability *(engineering, local government, central government, telecoms)*

Chapter 3 – Shaping and design

'The GlaxoSmithKline story: changing the way we change' authored by Kevin Holmes This chapter details a large-scale, long-term change initiative completed within GlaxoSmithKline. It describes the deployment of a company-wide management change innovation and aims to help other change practitioners with guidance in creating the conditions for the successful deployment for their own large-scale innovations.

Table 0.3

Industry Sector(s) Featured	Pharmaceuticals
Key change themes covered	This chapter also strongly relates to the following change chapters and opinion pieces
• The reasons to change • Implementing change • Innovation as change • Change value, impact and benefits • Leading change	1 – Why change? *(healthcare)* 5 – Change behaviour *(food)* 8 – Change leadership *(not for profit)* 9 – Change communication and engagement *(leisure and travel)* 10 – Change implementation *(telecoms)* 11 – Change readiness *(construction, ICT, electronics manufacturing)* 13 – Change: organizational capacity and capability *(engineering, local government, central government, telecoms)* 14 – Change: risk *(manufacturing, central government, logistics, energy, mining)* 15 – Change: sustainability *(food, marketing, engineering consultancy)* 16 – Change: innovation *(construction, transport)*

Chapter 4 – Shaping and design

'Shaping, scoping and designing a new total operating model' authored by Gillian Perry this chapter describes an organizational design (OD) change to a major utilities business to support an overseas company strategy following a number of company acquisitions. It focuses on the early-stage processes of shaping, scoping and designing the new 'total operating model' (TOM), detailing what went well and what could have been done differently, then reviews the implemented TOM to determine whether it would provide sustainable customer benefits and shareholder returns.

Table 0.4

Industry Sector(s) Featured	Energy
Key change themes covered	This chapter also strongly relates to the following change chapters and opinion pieces
• Organization design • Target operating model	2 –Vision *(energy)* 8 – Change leadership *(not for profit)*

(continued)

Table 0.4 *(continued)*

Industry Sector(s) Featured	Energy
• Organization design principles • Implementing change	9 – Change communication and engagement *(leisure and travel)* 10 – Change implementation *(telecoms)* 13 – Change: organizational capacity and capability *(engineering, local government, central government, telecoms)* 14 – Change: risk *(manufacturing, central government, logistics, energy, mining)* 16 – Change: innovation *(construction, transport)*

Chapter 5 – Change leadership and management: change behaviour

'The brain and adaptive change' authored by Paul Brown and Kate Lanz This chapter introduces the emerging field of applied neuroscience to address two fundamental issues at the heart of any change programme: the brain naturally resists change, and there is no agreed understanding of what 'an organization' is, which makes it extremely difficult to track where change is working and where it is blocked. A model is proposed that describes the 'vital organs' of any organization and suggests that tracking the way human energy is applied in organizations might be the key to mapping what is happening during change.

Table 0.5

Industry Sector(s) Featured	Food
Key change themes covered	This chapter also strongly relates to the following change chapters and opinion pieces
• The way the brain works • Human energy as the only source profit • Overcoming resistance to change • Seeing the whole organization and its dynamics clearly	1 – Why change? *(healthcare)* 6 – Change resistance *(financial services, electronics manufacturing)* 10 – Change implementation *(telecoms)* 13 – Change: organizational capacity and capability *(engineering, local government, central government, telecoms)*

Chapter 6 – Change leadership and management: change resistance

'Working with resistance to change' authored by Rod Willis, Anthony Burrows and Sarah Coleman This chapter looks at how resistance to organizational change works to hamper delivery of change, and so of benefits and value to the organization. We talk about 'resistance' as if it is a single and specific thing, but this is a generic term covering a spectrum of ways in which ambivalence, focus and energy diverted to other priorities, challenge, hostility and active opposition to change manifest themselves. People react to change in different ways given their own circumstances, ambitions and concerns, and it is not always helpful to use a single term to cover such a range of seemingly negative responses. This chapter explores resistance to change from different industry sectors and different perspectives.

Table 0.6

Industry Sector(s) Featured	Financial Services, Electronics, Manufacturing
Key change themes covered	This chapter also strongly relates to the following change chapters and opinion pieces
• Resistance to change • Implementation • Change adoption • Employee communication and engagement	1 – Why change? *(healthcare)* 2 – Vision *(energy)* 5 – Change behaviour *(food)* 7 – Change resilience *(pharmaceuticals)* 9 – Change communication and engagement *(leisure and travel)* 11 – Change readiness *(construction, ICT, electronics manufacturing)* 12 – Cultural approaches *(construction)* 15 – Change: sustainability *(food, marketing, engineering consultancy)*

Chapter 7 – Change leadership and management: change resilience

'Creating the resilient organization' authored by Tianne Croshaw This chapter highlights how critical it is to create and support a mentally and emotionally resilient workforce in the face of current and future change. It introduces foundation tools that can be used to better understand workforce resilience and why some people embrace change while others resist.

Table 0.7

Industry Sector(s) Featured	Pharmaceuticals
Key change themes covered	This chapter also strongly relates to the following change chapters and opinion pieces
• Impact change has on our behaviours • Why some embrace change while others resist • How to create a more mentally and emotionally resilient workforce and through them a more resilient organization • Spreading the message of resilience through your organization	1 – Why change? *(healthcare)* 6 – Change resistance *(financial services, electronics manufacturing)* 9 – Change communication and engagement *(leisure and travel)* 10 – Change implementation *(telecoms)* 14 – Change: risk *(manufacturing, central government, logistics, energy, mining)*

Chapter 8 – Change leadership and management: change leadership

'Leading change in a not-for-profit organization' authored by Jacqueline Mitchell This chapter focuses on an NFP organization whose culture had become dysfunctional and which was at a turning point in its evolution. It highlights the importance of a shared vision and confirms that successful leadership of change is not all about the executive level. The chapter also demonstrates that leading change is not always a smooth path, and that difficult and unpopular decisions are often necessary.

Table 0.8

Industry Sector(s) Featured	Not for Profit
Key change themes covered	This chapter also strongly relates to the following change chapters and opinion pieces
• The importance of a shared vision • Successful leadership of change is not all about the executive level • Change is not all about a smooth path	6 – Change resistance *(financial services, electronics manufacturing)* 9 – Change communication and engagement *(leisure and travel)* 13 – Change: organizational capacity and capability *(engineering, local government, central government, telecoms)* 15 – Change: sustainability *(food, marketing, engineering consultancy)*

Chapter 9 – Change communication and engagement

'Employee communication and engagement during change: insights from neuroscience' authored by Hilary Scarlett This chapter explores the impact that organizational change can have on the brain and sets out how organizations can plan their communication to help employees perform at their best at times of uncertainty. It includes a global award-winning case study from TUI UK & Ireland.

Table 0.9

Industry Sector(s) Featured	Leisure and Travel
Key change themes covered	This chapter also strongly relates to the following change chapters and opinion pieces
<ul><li>Impact of organizational change on the brain</li><li>Why our brains crave information and certainty</li><li>What influences the messages we hear during change</li><li>The role of storytelling, visuals and emotions in change communications</li></ul>	5 – Change behaviour *(food)* 6 – Change resistance *(financial services, electronics manufacturing)*

Chapter 10 – Change implementation

'Project Carpe Diem: the systematic journey of a multi-locational and multicultural transformational change programme in a large telecoms company' authored by Viren Lall This chapter explores the journey, leadership challenges and insights gained from a multi-locational and multi-cultural transformational change programme within the service delivery function of the global services division at one of UK's largest telecoms corporations. It explores the importance of leadership as a critical transformational skill, beyond the level of the sponsor and cascaded down levels of organization where change happens at the coalface. It also shares techniques to build a common purpose, generate goodwill and use transformation as an opportunity to develop future leaders.

Table 0.10

Industry Sector(s) Featured	Telecoms
Key change themes covered	This chapter also strongly relates to the following change chapters and opinion pieces
<ul><li>Leadership of change needs organization capability development</li><li>A change process is necessary but not sufficient for success</li><li>Delivering change in a new target operating model</li><li>Implementing transformational change globally (multi-locational, multicultural)</li></ul>	2 – Vision *(energy)* 3 – Shaping and design *(pharmaceuticals)* 4 – Shaping and design *(energy)* 6 – Change resistance *(financial services, electronics manufacturing)* 7 – Change resilience *(pharmaceuticals)* 8 – Change leadership *(not for profit)* 11 – Change readiness *(construction, ICT, electronics manufacturing)* 12 – Cultural approaches *(construction)* 13 – Change: organizational capacity and capability *(engineering, local government, central government, telecoms)*

Chapter 11 – Change readiness

'Operational readiness for change' authored by Rod Willis, John McLelland, Kevin Parry and Sarah Coleman This chapter looks at how organizations make themselves operationally ready for change, using diverse case studies drawn from an airport cargo terminal construction in South East Asia, an ICT outsourcing deal, new product introduction and its implications for the supply chain in an aerospace manufacturer, and a merger and acquisition in the electronic manufacturing sector.

Operational readiness for change is often regarded as an ambiguous concept, so it tends to be considered quite late on and is often under-represented within the change process. But any delay in the implementation of planned change will result in 'value decay', where the original anticipated value attributed to the change will not be transferred to the business. Operational requirements around process, structure and procedure need to be complemented by other people-focused components such as mindsets, values and skills.

Table 0.11

Industry Sector(s) Featured	Construction, ICT, Electronics, Manufacturing
Key change themes covered	This chapter also strongly relates to the following change chapters and opinion pieces
• Activity planning • Employee communication and engagement • Structure, process and people	1 – Why change? *(healthcare)* 6 – Change resistance *(financial services, electronics manufacturing)* 9 – Change communication and engagement *(leisure and travel)*

Chapter 12 – Change: cultural approaches

'Managing change in Asia and the West: different windows, different views' authored by Kevin Parry This chapter explores how our culture and perceptions affect how we approach organizational change and expect it to be implemented. It contrasts the management of change in Asia and the West and illustrates how our models of organization and leadership of change impact management and employee behaviour. It considers the effect of these cultural differences using case studies, and frames the challenge for tomorrow's leaders in how change is designed, scoped and implemented.

Table 0.12

Industry Sector(s) Featured	Construction
Key change themes covered	This chapter also strongly relates to the following change chapters and opinion pieces
• Multicultural change • Shaping and designing change • The impact of values and beliefs • Communications and engagement	4 – Shaping and design *(energy)* 8 – Change leadership *(not for profit)* 9 – Change communication and engagement *(leisure and travel)*

Chapter 13 – Change: organizational capacity and capability

'Developing change capacity and capability in organizations' authored by Robert Cole and Sarah Coleman This chapter addresses two basic concepts for successfully shaping, scoping, designing, implementing and embedding organizational change: having sufficient resources to do change (change capacity), and ensuring that people resources have the right skills and are working efficiently (change capability).

Table 0.13

Industry Sector(s) Featured	Engineering, Local Government, Central Government, Telecoms
Key change themes covered	This chapter also strongly relates to the following change chapters and opinion pieces
<ul><li>Strategic versus operational capacity</li><li>Resource planning and development</li><li>Portfolio management</li><li>Capability assessment</li><li>Change roles</li></ul>	1 – Why change? *(healthcare)* 2 – Vision *(energy)* 3 – Shaping and design *(pharmaceuticals)* 4 – Shaping and design *(energy)* 5 – Change behaviour *(food)* 8 – Change leadership *(not for profit)* 12 – Cultural approaches *(construction)* 16 – Change: innovation *(construction, transport)* 17 – The future and change

Chapter 14 – Change: risk

'Risk and organizational change' authored by Ruth Murray-Webster This chapter argues that risk and change are closely connected: a reciprocal relationship that it is important to manage as a whole rather than as two distinct parts. Change – a disruption of the status quo – triggers uncertainty about the future in the hearts and minds of the people in the situation. Written for the change management professional rather than the risk specialist, this chapter explores common challenges of understanding and managing risk during organizational change. Examples and practical tips that can be applied in any organization are offered.

Table 0.14

Industry Sector(s) Featured	Manufacturing, Central Government, Logistics, Energy, Mining
Key change themes covered	This chapter also strongly relates to the following change chapters and opinion pieces
• Securing funding for organization change • Engaging stakeholders to share perceptions of risk • Reporting progress and maintaining commitment • Overcoming systemic bias when making decisions about change when things are uncertain	4 – Shaping and design (energy) 6 – Change resistance (financial services, electronics manufacturing) 9 – Change communication and engagement (leisure and travel)

Chapter 15 – Change: sustainability

'Embedding and sustaining change' authored by Andy Wilkins and Kate Stuart-Cox This chapter shares an approach to 'embedding and sustaining change' that is effective but which will require many in change management to refresh their operating system, that is, the mindset needs to change from an over-reliance on a machine metaphor and rhetoric to seven keys to embed and sustain any change effectively.

Table 0.15

Industry Sector(s) Featured	Food, Marketing, Engineering Consultancy
Key change themes covered	This chapter also strongly relates to the following change chapters and opinion pieces
• People • Environment • Process • Outcome	3 – Shaping and design (pharmaceuticals) 5 – Change behaviour (food) 6 – Change resistance (financial services, electronics manufacturing) 7 – Change resilience (pharmaceuticals) 8 – Change leadership (not for profit) 10 – Change implementation (telecoms)

(continued)

Table 0.15 *(continued)*

Industry Sector(s) Featured	Food, Marketing, Engineering Consultancy
	11 – Change readiness *(construction, ICT, electronics manufacturing)*
	14 – Change: risk *(manufacturing, central government, logistics, energy, mining)*
	16 – Change: innovation *(construction, transport)*
	17 – The future and change

Chapter 16 – Change: innovation

'Change innovation' authored by John Pelton This chapter describes innovation in one of Europe's large change programmes, Crossrail. Innovation and change can be considered to be symbiotic, yet all too often the nature of the relationship between them is confused or in conflict. Recently Crossrail, currently the largest construction project in Europe, took a pioneering initiative and introduced an innovation programme, Innovate 18, to bring about change through a systematic approach to innovation. This chapter explores the impact that this innovation programme has had in terms of the changes that have resulted within the Crossrail organization and also whether the initiative has provided a catalyst for change in the industry as a whole. The conclusions from this experience may provide lessons for the management of innovation and change in organizations and industry.

Table 0.16

Industry Sector(s) Featured	Construction, Transport
Key change themes covered	This chapter also strongly relates to the following change chapters and opinion pieces
• Leadership • Vision • Behaviours • Benefits	5 – Change behaviour *(food)* 9 – Change communication and engagement *(leisure and travel)* 13 – Change: organizational capacity and capability *(engineering, local government, central government, telecoms)* 14 – Change: risk *(manufacturing, central government, logistics, energy, mining)* 15 – Change: sustainability *(food, marketing, engineering consultancy)* 18 – Leading the agile organization

Part 2 – The future of organizational change – opinion pieces from future thinkers

Part 2 of *Organizational Change Explained* consists of six short opinion pieces by future thinkers. These opinion pieces provide commentaries on and glimpses of how change might influence organizations in the future, the way organizations might change to accommodate this future and what impact this might have on industry sectors. In particular, these opinion pieces highlight that organizations can no longer rely on one-off, discrete change initiatives because change is now 'always on'. The summaries below show the change themes that each opinion piece addresses and how it relates to other chapters.

Opinion piece 1

'The future and change' authored by Ira Blake A complex set of factors is reshaping our understanding of organizational change and our practice of change management. New workplace paradigms are needed, and change practitioners must reinvent existing models, update competencies and develop new strategies for disseminating change. This opinion piece explores a future where successful change depends on releasing the change capability of employees and resolving associated challenges – such as the locus of control, innovation and purpose – while maintaining the strategic direction of the business.

Table 0.17

Industry Sector(s) Featured	All Industry Sectors
Key change themes covered	This opinion piece also strongly relates to the following change chapters and opinion pieces
• Emergent changes in an adaptive change environment • The changing role of change managers and practitioners • Creating the environment, opportunities and space for change • Evolution of change: from outcomes and ROI to individual contribution and purpose	7 – Change resilience *(pharmaceuticals)* 8 – Change leadership *(not for profit)* 9 – Change communication and engagement *(leisure and travel)* 13 – Change: organizational capacity and capability *(engineering, local government, central government, telecoms)*

Opinion piece 2

'Leading the agile organization' authored by Heather Bewers To date, organizational change has been a project or programme designed to effect an identified change. The programme will be planned, and may be substantial and take time, but there are boundaries and a specific goal. In a VUCA world, the ability to flex and to be agile will be a core competence of organizations and of leaders: change will be the norm, not an applied and separate exercise.

Table 0.18

Industry Sector(s) Featured	All Industry Sectors
Key change themes covered	**This opinion piece also strongly relates to the following change chapters and opinion pieces**
• External drivers of change • Consequences of drivers for organizations • Changing role of leaders – decentralized management, experimentation and failing, relationship and people management	3 – Shaping and design *(pharmaceuticals)* 7 – Change resilience *(pharmaceuticals)* 13 – Change: organizational capacity and capability *(engineering, local government, central government, telecoms)*

Opinion piece 3

'The shift from complicated to complex' authored by Heather Bewers Traditional change (and project) management has relied on a strong 'command and control' approach to achieve planned and predictable outcomes. A connected world makes that predictability more difficult, if not impossible, and a fresh perspective is needed to handle complex, emergent and unforeseen events and outcomes. This opinion piece explores what that perspective will need to cover.

Table 0.19

Industry Sector(s) Featured	All Industry Sectors
Key change themes covered	**This opinion piece also strongly relates to the following change chapters and opinion pieces**
• Issues with traditional change management approach • The implications of a VUCA, connected world	3 – Shaping and design *(pharmaceuticals)* 7 – Change resilience *(pharmaceuticals)*

Industry Sector(s) Featured	All Industry Sectors
• Experiments to understand emergent outcomes rather than planned change • A mindset focused on outcomes, not on specific deliverables or activities	13 – Change: organizational capacity and capability (engineering, local government, central government, telecoms)

Opinion piece 4

'The future and manufacturing' authored by David Caddle What are some of the key technical developments that have influenced, shaped and changed the manufacturing sector to the present, and how will the sector evolve and change in the future? This opinion piece highlights the manufacturing sector now and in the future.

Table 0.20

Industry Sector(s) Featured	Manufacturing
Key change themes covered	This opinion piece also strongly relates to the following change chapters and opinion pieces
• Use of technology • Increasingly dependent on highly skilled workforce • More sustainable – full lifecycle management of products • Innovation – use of 'internet of things'	6 – Change resistance *(financial services, electronics manufacturing)* 13 – Change: organizational capacity and capability *(engineering, local government, central government, telecoms)*

Opinion piece 5

'The future and local government' authored by Peter Glynne This opinion piece outlines six key factors driving the scale, pace and complexity across local government over coming years, exploring what this means for leaders of change across public services. It considers the three major political agendas driving significant and complex change throughout the sector: devolution (moving power to cities and local areas); the need for more joined-up government; and the imperative for continued cost reduction. It also focuses on digital change, specifically considering its impact on the sector's change agenda and how mature the collective approach is. It concludes by examining the collective impact of the six factors, what this means to leaders and how it challenges them on their readiness to deliver such fundamental change.

Table 0.21

Industry Sector(s) Featured	Local Government
Key change themes covered	This opinion piece also strongly relates to the following change chapters and opinion pieces
• Managing a portfolio • Delivering a national strategy • Overcoming barriers to change • Managing common change across multiple organizations	4 – Shaping and design *(energy)* 6 – Change resistance *(financial services, electronics manufacturing)* 15 – Change: sustainability *(food, marketing, engineering consultancy)* 19 – The shift from complicated to complex 22 – The future and healthcare

Opinion piece 6

'The future and healthcare' authored by Adi Gaskell Today, healthcare faces massive technological innovation against a challenging economic background where an ageing population is placing new demands on healthcare providers. This opinion piece features some of the more significant technological innovations and explores their early impacts in the healthcare industry today. It also focuses on the UK National Health Service by detailing some of its attempts to change in order to keep its head above water.

Table 0.22

Industry Sector(s) Featured	Healthcare
Key change themes covered	This opinion piece also strongly relates to the following change chapters and opinion pieces
• Demographic change • Rapid technological change • Open innovation	1 – Why change? *(healthcare)* 2 – Vision *(energy)* 3 – Shaping and design *(pharmaceuticals)* 6 – Change resistance *(financial services, electronics manufacturing)* 17 – The future and change 18 – Leading the agile organization 19 – The shift from complicated to complex

Finally, *Organizational Change Explained* brings together a wide range of perspectives on organizational change now and for the future. It has been written for those currently grappling with, or who are interested in, the practicalities of organizational change. We hope that the range of inspiring authors contributing their change experiences, insights, thoughts and perspectives from their own work within organizational change across multiple change themes and industry sectors will help the reader to explore and model solutions to their own organizational change challenges. We hope you enjoy reading *Organizational Change Explained*, but above all we hope you find the content useful and thought provoking.

References

Baer, D (2014) [Accessed 25 August 2016] How 16 of the oldest companies on earth have been making money for centuries [Online] www.businessinsider.com/oldest-companies-on-earth-2014-8?IR=T

Beinhocker, ED (2007) *The Origin of Wealth: Evolution, complexity, and the radical remaking of economics*, Random House Business Books, London

Chartered Management Institute (2014) *Management 2020*, CMI, Corby, UK

Daepp, MG *et al* (2015) [Accessed 16 August 2016] The mortality of companies [Online] http://rsif.royalsocietypublishing.org/content/12/106/20150120

Department for Business, Innovation and Skills (2015) [Accessed 16 August 2016] Business population for the UK and regions 2015 [Online] www.gov.uk/government/uploads/system/uploads/attachment_data/file/467443/bpe_2015_statistical_release.pdf

Dobbs, R, Manyika, J and Woetzel, J (2015) *No Ordinary Disruption: The four global forces breaking all the trends*, Public Affairs, New York

Greiner, LE (1972) Evolution and revolution as organizations grow. *Harvard Business Review*, 50 (4), pp 37–46

Greiner, L (1998) [Accessed 15 August 2016] Evolution and revolution as organizations grow [Online] www.hbr.org/1998/05/evolution-and-revolution-as-organizations-grow

Haeckel, SH (1992) From 'make and sell' to 'sense and respond'. *Management Review*, 81 (10), pp 3–9

Hannah, L (2009) *The Rise of the Corporate Economy*, Taylor & Francis, Abingdon

Hlupic, V (2014) *The Management Shift: How to harness the power of people and transform your organization for sustainable success*, Palgrave Macmillan, Basingstoke

Jae-kyoung, K (2008) [Accessed 25 August 2016] Centennial firms dry up in Korea, *Korea Times*, 14 May [Online] www.koreatimes.co.kr/www/news/biz/2008/05/123_24196.html

Kotter, J (1996) *Leading Change*, Harvard Business Review Press, Boston, MA

Laloux, F (2014) *Reinventing Organizations: A guide to creating organizations inspired by the next stage of human consciousness*, Nelson Parker, Brussels

Lewin, K (1947) Frontiers in group dynamics: concept, method and reality in social science; social equilibria and social change. *Human Relations*, 1 (June), 5–41

Mayson, S (2014) [Accessed 24 August 2016] Clementi 10 years on (and now for the next 10) [Online] www.stephenmayson.com/2014/12/19/clementi-10-years-on-and-now-for-the-next-10/

O'Hara, WT (2004) *Centuries of Success: Lessons from the world's most enduring family businesses*, Adams Media, Avon, MA

Robertson, B (2015) *Holacracy: The revolutionary management system that abolishes hierarchy*, Portfolio Penguin, London

Taleb, NN (2008) *The Black Swan: The impact of the highly improbable*, Penguin Books, London

PART 1
The reality of organizational change – practitioner case studies and insights

Changing culture through conversation

01

Organizational development in the NHS

KELLY ANGUS, KAREN DUMAIN AND PAUL TAYLOR

Introduction

Organizational development (OD) practitioners have a significant role in leading culture change initiatives by embedding theory into practice. The NHS OD community came together to develop a new digital resource (Do OD, 2014a) that focuses on culture change, learning much about the process along the way. Here we will describe that journey, illustrated by a case study from a successful NHS organization that explored and developed their culture despite complex and challenging circumstances. We'll conclude with reflections on culture change, and tips to help you in your own culture change work, as well as questions to help you reflect on your approach.

We take the view that it is possible to change culture. When you pay attention to organizational culture and take action, you can change it. Our stance assumes that organizations are socially constructed, meaning-making systems. Therefore, culture changes as the conversations in the organizations change. Culture is created in the interactions between people, in our relationships and our behaviour. Culture is everything we say and do. We are the culture of our organizations.

Background

The National Health Service is the largest employer in the UK. Over 1.3 million staff work in the NHS, with over a million patients being seen every 36 hours. Change in the NHS is constant, but in recent years the scale and pace of change have increased exponentially. In 2012, the then Chief Executive of the NHS described the changes needed as 'so big they could be seen from space'.

The NHS is a source of national and public pride in the UK. Public perception of the NHS remains high, despite challenging circumstances. An IPSOS MORI poll in 2013 showed 71 per cent of people agreeing that 'Britain's National Health Service is one of the best in the world'. In the opening ceremony of the 2012 Olympics, the NHS was showcased as a shining example of British culture. The NHS Five Year Forward View – the document that sets out the shared vision for the future of the NHS – notes significant progress in the last decade, including better outcomes in cancer and cardiac care, shorter waits and increased patient satisfaction. However, the Five Year Forward View also notes that the quality of care across the system can vary and that we need to be responding more effectively to the changing needs of our patients.

The changing needs of the population are set against a challenging financial backdrop, described by the Nuffield Trust as 'an unprecedented financial challenge'.

The London School of Economics has stated that the NHS needs to respond to the expectations of its patients, who want care delivered closer to home and their wellbeing to be prioritized.

Culture change

Culture change is one aspect of OD. While we focus here primarily on culture as the key factor, we recognize that aspects of organizations such as leadership, skills, structures, systems and staff engagement are also intrinsically connected. Leading culture change is, in itself, a significant challenge. It's widely acknowledged that organizational change is difficult and takes time. People respond very differently to change. Working in a people-centric context means acknowledging that change is a subjective experience and that there are many differing responses among individuals. One NHS ward manager told us: 'Change is difficult and staff perceive it as a difficult challenge ahead as it is the unknown', whereas another NHS team leader said: 'One of the things I don't like is when they use that phrase "people don't like change" because I love change. So if I hear somebody say "oh, nobody likes change", I say I do.'

Despite a continual cycle of change over recent years, helping staff to embrace change, and in particular culture change, is key to the future success of the NHS.

Why do we take culture seriously in the NHS?

Over the past few years, culture and culture change have been at the top of the NHS agenda. Turn on the radio, watch the news, and there is very likely to be a discussion on the state of the NHS and invariably on how the culture of the top team, or the organization, has played a big part. While the NHS is used to being in the media, underneath this public scrutiny sits a very real concern and understanding of the need for ensuring a compassionate culture across the NHS.

What do we mean by a *compassionate culture*? Following the extensive inquiry into failings at Mid Staffordshire NHS Foundation Trust, Robert Francis QC published his final report in February 2013. It told a story of suffering of many patients, in a culture of secrecy and defensiveness. The inquiry highlighted a whole-system failure, one that should have had checks and balances in place to ensure that patients were treated with dignity. The 1,782-page Francis Report that was the outcome of investigations into Mid Staffordshire Hospitals NHS Trust had 290 recommendations, with major implications for all levels of the health service across England. It called for a whole-service, patient-centred focus. The detailed recommendations did not call for a reorganization of the system, but for a re-emphasis on what is important. The report noted that the extent of failure of the system suggested that a fundamental culture change was needed, and there were four key messages:

- This was a system failure as well as a failure of an organization.
- No single recommendation should be regarded as the solution.
- A fundamental change in culture is required across the NHS.
- There is a need to secure the engagement of every single person serving patients in the change that needs to happen.

Mid Staffordshire was, of course, only one Healthcare Trust, but it was a call to action across the NHS to ensure that such a situation as this was not repeated and that a culture of compassionate care should be the standard for all NHS healthcare organizations. This is amid a changing, complex world and an NHS that strives to support healthcare in the 21st century. The Five Year Forward View recognized that the NHS was at a crossroads and needed to change to move forward.

Meeting the healthcare challenges of the 21st century and of the Francis Review and others has put culture to the fore as a key determinant in what creates safe healthcare systems.

So what's the evidence that culture change is possible? Increasingly there has been a wealth of evidence, most significantly from the work of West and Dawson (2012) on positive links between organizational culture, leadership and reduction in patient mortality. Many definitions of culture – see Schein (1984, 2010) – have in common an emphasis on the shared basic assumptions, norms and values and repeated patterns of behaviours of particular groups and teams. Culture becomes 'the way things are done around here'. Edgar Schein and complexity experts such as Glenda Eoyang at the Human Systems Dynamics Institute (www.hsdinstitute.org) suggest that identifying these patterns, similarities and differences is the first step to changing culture.

Also highly influential in the NHS has been the work of West et al (2001), who have analysed data and information from annual staff surveys in which all NHS healthcare organizations are required to take part. Professor West has been able to evidence very clearly that high staff engagement, and creating the right culture and conditions, lead to better patient care and lower mortality. As we look at whole systems and what makes a healthy organization, we know that organizational culture is one of the key variables or elements that contribute to high-performing and effective healthcare organizations.

Leading global experts in the field of organizational development have developed 'big system' models that identify the vital components that, working together, make effective high-performing organizations. Two well-known and well-used models, Dr Mee-Yan Cheung-Judge's four frames model (2015) and the Burke–Litwin (1992) model, both identify culture as a key component.

OD practitioners leading culture change

The NHS has a rich history of OD practice as a lever for change. Here we turn our attention to the role of OD practitioners leading and facilitating culture change. In the NHS we describe one of the characteristics of OD practice as enabling people to transform systems. We highlight the importance of using an OD model to diagnose issues and respond by structuring interventions that go beyond culture change as well as looking at the capability of OD practitioners leading change.

Culture change sits firmly in the domain of OD – a field of practice rooted in behavioural science that enables people to transform systems. Practitioners of OD think systemically about how an organization can improve its abilities to deliver strategic goals by examining the levers of change as well as how organizations can sustain the culture they need. Culture change is a key component of our work in OD within the NHS. Does the organization have a strategically appropriate culture that facilitates high performance? For the NHS this is about high-quality patient care.

Using OD theory in practice

Understanding your organizational culture is a key determinant in both knowing 'the way things are done around here' and looking to what you may need to change in the future. For the NHS, ensuring a compassionate culture means both identifying the current culture and asking the curious questions to enable a vision of what a compassionate culture could be like. And then, of course, the important 'how' and 'what' to make this happen. It's everyone's business – senior leaders and boards, clinical leaders, team managers and front-line staff who together can make a significant difference to patient care.

Building a new OD intervention

To support the national response to the Francis Report, we undertook a project to develop a new resource for OD practitioners, showing how the community could contribute to a major shift in the culture of the NHS. We saw this as an important call to action for OD.

Members of the NHS OD community collaborated to design and build a new resource that would support OD practitioners with their culture change work. Ten organizations were supported by the national team to share their OD experience and stories, with the goal of co-creating a brand new culture change tool. The finished product was turned into a digital OD intervention that is accessed through smartphones and tablets.

Our work on culture change was triggered by two key questions: How do we develop compassionate cultures? How do we create organizational conditions that encourage openness and transparency?

The first outcome of our work was created by a group of OD practitioners who worked to curate and develop tools, resources and guidance. This was made available as an offer of support to the OD community.

The next stage of the project involved us working collaboratively to think more deeply about culture change on a system level. Using action research methodology, we worked with ten NHS organizations, who self-identified either as a 'beacon' or as a 'pilot': beacons were organizations that had undertaken culture change work with significant OD activity and reported good progress in their efforts; pilots were organizations who identified as being at the early stages of their culture change journeys. Our intention was to provide those organizations with support and help to understand why things work and why things don't when it comes to culture change.

One of our initial goals from the project was to develop an OD tool that would identify the conditions that need to be created to achieve maximum impact from culture change interventions. Two questions focused our approach: How can we create cultures where compassionate care is the norm? How can we best make use of new technologies in our OD practice?

Our work was supported by Southampton University Business School (www.southampton.ac.uk/business-school/). Dr Stefan Cantore worked with us to shape and develop the culture change project, bringing both academic rigour and a fresh perspective to our culture change challenge.

Theory and practice

In creating our culture change tool we drew on principles of dialogic organizational development, based on the work of Bushe and Marshak (2015). In more traditional OD approaches, change is seen as linear and planned. Organizations are viewed as machines, and when they 'break' they can be 'fixed'. We look for problems and identify solutions, but this can often be slow. On the other hand, dialogic OD accepts that organizations are complex, living human systems. Using an inquiry approach, predominantly based on strengths instead of weaknesses, change can be implemented rapidly. We chose to adopt a dialogic mindset in support of the culture change project. The dialogic mindset is based on a set of assumptions that underpin the approach. This includes an acceptance that reality and relationships are socially constructed and that the organizations we work in are meaning-making systems. In these systems, language matters, and the creation of change necessitates a need to change our conversations.

Alongside the principles of dialogic OD, we also drew on the principles of appreciative inquiry (Cooperrider and Srivastva, 1987). This is an approach to change, often known as AI, that focuses on strengths, successes and positives rather than problems and negatives. It is the art and practice of asking questions that strengthen a system's capacity to learn and develop its potential. It is based on the premise that organizations change in the direction in which they inquire. So an organization that inquiries into problems will keep finding them, but an organization that attempts to appreciate what is best in itself will discover more and more that is good.

Part of our project was inquiring into what had worked well in changing culture in organizations. We reflected on the interventions and practices that had generated success. From this, using action research, we were able to build generative thinking and ideas to inform the shape and content of the emerging OD tool.

Early on in the process we had a conversation with an OD practitioner who was keen to be involved in the culture change work. However, when we explained our approach of collective inquiry, they decided not to continue with the selection process, stating 'we just need you to give us the answer. We don't have time to work it out.' We noticed that the prevailing culture in the system appears to be finding quick answers that suit the one-size-fits-all approach. Our response was to be counter-cultural and bring some difference into the discussion.

This conversation helped to shape the tone of the project. We had been picking up a sense of urgency in the system, a need to find solutions and to find them now. This spoke of the traditional approach detailed above – the machine has broken and we need a fix. While we didn't naturally agree with that approach, it can be seductive to believe that there is a single answer that will fix everything. We took a decision at that point to avoid walking that path. We also realized that there were already great examples of OD practice and culture change in the system, and we wanted to build on this. Our work would be focused not on providing answers but on creating the conditions of inquiry where questions can be asked that will enable organizations to reach their own conclusions about what they need to do about their organizational culture. If only there was a single silver bullet that would work for everyone! Unfortunately, it's more complex than that, and the tone of our project was established. We would ask questions, not provide answers.

We developed three principles to underpin our approach:

- Change happens through action.
- Conversations spark action.
- Good questions start great conversations.

The 10 organizations working with us on the project had come together so that they could meet each other, share ideas for the work and contribute to the design of the end product. We worked collaboratively, in the spirit of appreciative inquiry, using dialogic OD methodology to deliberately stimulate our thinking about culture change and help us explore our individual and collective narratives. As the people in the room told their stories of culture change, we noticed something surprising. The pilots had all done some good work with culture change. Even though they may have been early on in their journey, they still all had useful stories to share.

The OD culture change tool

The main outcome of the collaborative appreciative inquiry was the development and release of a new OD culture change tool (2014b). We decided to launch the tool as a digital resource, available on iOS and Android platforms. This would enable practitioners to literally have the tool in their hands whenever it was needed, and it is available as part of a free Do OD app that can be downloaded by anyone, anywhere. This culture change tool is a conversation stimulator. It can be used by individuals, teams and organizations (NHS and non-NHS) as a method for having conversations about culture. The tool consists of 144 questions focused across four areas: you, your team, your organization and your stakeholders. There's no right or wrong way to approach the questions. You start wherever you need to start and work your way through the questions in the order that suits. As you get to the end of a section, the app gives you a visual representation of your responses so that you can track progress. Alongside the OD culture change tool, we developed a set of accompanying resources called *Pointers* and *Practice*. Pointers consist of academic articles, culture theory, models and frameworks that can help to shape thinking about culture change. Practice resources are tried and tested practical OD tools and interventions that can be used to host dialogic spaces in organizations. The Pointers and Practice resources can be accessed via the app. We invite you to explore the tool and the app to consider how you might use it to stimulate conversations about culture change in your own context.

One of the 10 organizations, Northumbria Healthcare NHS Foundation Trust, has shared their culture change story.

CASE STUDY   Northumbria Healthcare NHS Foundation Trust

Northumbria Healthcare NHS Foundation Trust (NHFT) provides acute and community care to the population of North Tyneside and acute, community care and adult social care to the population of Northumberland. The Trust covers a population of around 500,000 people in the most rural county in England with approximately 9,300 staff.

The Trust had a proven track record and long-standing investment in OD, and the Do OD project around culture change came along at a time when the Trust's senior leadership team was focused on developing its organizational culture in response to the Robert Francis enquiry. We expressed an interest in sharing our experiences with the Do OD team and other organizations following a call to action from the Do OD project for organizations to get involved, but also to learn from others and explore in more depth what our intrinsic organizational evidence was telling us about our culture. Questions we started to ask ourselves were:

- What is our organizational culture?
- What influences our organizational culture?
- Can we describe our organizational culture?

All these questions produced much debate and discussion, not only within the HR/OD function but also with wider colleagues across the organization. NHFT was successfully chosen by the Do OD team as a beacon site to share our experiences with others. Our evidence was telling us that NHFT had a strong foundational base of robust patient experience and staff experience data over a number of years and we knew that this was a fundamental factor of our culture. Based on the research from Professor Michael West, the Trust strongly believed that, strategically, culture can make, and was making, a difference to its organizational outcomes, most importantly the quality of care that was being delivered to patients.

At this time, NHFT had a number of key organizational challenges that were recognized as potential strong influences on its organizational culture. These included:

- a wide geographical area of service delivery covering the most rural county in England, Northumberland;
- understanding its changing patient demographics and recognizing that elderly care was its core business;

- development of a new specialist emergency care hospital (the very first of its kind nationally) and the redevelopment of its existing sites;
- a cost improvement programme to deliver significant savings.

A strong ethos and associated support for staff development and OD interventions has been championed at board level for a significant period of time by the Chief Executive and the Executive Director of HR/OD. With their support, the HR/OD team started to consider what cultural intelligence it already had in terms of data/information and used this information to describe and articulate the elements that were strong influences and possible enablers to facilitate positive organizational change. Using a variety of culture intelligence surveys, such as the findings from a bespoke 'culture survey', the Staff Survey and the Friends and Family Test, as well as analysing the data from its real-time Patient Experience programme, the Trust was able to correlate and sense-check its organizational culture using thematic analysis to consider trends and areas requiring further exploration. This initial piece of scoping work revealed that the organizational culture narrative for the organization was supported by four key themes of activity, which have a significant impact on what staff, patients and stakeholders tell us about our organizational culture.

These four key themes were:

1 *Engagement*. Data from multiple sources told us that communication and engagement were of vital importance to staff. The NHFT purposely works in partnership with staff, trade unions, governors (staff and public) and its wider partners to ensure that they are involved in issues that may affect them, but also that they are involved and informed about operational matters as well as key strategic projects such as the new specialist emergency care hospital.

2 *Patient and staff experience*. The NHFT had successfully implemented Dr Kate Granger's #hellomynameis campaign. This campaign had enhanced a programme of training and support for staff to focus on quality and safety and to deliver compassionate care and kindness to patients. From the Staff Survey, staff told us that providing high-quality care for patients was significantly important to them in relation to how satisfied they felt in their role. Our staff also strongly stated that NHFT 'put patients first'.

3 *Values*. Our data were telling us that the values of the organization, which were shaped by staff across the Trust through engagement events, resonated with staff and our wider stakeholders across the organization. Developing the values was the start of a journey; NHFT has since built a plethora of its activities around the values of the organization. One example is that the Trust

worked with clinical and non-clinical staff to develop and refine its value-based recruitment process, aiming to identify candidates whose personal values are aligned to the organizational values. Staff training is also values focused, and the annual Trust staff awards recognize staff who advocate and embed the organization's values. Values were a strong feature across multiple sources of data that we examined.

4 *Communication*. The data evidenced that both internal and external communications for the Trust are well focused and that there is regular contact to and from the executive team through a variety of channels. Chief executive face-to-face road shows regularly take place; these enable staff to feed back and share ideas to facilitate improvement at the most senior level. It was clear that where action is taken as a result of such communications, this has a significantly positive impact on organizational culture; for example, the hospital parking system was changed following feedback from staff during these road shows. Similarly, using digital communication has proved to have a positive impact with staff: using social media, staff communications focused on a #proud campaign to encourage staff, patients and carers to feel proud in relation to the care received and/or behaviours demonstrated at NHFT. This has enhanced and grown since its inception.

One of the key strategic challenges for NHFT was to open the first specialist emergency care hospital in the country in June 2015. It was recognized during the early stages that team culture was a key component of the preparatory work required to lead staff through this significant change. Introducing the new specialist emergency care hospital was well planned, and the model of care has considerably changed the way that care is delivered to patients. Throughout the pre- and post-opening activities of the specialist emergency care hospital, the Trust remained focused on developing and maintaining a positive culture by ensuring that its values remained at the centre of communications with staff. Embarking on a journey to develop its values base, the Trust formulated areas of work to develop and embed the values further into the organization; these were focused on the employee journey, and a conscious decision was made to engage with staff and patients to ensure that the values represented the heart of the organization's purpose and being. This approach contributed to the successful opening of the new specialist emergency care hospital.

Following on from this work, organizational culture remains a key component of the Trust's HR/OD strategy. The Trust has continually engaged with staff and stakeholders through a variety of methods to seek their views in order to ensure that its cultural intelligence remains robust and that it has continual action planning in place to support its ongoing cultural development.

The completion of the NHS Employers case study enabled us to focus on what our cultural themes were and to provide a platform for future ongoing cultural development. Our case study and video can be found at: http://www.nhsemployers.org/campaigns/organizational-development/do-od-culture-change-app/storyofenquiry.

The Trust has won a number of local, regional and national awards and most recently has been awarded the HSJ Best Place to Work Award (2015) within the NHS, and regularly receives a highly scoring staff survey.

Conclusion

What did we learn along the way? Our 10 healthcare organizations, our academic partner and the Do OD team reflected on what we have learnt, and below are some of our top tips on culture change:

- Support and commit: at the highest levels (senior leadership team and board level), this is crucial to success and senior sponsorship is essential. This support is key; staff will 'look up' and look to the people at the top to become role models and demonstrate 'the way we do things around here'.

- Leadership: encourage leaders to think about their own behaviours, and about what they need to role-model and demonstrate. They are always visible, as is what they say and what they do.

- Involve, engage and empower: staff need to be at the centre of everything you do; they will take care of the organizational key purpose (in the case of the NHS it is the patients) and the organization if you take care of them.

- Communication: having good links with the communications team and a robust plan for sending messages into the organization is fundamental. The message needs to be consistent and repeated often with a variety of communications to communicate opportunities and successes.

- Use of language: when communicating about OD, use language that resonates with the organization. Within the NHS, patient and staff stories are the most powerful engagement tools.

- Develop bespoke interventions: understand and customize what works for your organization and your context. There is no 'one size fits all' approach, and focus and activities will change over time.

- Clarify: be clear about what the OD team is about and its purpose. This helps to develop greater organizational presence, credibility and confidence in OD as a powerful enabler of change.

- Space: changing culture is challenging, and so creating safe places for OD practitioners to reflect on experiences and practice is vital to ensure resilience. Protect time to create space for both the OD team and the organization; for example, through a culture steering group if required. Include some of the dissenting voices if possible, as they are very helpful when engaged as change agents.

- Stakeholders: map your key stakeholders and engage with as many professions as possible, keeping a clear line of regular communications with these at all times.

- Resourcing: ensure that adequate resources are available and that you use the skills and talents of your people to the best advantage.

- Expertise: ensure that the OD team have the expertise in culture to promote confidence and competence.

- Networks: use internal and external networks and resources to gather as much information about best practice and learning as possible.

For those leading culture change in organizations, there are particular points that became significant to us throughout our journey. We offer these as words of encouragement, support and advice:

- Keep going. There will be obstacles, but be clear about your vision and strategy, which should align with the organization's overall objectives.

- Build a network of engaged and positive colleagues to support your initiative.

- As consultants, recognize the inherent difficulties of being part of the system you are helping change, and know where your support is in the organization.

- Recognize that you, as part of OD, are a role model for whatever future culture you're looking for; if you don't embody it, why would others?

- The work is emergent and you must have an agile and flexible approach.

- Don't try to eat the elephant in one sitting.

- Don't wait for all the conditions to be perfect – start somewhere and demonstrate value.

- Be the change you want to see.

Key questions

To end, we offer 10 questions for you to consider as you embark on your own culture change journey:

1 What are your own beliefs about culture change?

2 What are the contextual conditions that shape your organization?

3 What assumptions do you make about change in your organization?

4 What intrinsic organizational intelligence do you have that could help you describe a narrative for culture change?

5 What is your trigger for culture change?

6 What does organizational development look like in your organization?

7 Which OD theories and models shape your culture change efforts?

8 What practical tools and resources do you draw on to support your work?

9 What is your organizational culture change story?

10 What is the conversation you need to have?

References

Burke, WW and Litwin, GH (1992) A causal model of organization performance and change. *Journal of Management*, **18** (3), pp 523–45

Bushe, GR and Marshak, RJ (2015) *Dialogic Organization Development: The theory and practice of transformational change*, Berret-Koehler, Oakland, CA

Cheung-Judge, MY and Holbeche, L (2015) *Organization Development: A practitioner's guide for OD and HR*, Kogan Page, London

Cooperrider, D and Srivastva, S (1987) Appreciative inquiry in organizational life research. *Organization Change and Development*, **1**, pp 129–69

Do OD (2014a) [Accessed 29 June 2016] Culture, behaviour and values resources [Online] http://nhsemployers.org/campaigns/organisational-development/do-od-tools-and-resources/culture-change

Do OD (2014b) [Accessed 27 June 2016] OD culture change tool [Online] www.nhsemployers.org/DoODapp

Schein, E (1984) Coming to a new awareness of organizational culture. *Sloan Management Review*, **25** (2), p 3

Schein, E (2010) *Organizational Culture and Leadership*, 4th edn, Jossey-Bass, San Francisco

The Mid Staffordshire NHS Foundation Trust Public Inquiry (2013) *Report of The Mid Staffordshire NHS Foundation Trust Public Inquiry*, chaired by Robert Francis QC, The Stationery Office, London

West, MA *et al* (2001) The link between the management of employees and patient mortality in acute hospitals. *International Journal of Human Resource Management*, **13** (8), pp 1299–310

West, MA and Dawson, JF (2012) [Accessed 27 June 2016] Employee engagement and NHS performance. The Kings Fund [Online] www.kingsfund.org.uk/sites/files/kf/employee-engagement-nhs-performance-west-dawson-leadership-review2012-paper.pdf

Sparking change

A world of change in electricity transmission

STEPHANIE McGREGOR

Introducing OFTO – a spark of change

Energy is possibly the sexiest it's ever been. A quick internet search for images of 'Paris Climate Change Conference' shows the leaders of 196 nations, hands raised in celebration, 'clapping, cheering and whistling wildly, embracing and weeping' (Harvey, 2015) at achieving agreement to new future goals to combat climate change. With the utmost respect for their considerable efforts, I'll defer celebrating until aspirations are followed with tangible industry-, sector- and country-level change.

As the driving force of progress, energy is at the centre of the climate change challenge. The challenge goes beyond plugging in more renewables and simply getting you and me to commit to 'greener' habits and technology. The challenge is one of time, investment and infrastructure at every industry level. Can we, as an industry, invest enough in markets, infrastructure, technology and education in order to achieve the best outcomes for future generations? The industry faces a plethora of hurdles, such as ageing and no longer fit-for-purpose assets, growing technical complexity and timetables for delivering change which are longer than political tenures and shareholder-return windows.

The change challenge requires rethinking the fundamentals and a focus on achieving positive generational impacts. The UK Offshore Transmission Owner (OFTO) regime represents one such rethink: a disruptive market redesign in the electricity industry that has sparked sizeable change, unlocked investment into energy and delivered benefits for consumers today and tomorrow. It offers a new model for further industry change if its achievements and lessons are properly understood and embraced.

This is the progressive story of how the OFTO regime triggered significant change in the electricity networks industry. This chapter looks at how the OFTO regime disrupted the industry, what the change drivers were, what made the change possible and what lessons this disruption offers, from my perspective at the time as the then Director Offshore Transmission with the Office of Gas and Electricity Markets (Ofgem). The views in this chapter are personal and do not necessarily reflect the views of the government or Ofgem.

The story before OFTO: the status quo

Networks and transmission

Fixed networks are the major building blocks of communities and economies, be they gas pipelines, water pipes, sewerage waste systems, rail lines, telecommunications, fibre networks or electricity lines. Networks underpin the basic services we deem necessary for modern, healthy and acceptable development.

In the electricity industry, networks are the fixed lines and connections of cables, carrying power from the producers (eg wind farms, nuclear power stations) to users (eg our houses, schools, businesses). There are two different types of cable in a network – transmission and distribution. Transmission lines do the 'heavy lifting' by carrying bulk volumes of high-voltage power over long distances very quickly – a bit like highways. These lines can be strung on pylons, buried underground or laid underwater. The rest of the network is made up of distribution lines, which carry power from the bigger transmission lines to the front doors of homes, work and schools – a bit like feeder roads and streets for the network. Without the transmission lines there wouldn't be enough power to carry to all our homes and businesses.

To understand the scale and importance of UK and European transmission networks, consider a few facts:

- The UK uses enough electricity every year to boil 2 trillion kettles (Ofgem, 2016).
- The UK has 813,000 km of electricity lines, including just 20,000 km of transmission lines (Ofgem, 2016).
- Over one-fifth of the average UK consumer electricity bill annually goes towards the cost of the electricity network (Ofgem, 2016).
- The EU has 10 million km of power lines and 298,092 km of transmission lines (Eurelectric, 2013).

The status quo

Before OFTO, the UK electricity transmission industry:

- was a network of fixed assets designed to serve a stable range of land-based fossil-fuel and nuclear generators – with a new generation coming along infrequently;
- had assets grouped in geographic portfolios for ownership, with large portfolios for operational, funding and cost economies of scale;
- viewed future development investment as being best done through the existing large portfolios.

Until the 1980s, the UK had a publicly owned, centrally controlled electricity market. By 1990 the industry had been privatized. Because of the characteristics described above, transmission lines became the sole responsibility of three monopoly-style privatized and regulated transmission owners (TOs): National Grid Electricity Transmission, Scottish Power and SSE. To help the model work, National Grid set up a separate subsidiary entity to take the additional responsibility for overall network system operation across all assets, that is, controlling the flows of power across the whole network.

In this landscape, a new power generator would apply for a connection point to the transmission network and they'd be given a location and a date for connecting and advised of the connection fees. The generator would also pay ongoing user charges to enable TOs to recover their ongoing costs of delivering and developing the network.

Ofgem (the UK electricity and gas market regulator) sets the user charges that TOs levy on generators for using the network. Ofgem also sets the regulated allowance and return on investment that TOs make under a periodic assessment (price control). Prior to 2008, any new transmission investment was delivered by the incumbent TOs and funded under the price control model. New forms of generation came along infrequently and there was no obvious need to change the industry model, until the 2000s when it became clear that electricity transmission could not stay the same.

Designing a new industry model

The new industry model for electricity transmission, the OFTO regime, was established as a result of a disruptive journey of change (Figure 2.1):

Figure 2.1   Change process resulting in the OFTO regime

Drivers

The drivers that pushed the electricity transmission industry to disruptive change, by introducing the OFTO regime, occurred nearly nine years earlier than the change itself. They led to an unexpected level of change, explaining why it later proved to be so disruptive.

My interviews with leading electricity transmission industry players revealed different views on the forces that led to the creation of the OFTO regime. New industry players, who came into the market because of the change through the creation of the OFTO regime, and who had far stronger perceptions that formalized government policy and targets within the UK and Europe, such as emissions targets, energy efficiency and competition policies, drove the change. However, existing players differed in their views – the drivers for change evolved over time and began quite differently. What distinguished enablers was whether something could be a forceful driver or trigger for change in its own right, or whether it was simply a crucial factor for making change possible and shaping its ultimate form.

The two drivers for the creation of the OFTO regime were (1) rapid change in a related industry: wind farms and related technology; and (2) industry players' needs and behaviours.

Driver 1: Rapid change in a related industry: wind farms and related technology

Wind farms have been the leading growth story in UK renewable energy. Fed by continuously evolving government subsidies, the renewables industry has grown from contributing 1.7 per cent of UK energy provision in 1997 to 7 per cent in 2014 (House of Commons Library, 2008), and is still growing. Since 2004, the growth in renewables, particularly offshore wind, has created demands for new electricity transmission infrastructure and pressures on existing land-based transmission infrastructure.

The fast growth in new offshore wind farms represented more new generators plugging into the onshore system than ever before. This presented three major challenges:

- The onshore network didn't have enough existing physical capacity to easily provide all these new connection points.

- The onshore network was designed for predictable and controllable fossil-fuel power sources. Wind power is vastly different; it's variable – due to when, and how strongly, the wind blows. It can't be drawn on at will to meet demand. Hence it is referred to as being 'intermittent' and creates unique pressures for networks, such as variability and 'noise', that networks weren't originally designed to handle.

- The 'rule books' – codes, standards, frameworks – that govern the obligations and technical standards for participants (the TOs) in the electricity transmission network were established over a decade earlier and hadn't foreseen the need to connect generators sitting out in the ocean. At the physical point where the offshore wind farm's cable connected to the onshore system they needed to comply with the 'rule books'; however, up to that point their design, standards and controls could be designed according as then felt suited their project, as they were large and costly private links.

Rapid expansion of offshore wind development in the UK created significant pressures and demands, which forced TOs, the developers, the government and the regulator to consider the question: How best to connect this growing volume of new offshore wind power to the existing UK electricity network in the most cost- and time-effective way?

Driver 2: Industry players' needs and behaviours

The needs and behaviours of the early offshore wind farm developers inadvertently drove the *industry* change that led to the OFTO model. The earliest UK developers of offshore wind farm projects were entrepreneurial, broke new ground and in regulatory terms were in unchartered waters (pun intended). They built their private offshore cable links focused on selling their 'cleaner' power. However, as project scale grew, developers worried about the significant cost and resource burden ahead, particularly for longer, bigger, private transmission cables to plug their power in onshore. They were also concerned about the traditional TOs' capacity to provide the new onshore connection points in time.

These early developers could see how the onshore TOs were funded and rewarded to maintain and develop the onshore transmission network. Cost and delivery risk for the onshore network was on the TOs' balance sheets and ultimately recovered from consumers, even with generators' user charges. Onshore network costs were shared. Onshore generators could also be paid compensation when they were constrained off the network by TOs when their energy was surplus to needs. To the offshore wind farm developers, building private offshore cable links, there was great appeal in finding a new way to access some of the onshore network benefits and support.

Hence, in the early to mid-2000s, a number of early developers began lobbying the government and Ofgem for their offshore transmission assets to be shifted to some form of competitively regulated transmission ownership. I'm told they were unrelenting in their lobbying. Their varied arguments included that lifting the cost burden off their shoulders would ensure faster development of the offshore wind farm industry, bringing forward economic and climate change benefits. The government, focused on supporting renewables, listened.

Other successes gave the government confidence that new models for infrastructure funding and delivery could work, but none that had been applied in regulated electricity networks. So the government and the regulator opened the door for potential changes by creating offshore transmission competition in the 2004 Energy Act. While detail about what 'competition' might look like was thin on the ground, this change was the beginning of regulatory and policy momentum for change.

By 2007 the government had been emboldened by further infrastructure success in other sectors and renewed commitments to EU targets on decarbonization and renewables. The groundwork was there for the creation of the Department of Energy and Climate Change the following year. The government and regulator built on the idea of offshore transmission competitions, by fully exploring and developing options to support the offshore renewable sector.

Opportunities and circumstances in government and Ofgem in 2007 drove the evolution of offshore transmission. There was a transition in thinking at the highest levels of Ofgem. The launch of the RPI-X@20 review (2008) of the approach to network regulation indicated a desire to see the tradi-tional approaches evolve. Interviewees used the words 'committed' and 'open-minded' to describe mobilization of civil servants and senior politicos around the idea of developing a form of competition in offshore transmis-sion based on the legislative door opened back in 2004.

There were fruitful alternative models for competition seeing results in other industries and new transmission assets coming forward that were different enough from the onshore network, due to operating in offshore environments, to merit closer examination of options for a new approach.

While providing a seemingly neat separable sequence, these drivers created a force for change during a complicated decade of overlapping developments and growing industries running to catch up.

Enablers

At the chapter outset I stated that agreement to future climate change goals by world leaders is a considerable achievement: therein lies a major change driver. But the effectiveness of change will be in the conversion to tangible industry-, sector- and country-level goals. These must be measurable in time and outcomes, and the key is in the change enablers.

The powerful drivers above weren't going to shape the OFTO change alone. These enablers shaped and propelled the scale and nature of change (Figure 2.2):

Enabler 1: Active policy development

The broad consensus among interviewees was that the policy development and industry engagement by government/Ofgem was deep, responsive and considered. My first impression upon joining Ofgem in 2008 was that in two decades working in public and private infrastructure sectors, I'd never seen this level of depth and reflection documented in policy development.

The government/Ofgem partnership in policy development was focused on answering the following critical questions: How should the industry framework support the growing and faster-paced roll-out of offshore generation? What are the potential models, including funding structures?

The main policy development and the stakeholder engagement activity was lengthy, over five years from 2004; it shaped the final OFTO regime such that it would change the industry landscape, and later create wider,

Figure 2.2   Enablers helping shape the OFTO change

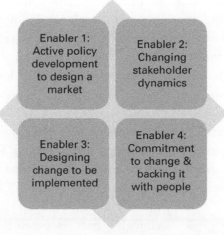

Figure 2.3   Active policy development for offshore transmission

2003
- Energy White paper on low carbon economy.
- Government of Ofgem commit to adressing offshore transmission needs of offshore wind farm developers.

2004
- Changes to the Energy Act 2004 create the legal ability to develop regulatory and competition arrangements for offshore transmission.

2005/06
- Government of Ofgem initiate studies and consultation on offshore grids, models for regulated competition and charging, including workshops and forums.
- Government extend the regulation framework for onshore transmission ie 'rule books' to cover offshore transmission.

2007
- Government decide on a non-exclusive competition for awarding licences for ownership of offshore transmission, offshore distribution links were exempt and EU third package, with unbundling provisions affecting transmission and generation, proposed.
- Policy and regulatory developments underway on the regulatory framework.

2008
- Consultations and refinement by Ofgem and Government on detailed design of legal aspects of a competitive regime including licences, codes, frameworks, execution structure, costs and comparative competitive models.
- Substantial conclusion of the design of the OFTO regime.

2009
- Creation of secondary regulations and cost recovery models to support execution of OFTO competitions.
- OFTO regime launched.
- Funding support from EIB secured.

albeit unexpected, change. The history of active policy development around the question of what to do about offshore transmission is summarized in Figure 2.3.

Looking back at published industry responses to consultation and development from 2005 onwards, the government and Ofgem worked with industry stakeholders to genuinely test and evaluate options while shaping the solution for offshore transmission. Key challenges that arose over the course of policy development were to:

- challenge whether simply extending the traditional status quo model was the best solution against the value of change;
- debate and assess the value metrics in doing something new;
- assess the need and opportunity to bring additional operator capacity, finance and expertise into the market to support high rates of growth;
- satisfy the European Directive called the Third Energy Liberalisation Reform Package [aka Third Package] by the European Commission. Published in 2009, this required the ownership of transmission assets to be unbundled from that of generation assets.

The change was to design an effective new market. By the time change was ignited with the OFTO regime launch in 2009, it was based on robust, well-debated and considered foundations.

Enabler 2: Changing stakeholder dynamics

The stakeholder landscape notably expanded and diversified from 2004 through to implementation in 2009.

The level of engagement, high-quality contributions and competing views over time (documented in the Ofgem and Department of Energy & Climate Change (DECC) online publication archives) clearly influenced the design of the OFTO regime and how it came to be implemented. Without it, fewer and less impactful leaps in the market design would have been made. The stakeholders (Figure 2.4) could be characterized as the existing TOs and fossil-fuel/nuclear generation players, plus:

- new generators with a greater variety of multi-national/multicultural participants;
- potential new transmission owners and operators with no previous transmission experience;
- greater numbers and variety of financiers and funders at the direct engagement level.

Figure 2.4   Stakeholders engaged in the OFTO design

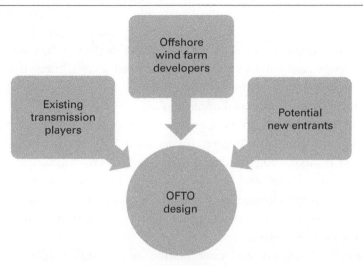

Stakeholder dynamics – existing transmission players   As the main existing stakeholders, the three TOs and the System Operator (SO) faced a triple whammy of challenges, while also considering the OFTO design:

1 *More new generator connections being sought post 2005 than ever before, beyond their planned administrative and technical capacity*: increased the demand on TOs to create and deliver new connections and to forward plan and forecast in new ways. This created the potential to challenge any case made to take over a growing pipeline of offshore transmission assets.

2 *Technical consequences of increasing volumes of intermittent wind power coming into the onshore network*: resulting in the need for rapid network, systems and technology upgrades by the existing TOs.

3 *The risk that the existing TOs' traditional transmission line mandate might be undermined by government and regulator decisions to address offshore wind farm developer needs*: Since privatization there had been little challenge to the notion that monopoly structures were a necessary and natural part of the transmission industry. Yet here the emerging offshore transmission need was challenging that notion. TO submissions to Ofgem and government consistently show preferences for extending the status quo, ie their responsibilities extended to cover offshore transmission, albeit with tweaks to reflect the new demands of offshore transmission.

Stakeholder dynamics – offshore wind farm developers In the early years, wind farm players were a group of early adopters with a disparate mix of entrepreneurial starts-ups like Warwick Energy (Barrow and Thanet wind farms), larger consortia and solo players like E.ON (Robin Rigg wind farm). One interviewee involved at the time described it as a 'time of intensely driven project-oriented behaviours fuelled by limited resources and significant worries of early financial implosion'.

In the early days of lobbying government for an alternative solution to the offshore transmission burden, it was a more a collection of individual voices. As projects progressed and new waves of larger projects emerged, the mix of developers and investors changed as newer parties joined the industry. Developers looked above their own project horizons, became more active in industry bodies and began to challenge each other and cultivated joint views on key issues.

A greater coherence and coordination among stakeholders coincided with the finalization of the OFTO concept in 2007. With details on the mechanics of the OFTO regime being developed through to 2009, while the wider comfort with the concept lifting the cost and ownership burden remained, some serious concerns raised were:

- loss of control of the transmission assets that their wind farms would solely rely on to transport power to shore;
- inability to gain profit from transferring ownership of the offshore transmission assets they had built;
- complexity, cost and timing of the regime;
- the level of influence they would have on the design of future links;
- inability to access all the benefits enjoyed by onshore generators, such as compensation payments for being 'constrained off';
- potential consequences of mismatching asset life of the wind farm versus offshore transmission assets.

Stakeholder dynamics – potential new entrants There were a few new entrants to the wind farm developer market by 2007/08. However, more significant was the creation of a stakeholder group that didn't yet exist – future OFTOs. The OFTO regime design allowed for entirely new entrants with no previous exposure to either generation or electricity networks.

Government and Ofgem managed to flush out some potential new entrants' perspectives through examination of competition models in other industries. Over time, a small and disparate range of potential new entrant 'stakeholders' emerged, but it wasn't really until late 2008/09, with the commencement of the first OFTO regime competition close at hand, that potential new entrants started to emerge more strongly.

A great many of these new players had a steep learning curve, but their primary focus was on:

- entering the market on a level playing field if the onshore TOs chose to tender through the competitions;
- understanding what risks they would be expected to take;
- ensuring that project finance could be matched against corporate balance sheet solutions that existing utilities might bring.

The growing presence of potential new entrants in 2008/09 also created greater pressure for other stakeholders such as the TOs. It also gave stronger comfort to wind farm developers who were concerned about OFTO numbers.

Enabler 3: Designing change for implementation

Beyond policy development and stakeholder engagement, experience has led me to believe that the most important enablers are designing implementation and the commitment of the right people.

Design for implementation requires a concept to be worked through into detailed mechanics, that is, how it will work practically at the front line. This involves collaboration, detailed mapping, testing/re-testing, the laying out of precise pathways, reiteration of lessons and understanding, actions consistent with design, and continuous measurement during implementation. Without this, the risks are prolonged engagement loops, marginal steps of action, poor measurement and higher odds of failure in taking leaps to deliver actual change.

By 2007 the OFTO regime concept was:

- Offshore transmission links would be built, operated and financed by new offshore transmission owners – aka OFTO Build.
- Transitional arrangements, to deal with generators already constructing assets, would transfer assets to OFTOs for financing and operations – Generator Build.
- All OFTOs would be appointed by competitive tender process and open to any entity able to meet the criteria.
- Tenderers would bid a regulated revenue stream to recoup construction, finance and operations costs.

Figure 2.5 OFTO assets

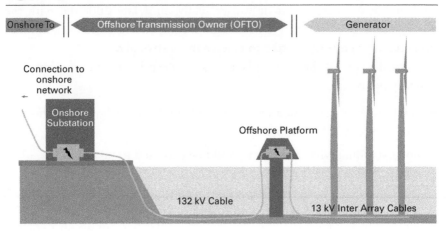

SOURCE Ofgem (2009)

- Wind farm developers would pay for using the assets via an annual charge.
- UK consumers would continue to pay for these assets even if a wind farm ceased operating.
- As Figure 2.5 shows, OFTO assets would include the offshore platform and subsea transmission lines up to the onshore substation connection.

Ofgem and DECC spent from late 2007 until 2009 designing the incredibly complex detail of how to make the OFTO regime happen. This led me to joining them in 2008 to focus on designing implementation mechanics and processes and build a resource composition capable of delivery.

In an open letter, DECC and Ofgem (2008) acknowledged that debate continued, among some, about the overall direction of change; however, they made it clear that the sound policy and stakeholder engagement of prior years created a solid implementation foundation.

Enabler 4: Commitment and people

Reading back over hundreds of consultations and responses from 2004 through to implementation in 2009, unwavering commitment was evident, exemplified when DECC decided in 2007 that Ofgem would run the offshore transmission competitions. It was clear again in 2008 when Ofgem began to consider resourcing required to implement.

Some stakeholders raised concerns that the regime would be too different from Ofgem's core business activity. While it would operate within the electricity regulation framework, its non-traditional features and execution would require different support from that of Ofgem's other activities.

People resource challenges emerged and industry players raised questions:

- With a predominant economic regulatory and enforcement profile, would there be a skills gap around running competitions, understanding offshore construction details, managing intensive project due diligence and executing complex financial transactions?

- With no track record, and thus no in-house experience, of promoting infrastructure projects and competitions, could existing resources and processes adapt to a new model of delivery?

Ofgem proposed options for structures to run the regime, and costed and tested them via consultations.[1] They established a board sub-committee to provide supervision, challenge and guidance to the team running the regime. Policy development staff were included as part of the delivery team.[2] The organization recruited staff with commercial and transactional experience. Extensive use was made of expert advisers to inform the internal team during implementation. The new regime was aligned with Ofgem E-Serve, a new branded delivery arm for activities requiring a dedicated focus and deemed separate from Ofgem's traditional core activities. Ofgem handled uncertainty in delivery of competition, built credible committed resources and focused on making things happen.

Chris Veal, Managing Director for Transmission Capital, was questioned by the Public Accounts Committee in 2012 on what dealing with Ofgem for the OFTO process was like. He viewed 'the Ofgem team to be very good... a better experience than we might have expected... They found the Ofgem team to be constructive, well educated and well informed, and it knew what it was doing'.

Long-term change is created

Ofgem launched the first OFTO regime tender round (TR1) in June 2009, with nine projects worth an estimated £1.1 billion capex, connecting 1.5 GW of offshore wind generation. Ofgem also assessed all of the transmission development costs that the offshore wind farm developers could

Figure 2.6   Key OFTO regime figures

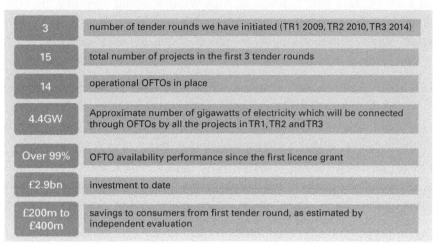

3	number of tender rounds we have initiated (TR1 2009, TR2 2010, TR3 2014)
15	total number of projects in the first 3 tender rounds
14	operational OFTOs in place
4.4GW	Approximate number of gigawatts of electricity which will be connected through OFTOs by all the projects in TR1, TR2 and TR3
Over 99%	OFTO availability performance since the first licence grant
£2.9bn	investment to date
£200m to £400m	savings to consumers from first tender round, as estimated by independent evaluation

SOURCE Ofgem (2016)

recover through the transactions. These projects were run as generator build under the transitional arrangements.

The effects of the global financial crisis in early 2009 led to real risk of limited turnout for the first competition. Ofgem, with adviser support, proactively targeted the widest market possible through promotion activities more typical of commercial asset or company sales. This effort, combined with the dearth of alternative opportunities in the wider infrastructure market at the time, led to a far greater response than expected when the first round of OFTO launched.

The result was successful appointment of a preferred bidder and a reserve bidder for all projects and offers of £4 billion in funding against £1 billion in assets, in addition to £300 million in funding from the European Investment Bank secured by Ofgem. All preferred bidders were new entrants and offered project finance solutions. This was the first time project finance entered the UK regulated transmission industry. New funders, transmission owners and advisers, all with different and new ideas, came into the electricity transmission market.

A new market model was established

The OFTO regime continues to support the delivery of offshore transmission, the demand for which will continue while the two main drivers continue to create the need.

It's not often a new market is created, let alone in a sector like transmission where new entrants have been scarce. The proof of the new market, and the permanent change in the transmission industry landscape, has been the success of subsequent rounds. Key OFTO regime figures from launch in 2009 to early 2016 are shown in (Figure 2.6).

In March 2016, Ofgem announced Tender Round 4 with a single project estimated at £230 million, as well as suggesting launch of Tender Round 5 in late 2016 with four projects. Various sources estimate that future OFTO rounds up to 2020 could be worth between circa £5 billion.

Consumer savings have been achieved

Ofgem commissioned independent consultants to examine savings from each tender round when compared against a range of merchant and regulated counterfactuals for transmission delivery. A recent report (Cambridge Economic Policy Associates, 2016) estimates that savings for consumers in total across the three tender rounds 'range from £683 million to £1,092 million (NPV 2014/15 prices)'.

Extending the new market model into other areas

The intention back in 2003/04 was to solve the offshore transmission dilemma first raised by wind farm developers. In doing so, the government and Ofgem created a new market and changed the electricity industry transmission landscape forever. With this industry change, the true disruptive impact of the OFTO model has begun. The regime provides strong proof of concept for a new form of regulated competition for large-scale projects creating value and savings for customers.

With this proof in hand, DECC and Ofgem have keenly embraced the potential to adjust the model to apply to new, separable and high-value onshore transmission assets under the Competitively Appointed Transmission Owners (CATOs) model. This swiftly translated into draft legislative proposals for 2016 that would create powers for CATO to be rolled out in future.

Dann (2016) reported that in response to the Ofgem consultation in January 2016 on CATO proposals, the National Grid TO said: 'the proposals have an over-reliance on analogies to the offshore transmission owners' (OFTO) regime and do not take into account the differences between offshore and onshore assets'. Should CATO proceed, it may be the greatest disruption to the traditional mandate of onshore transmission owners since privatization.

The regime continues to evolve

In June 2012, the National Audit Office reported on an early review of the OFTO model based on the first four licences awarded by Ofgem under OFTO TR1.

> 'These new [OFTO] deals bring the benefit of competition but lock consumers into 20-year deals to pay prices increasing each year with inflation, whether the assets are used or not. Competition brings pressure to bear on the levels of those prices, but the terms of future deals will have to be refined to make sure consumers get best value in return for these long-term commitments.'
> (Amyas Morse, Head of the National Audit Office, 22 June 2012)

The NAO (2012) report concluded that there were benefits from the 'innovative use of competition to award companies licences to transmit electricity to offshore wind farms' and the potential for more benefits. It noted the good levels of interest, despite financial market difficulties, with competition 'holding prices down in these [four] deals', with costs of debt representing 'a competitive deal for licensees in the prevailing banking environment'.

On the flipside, the NAO also warned of the potential for consumers to be left with significant risks, including the cost of inflation, high transaction costs and lack of clawback provisions. They flagged that there was scope for improving financing costs and robust benchmarks for transmission construction costs.

In respect of early lessons, the NAO highlighted that its review of the (then) new arrangements created the opportunity for the government and Ofgem to learn lessons for future transactions, while noting that there were 'also lessons for other public authorities in developing new commercial models'.

The Public Accounts Committee, based on the NAO review, that same year more heavily criticized the regime based on concerns stemming from the experiences in the UK Private Finance Initiative (PFI) market. Their criticisms, based only on the first four projects at the time, were:

- Doubt that the new licensing regime will deliver savings for consumers.
- Fundamental weaknesses with the model applied to the first licence competitions.

- It is not clear that a diverse and competitive market has been created.

- It is unacceptable that HM Treasury has allowed the Department and the Authority to proceed with the new regime without incorporating lessons from previous government experience on PFI.

However, Ofgem has constantly reviewed and refined the regime since these early rounds, with feedback considered. While a review of the Oral Evidence to the Public Accounts Committee suggests that Ofgem may not agree with all its conclusions, nor those of the NAO, it is clear that it addressed treatment of indexation and clawback of future gains via consultation related to later tenders. Reviews and assessment from the investor market of OFTOs have proven to be favourable overall.

Lessons learnt

Based on my own views and experience and that of my generous interviewees, I can conclude that many lessons have been learnt:

1 *Implementation.* Implementation ultimately worked because:

- Commitment to change over an extended policy and design duration was maintained.

- Extensive policy development and stakeholder engagement created a strong framework for change.

- Aspects of the traditional onshore regulatory regime and its balance of risks were preserved.

- There was a focus on identifying and unlocking value for consumers.

- Action sooner rather than later was critical to implementation, as was designing the creation of a market with the implementation detail required.

- Ongoing transparency and confidence in the details that required resolution in later stages of implementation was achieved.

- Government and Ofgem accepted that education was necessary.

- An acceptance that implementation would push comfort zones to the limit was fostered.

2 *Agility during change and disruption.* Change progressed from a concept to reality because:

- Change proponents and stakeholders were responsive and engaged.

- The model for change was responsive to ongoing demands (eg wind farm developers lobbied to retain transitional OFTO features permanently).

- The clear and firm implementation commitment fostered a culture of 'how do we progress' not 'why'.

- The proponent organizations (DECC and Ofgem) gave their people strong backing to progress and maintain change momentum.

- The change was designed to allow new stakeholders to enter the market, bringing with them lively questioning, new demands, new expectations and a drive to find a way for change to happen.

3 *Keeping ahead of future market change.* The OFTO regime continues to be an effective change because:

- The vision and model for change is not viewed as static, but instead as one subject to a dynamic world and requiring ongoing monitoring and review by the leading change proponents (Ofgem and DECC).

- Proponents and stakeholders have bought into the model and are now motivated to keep it relevant by proactively identifying issues still needing to be addressed, such as:

  - options for increasing model flexibility;

  - how to find a way to use mechanisms designed to anticipate future requirements and incorporate that future proofing into projects;

  - unintended consequences of the change and the need for swift movement in related industries where impact can be felt, such as the transmission insurance market, which seemed unprepared for the change in nature of demand.

- Government desire to achieve further even further consumer value, such as:

  - delivery of the OFTO Build model, rather than current generator build model;

  - creation of an equivalent model of change for the onshore transmission market.

- Lessons learnt are being actively taken into new but related markets, such as onshore transmission.

- Proponents actively monitor and manage the risk of the new market failing to fulfil project growth through redesign and expansion into related markets.

- Proponents and stakeholders continue to engage and participate, as entry into an established but evolving market can reap significant rewards and innovation if risks are identified and addressed through change design.

- The change proponents have designed into the model the mandatory obligation for the key party to regularly take a ten-year view on future demands and market changes and report it to the wider world.

As the OFTO regime is now firmly established as a market- and an industry-changing model, the key lessons above will continue to be fertile ground for future developments.

Conclusion

It was a great privilege to lead the delivery of a change model that arguably represents the most significant change in the industry structure since privatization in 1990. The OFTO model has:

- proven to be a viable new model for electricity network investment, with the potential for fostering change beyond its original design intent;

- brought multiple new players into a traditionally closed market;

- disrupted the historic conventions and status quo;

- offered a new model to consider to aid growing demands for critical infrastructure.

My conclusion, after many months' research and interviews for this chapter, is that formulaic methodical paths of creation are very rarely how industry-level change of real consequence happens. In the UK electricity transmission industry we have seen fired-up disruptive change that may yet create further changes to the structure of the industry in the future, if CATO proceeds.

If policy makers can open their minds to new models at industry disruptive levels, perhaps the challenges arising from the Paris Climate Change Conference may not have to be as insurmountable as they feel today.

Change is an iterative process requiring long-term commitment to end users. It requires extensive engagement and a focus on the value sought rather than the process itself. We can only drive change through a clear articulation of the value it can bring and having solutions designed for delivery – practicality is often overlooked. For change to be effective, strategic vision must be driven through to delivery by focusing on the detail.

Notes

1 Ofgem, various Tender Round 1 consultations from 2008 to 2011 [Online] https://www.ofgem.gov.uk/electricity/transmission-networks/offshore-transmission/offshore-transmission-tenders/tender-round-1
2 Department for Business, Enterprise & Regulatory Reform and OFGEM (2008) *Offshore Electricity – Open Letter to Industry.* Available at www.ofgem.gov.uk/sites/default/files/docs/2008/02/offshore_electricity_transmission_open_letter_to_industry.pdf [Last accessed 2.6.16]

References

Cambridge Economic Policy Associates (2016) *Evaluation of OFTO Tender Round 2 and 3 Benefits: Report for the Office of Gas and Electricity Markets.* Available at https://www.ofgem.gov.uk/system/files/docs/2016/03/ofgem_tr2_tr3_evaluation_final_report.pdf [Last accessed 2.6.16]

Dann, L (2016) DECC backs transmission competition despite industry concerns, *Utility Week*, February

Department of Energy & Climate Change and OFGEM E-Serve (2012) *Offshore Transmission Co-ordination Project Report – Conclusions Report.* Available from www.ofgem.gov.uk/ofgem-publications/51614/20120103otcp-conclusions-report.pdf [Last accessed 1.6.16]

Eurelectric (2013) Power Distribution in Europe Facts and Figures. Available from www.eurelectric.org/media/113155/dso_report-web_final-2013-030-0764-01-e.pdf [Last accessed 01.06.16]

European Wind Energy Association: Wind in Power 2015 European Statistics, February 2016 available online at https://windeurope.org/wp-content/uploads/files/about-wind/statistics/EWEA-Annual-Statistics-2015.pdf

Harvey, F (2015) Paris climate change agreement: the world's greatest diplomatic success, *The Guardian*, 14 December. Available from www.theguardian.com/environment/2015/dec/13/paris-climate-deal-cop-diplomacy-developing-united-nations [Last accessed 01.06.16]

House of Commons Library: Renewable Energy Statistics Standard Note SN/SG/3217, August 2008 and Department of Energy and Climate Change: Special Feature – Renewable Energy in 2014, June 2015 available online at https://www.gov.uk/government/uploads/system/uploads/attachment_data/file/437953/Renewable_energy_in_2014.pdf

National Audit Office (2012) Offshore electricity transmission: A new model for delivering infrastructure, Report by the Comptroller and Auditor General HC 22 Session 2012–13, June

Ofgem (2008) RPI-X@20 Review. Available at www.ofgem.gov.uk/network-regulation-riio-model/background-rpi-x20-review [Last accessed 2.6.16]

OFGEM: Preliminary Information Memorandum: London Array (Phase 1) Offshore Transmission Assets, November 2010 and Fehrenbacher, K (2013) The massive London Array offshore wind farm is finally done and it's awesome, GIGAOM.com, July

Ofgem (2009) City Briefing: Offshore Transmission Presentation. Available from www.ofgem.gov.uk/sites/default/files/docs/2009/04/city-briefing-event—slides-150409_0.pdf [Last accessed 1.6.16]

Ofgem (2016) Infographic: The energy network. Available from www.ofgem.gov.uk/publications-and-updates/infographic-energy-network [Last accessed 1.6.16]

Public Accounts Committee, Oral Evidence Taken before the Committee of Public accounts on Wednesday 17 October 2012, Twentieth Report Department of Energy and Climate Change: Offshore Transmission-a new model for infrastructure, 6 December 2012

The GlaxoSmithKline story

03

Changing the way we change

KEVIN HOLMES

This is a narrative of change – albeit change on a large scale, across 110,000 people and 150 countries – in GlaxoSmithKline (GSK). It's also a narrative of management innovation, and our intention in sharing it is to help other change practitioners with guidance in creating the conditions for the successful deployment of their own large-scale change. In the case of GSK it was about 'Accelerating Delivery and Performance' – a concept invented by GSK – otherwise known as ADP.

Why did GSK need ADP?

GSK is a science-led global healthcare company that researches and develops a broad range of innovative products in the three primary areas of Pharmaceuticals, Vaccines and Consumer Healthcare. In 2008 GSK appointed a new CEO. At the time, the pharmaceutical industry was entering what the new CEO described as an incredibly turbulent and stormy period, with pharmaceutical companies likely to be here one day and gone the next unless they innovated. In his first months he refocused GSK on a set of five strategies: (1) growing a more diversified global business; (2) delivering more products of value from R&D; (3) simplifying the way in which the business operates; (4) empowering the workforce; and (5) building trust with society.

However, by 2009 the new CEO was expressing his continuing frustration with a lack of progress on both 'simplification' and 'empowerment' and reminding employees that existing complex ways of working needed to change because they were expensive and slowing GSK down. He requested that all 110,000 employees focus on these as critical issues, and asked all managers and supervisors to lead by empowering their teams rather than simply trying to be maintainers of the status quo.

An internal executive report from that same period identified GSK's strategic plan as highly ambitious and dependent on an unprecedented level of enterprise-wide change. It also pointed to a significant risk area of inadequate change management leading to potential failures in the implementation of major business initiatives.

What is ADP?

At its heart, ADP is a fusion of simple approaches from LeanSigma or continuous improvement (CI), organizational development (OD) and project management (PM), with the objective of accelerating delivery of the business strategy. Very quickly we realized that, by themselves, these approaches were insufficient to manage and implement change effectively, and that additional components were required. The first of these was the internally developed *GSK Change Framework* (see Figure 3.1), which became an instantly recognizable and universally used model across GSK, not just for managing change but also as a template to use in running projects and even solving problems. The Change Framework was designed as a process that provided phases, objectives, tasks and activities that link to learning as well as the GSK Leadership Behaviours.

The second component was *Principles for Accelerating Change (PACE)* – this was a simple set of six principles, associated with successful change, that were intended to serve as 'accelerators' by underpinning the Change Framework but not embedded in it. They were:

1 Any change starts with 'self' first.
2 There must be clear, active, committed and visible sponsorship by key stakeholders (at all levels).
3 There must be a set of simple time-bound measures tied to financial/ business results.
4 The people impacted should own and design the change.
5 Focus on the vital few things that can be changed right now.
6 Use fit-for-purpose solutions that address customer needs.

Figure 3.1 GSK change framework. © 2016 GlaxoSmithKline group of companies

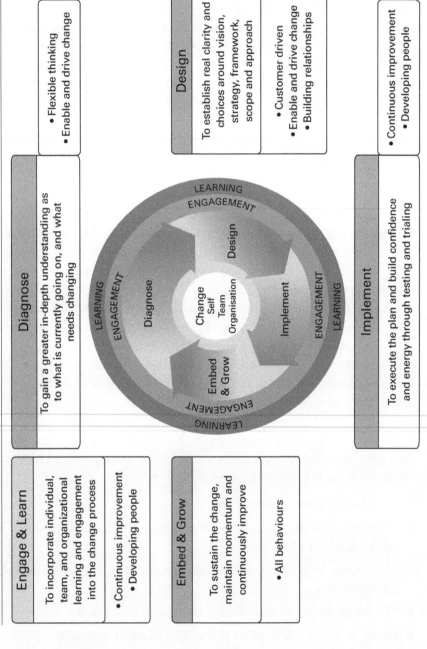

Engage & Learn

To incorporate individual, team, and organizational learning and engagement into the change process

- Continuous improvement
- Developing people

Diagnose

To gain a greater in-depth understanding as to what is currently going on, and what needs changing

- Flexible thinking
- Enable and drive change

Design

To establish real clarity and choices around vision, strategy, framework, scope and approach

- Customer driven
- Enable and drive change
- Building relationships

Embed & Grow

To sustain the change, maintain momentum and continuously improve

- All behaviours

Implement

To execute the plan and build confidence and energy through testing and trialing

- Continuous improvement
- Developing people

LEARNING
ENGAGEMENT
Design
Diagnose
Change
Self
Team
Organisation
Implement
Embed
& Grow
LEARNING
ENGAGEMENT
ENGAGEMENT
LEARNING

Figure 3.2   GSK fundamentals for delivery. © 2016 GlaxoSmithKline group of companies

GSK Fundamentals for Delivery

Choose to do the right things   •   Get better at getting the right things done

	I seek the **Voice of the Customer** to understand what they really need and value. *Typical tools and practices: Gemba, Interviews, Strategy Development*
	I **'go and see'** to understand processes, accountabilities and performance. *Typical tools and practices: GEMBA Walks, Process Mapping*
	I carry out **Problem Solving** in order to identify **Root Causes** and implement sustainable solutions. *Typical tools and practices: Change Framework, Problem Statement, Root Cause Diagnosis*
	I effectively define the **benefits** and **scope** of work to ensure alignment with strategy. *Typical tools and practices: Project Charter, Project Mural, KPI's, Return on Change*
	I make a conscious decision about the **Approach to change** to ensure successful implementation. *Typical tools and practices: Change Approaches, Change Curve*
	I carry out **Implementation Planning** to accelerate execution and deliver benefits. *Typical tools and practices: Joint Planning Session, Risk and Issue Management*
	I carry out **Visual Performance Management** to engage and align teams. *Typical tools and practices: KPI's, Comms. Cells, Accountability Boards*
	I take responsibility for **continuously improving** my part of the business. *Typical tools and practices: Sand-Pebbles-Rocks, Standard Work, Change Framework*
	I effectively **engage** the right **stakeholders** and sponsors to accelerate delivery. *Typical tools and practices: Stakeholder Map and Management Plan*
	I am **personally accountable** for my own effectiveness, learning and development. *Typical tools and practices: Reflection, Journaling*
	I **coach** individuals and teams to improve performance. *Typical tools and practices: Feedback, Coaching, Inverted Triangle*
	I focus on our **Ways of Working** in order to increase team effectiveness. *Typical tools and practices: IPO, Advocacy I Inquiry, Fist or Five, AAR*

Phase labels (right side): Diagnose · Design · Implement · Embed & Grow · Engagement · Change Self, Team, Organisation · Learning

Note: This illustrates the primary Fundamentals for each phase of the Change Framework; however **all** Fundamentals can be relevant in any phase.

©GSK 2011

The third and most critical component was the *GSK Fundamentals for Delivery* – these are shown in Figure 3.2. In plain language, these are the 'simple sticky things' that improve performance in everyday work, not just for strategic projects. The intent behind these was that they acted as a set of 'behaviours' or 'things that people do' – note that each starts with 'I' – rather than a list of tools and techniques. Each Fundamental is linked to a phase of the Change Framework, and they also provided the definition for the development of ADP 'practitioners', that is, people who apply all of these practices and teach some of them in their daily work.

There were 12 Fundamentals:

- The '*Voice of the Customer*' refers to a continuous process that aligns the work that teams do and provides insights on customer needs and how well those needs are being met. The goal of '*Go and See*' is to identify improvement opportunities, and this Fundamental is also intended to be used by leaders in coaching their teams. The focus of '*Problem Solving*' is on finding 'Root Cause' rather than implementing solutions, and is intended as a team activity that also drives alignment and understanding within a team.

- '*Benefits and Scope*' helps ensure alignment of projects with the high-level goals of the organization, helps engagement and alignment in the project team and increases chances of project success. The focus of '*Approach to Change*' is on people's commitment rather than compliance, and acknowledges that the more effective change approaches are those that involve those individuals impacted in designing the change. There are different 'Approaches to Change' and, in general, organizations do not consider which would be most appropriate. '*Implementation Planning*' makes plans and planning visual, using simple tools, and focuses on the process of planning rather than the plan itself. It is also about the engagement and alignment of project teams.

- '*Visual Performance Management*' answers the 'are we winning?' question and identifies further improvement opportunities. It is first and foremost 'visual', using 'walls rather than in desks', and can also require a cultural change or a mindset shift as performance becomes visible to all. '*Continuous Improvement*' refers to the small-scale day-to-day improvements made by individuals that have to be owned and initiated by individuals and requires 'standards' to assess performance. Effective '*Stakeholder Engagement*' is a key part of ADP and can make or break a project. It suggests that stakeholders' have to be engaged and re-engaged as they change through the life of a project.

- '*Personal Accountability*' is about owning one's personal learning and development rathr than it being the responsibility of a line manager or supervisor. It requires taking a detached, more objective view of oneself such that the subsequent reflection is a way of amplifying learning about oneself. '*Coaching*' helps individuals and teams be 'the best they can possibly be' by driving 'change starts with self' – at the heart of the Change Framework – and is a key part of a leader's and manager's responsibilities. '*Ways of Working*' helps teams do the right things and work on how they do them. It contains some simple tools that will help team and meeting effectiveness, the consequences of not doing this being longer meetings and less effective teams.

In our research we also asked the same question – What is ADP? – to the wider ADP community or 'users' of ADP. Responses fell into four categories:

1 '*Ways of Working*' is about teams doing the right things and using simple 'soft' tools to help team and meeting effectiveness. 'Users' reported their teams to be functioning more effectively, with greater levels of engagement as well as fewer and shorter team meetings.

2 '*Personal Accountability*' linked with the concept of self-empowerment not only as a process requiring courage and personal change at a beliefs level but also as an outcome producing benefits from the application of ADP. Users also commented on their own willingness to change, the feedback and coaching they received and the benefits of becoming more thoughtful and focused.

3 '*Coaching*' referred to the changes in an individual's leadership style, where leaders take accountability for the performance of their teams, coaching them in ADP, and the personal courage that those changes required. 'Users' noted that the personal coaching they received was an important enabler.

4 '*The Fundamentals*' provided structure, process and a set of common-sense tools to take ADP 'users' into practical implementation. 'Users' referred to the power inherent in not only combining tools from the three disciplines but also in bringing the soft skills or change management tools to the fore. There were also comments that praised the completeness of the tools and, at the same time, complained that the quantity of tools was overwhelming and that a degree of simplification of the toolkit was required. Although the intent of the Fundamentals was always as a set of 'principles' rather than tools and practices, much of the ensuing debate among 'users' focused on 'using the right tool in the right way'.

How did ADP come about?

Phase 1

In 2009 – for the CEO – the realization was simple: (1) GSK needed a fundamental rethink of its approach to change management with a view to '*change how it changed*' and (2) GSK's competitors had a very similar set of strategies, so the differentiator would be accelerating the delivery of those strategies through '*disciplined execution*' to out-perform GSK's competitors. GSK has a long history of embedding management innovations – for example, Total Quality Management (TQM), Lean, Six Sigma – usually using external consultants to implement these into an individual business unit or function. However, in this case, the focus of change needed to be on enterprise-level performance improvement, and the CEO decided that existing management innovations would, by themselves, be insufficient to meet the challenge. Instead, he elected to sponsor a small internal team who identified simple approaches from OD, CI and PM to accelerate delivery of the business strategy. The fusion of these approaches was Accelerating Delivery and Performance (ADP), which had a simple set of objectives:

- Accelerate delivery of the GSK Strategy.
- Embed a structured, disciplined way of working.
- Use a pragmatic approach to build skills and capabilities in leadership, OD, PM and CI.
- Embed the GSK values and behaviours to deliver excellence.

The ADP team started working in mid-2009 on an 'experimental' phase of 10 projects that had been identified by senior management. The intent was to use these not only to further develop the ADP 'approach' and demonstrate the benefits but also to create a 'pull' to continue. As a result of these early successes, the ADP team supported a further 40 change projects applying ADP in 2010. These projects reported not only improved internal and external relationships – with teams and stakeholders – but also an enhanced project management and planning capability after working with the ADP team. They also found that ADP accelerated the delivery of project objectives, supported the adoption of disciplined ways of working and used action learning to build sustainable capability and embed GSK values. However, this phase was not all smooth sailing – there were problems to do with the initial engagement between ADP and the project teams.

Some projects were already under way before the ADP team arrived, and that arrival was perceived not only as disruptive but also as occasionally conflicting in terms of the methodologies associated with external consultants.

Phase 2

The shift in 2011 was to move from 'working on projects' to applying ADP at a business unit level; the scale-up was dependent upon developing in-business expertise and the effective transfer of accountability. By intervening at the level of leaders and teams in individual business units, ADP was applied to their specific business problems, resulting in tangible benefits, for example in market share in Europe, acceleration of product launches, increased sales in pilot regions of the United States. Those leaders and teams were taught and coached so that they not only solved their current business problems but developed the skills to do that again and again. This self-motivated development of expertise also required a focus on building leadership belief and trust in the approach. At the outset GSK leaders were at best neutral and at worst deeply cynical, so these activities served as 'guiding lights' or 'beacon projects' that helped to establish the 'proof of concept' of ADP as fusing the disciplines of OD, CI and PM to produce 'hard' and 'soft' benefits. This attracted the attention and support of leaders who wanted *both*.

Business units and functions who 'opted in' to ADP became part of the ADP performance management system – this has its roots in the Toyota production system and also links to the quality function deployment (QFD) house of quality. Others refer to this as Hoshin Kanri – a quality planning and management method that was developed in Japan by Yokogawa Hewlett-Packard in the early 1970s. Different authors have given different interpretations; however, the following by Jolayemi (2008) is generally believed to be the most accurate: (1) Hoshin – a compass, a course, a policy, a plan, an aim; (2) Kanri – management control of the company's focus.

An important component of this was its visual representation as a 'strategy house' – the content of which was 'refreshed' on an annual basis and so evolved over the period from 2010 to 2015. A consolidated 'thematic' ADP strategy house is shown in Figure 3.3 with its four levels.

The first level of the strategy house is the ADP Mission and acts as a portrait of its future – defining its direction and aspiration by linking a 'what'

Figure 3.3 ADP strategy house. © 2016 GlaxoSmithKline group of companies

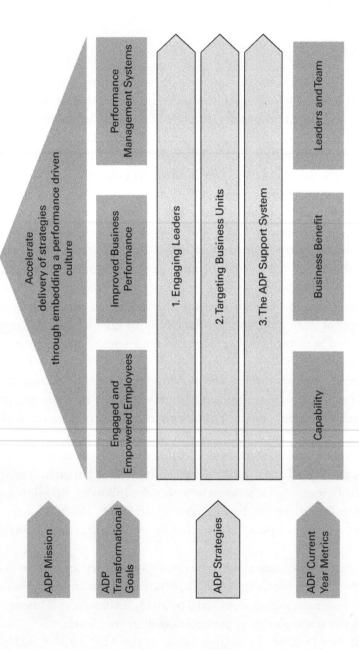

to a 'how' and fulfilling the original brief from the CEO. This was sometimes referred to as 'True North' – from the work of FranklinCovey (2014).

The second level shows a set of Transformational Goals or medium-term three- to five-year objectives that must be accomplished in order to achieve the Mission. These were grouped around three themes:

1 Engaged and empowered employees – this evolved into a specific measure linked to the Engagement and Empowerment scores on the internal GSK employee survey.

2 Improved business performance – this evolved into a financial measure of total shareholder return exceeding external analysts' expectations.

3 Performance management systems – this evolved into a target of 10,000 functioning performance management systems across GSK, evidenced by the number of performance review meetings or Comms Cells.

Using 'systems thinking' (Checkland, 1981), it is feasible to characterize these as an 'Input–Process–Output' systems model, with 'empowered employees' as the 'Input', 'how leaders – and their teams – operate' as the 'Process' and 'delivery' of the GSK strategies as the 'Output', with ADP characterized as the embedding of a performance management system. This is shown in Table 3.1.

The third level of the strategy house shows the annual plans or 'strategies' that describe the activities that were being worked on for the current year. These were also in three themes:

Table 3.1   Input–Process–Output systems model © 2016 GlaxoSmithKline group of companies

Input	Process	Output
Every employee is empowered, motivated and capable of driving business performance improvement. This measure is linked to improvements in the Engagement and Empowerment sections from the internal GSK employee survey.	Leaders institute a culture of business performance improvement through coaching their teams in the use of the performance management system. This measure is linked to the number of Comms Cells operating across GSK. The target was 10,000.	GSK is excellent at rapidly executing strategic priorities. This measure is linked to the business performance improvement rate where total shareholder returns exceed external analysts' expectations.

1 Engaging leaders – a strategy which consistently linked to increasing the number of influential leaders role modelling and teaching or coaching ADP.

2 Targeting business units – this strategy consistently referred to the goal of targeting business units in developing their self-sustaining momentum and discipline in the application of ADP.

3 The ADP support system – this strategy evolved from developing simple summary packages of ADP tools and systems in 2010 to supporting the embryo ADP communities of practice and maintaining capability and performance standards in 2015.

The fourth level shows the 'current year lag goals' that describe the metrics and targets for the current year, and should be delivered – in the current year – through execution of the ADP strategies. These also fell into three categories:

1 Capability – this refers to the numbers who reach a particular level of capability in using and teaching/coaching ADP. It links to the Transformational Goal of 'empowered employees'.

2 Business benefit – this evolved from a simple measure of the number of projects into an equally simple measure of 'hard benefits' or 'cash'. This is linked to the Transformational Goal of 'Improved Business Performance'.

3 Leaders and teams – this category links to the transformational goal of performance management systems or 'how leaders – and their teams – operate'. It evolved over time from a simple count of leaders using ADP to leaders 'owning' a 'mature' performance management system.

The definitions of metrics linked to the 'capability' and 'business benefits' categories are quite consistent from year to year, while there is much more variation with the 'leaders and teams' category. In fact, there are more goals linked to 'leaders and teams' than to the other categories – this may be because the ADP team was unclear about what aspect of leadership ADP should or will impact.

Business units and functions who 'opted in' to ADP typically followed the process shown in the Business Unit ADP Transformation Roadmap (Figure 3.4), which illustrates the journey from 'prove it works' through 'build capability' to 'way of life'. Based on a 'lean capability framework', this was able to provide a sense of 'journeying' and 'destination' for participating business units and leaders. It also illustrates the activities and roles of

Figure 3.4 ADP transformation roadmap. © 2016 GlaxoSmithKline group of companies

Business Unit ADP Transformation Roadmap

	Prove	Build understanding	Build Business Improvement capabilities and begin deployment	Full deployment at all levels – 'In place'	Way of life – 'In use' convert to benefit
Capability & Business Performance	Prove the approach is transferable to targeted business unit	Build understanding in the organisation	Build capability in the organisation	Business improvement starting to happen at all levels of the business	Business improvement is the process and mindset by which the business is run
ADP is doing (engagement and delivery of standard offerings)	• Driving pilot projects	• Building capability through experiential learning • Project coaching	• Coaching of leadership • Deployment of management system	• Facilitating strategy/deployment	• Facilitating business unit diagnosis
BU Leaders are doing	• Test the water • Learning where and how ADP approach can help meet business challenges	• BU executive team *expressing* commitment to: personal change and development; ADP approach/ principles • Committing resources	• BU executive team *modelling* commitment to: personal change and development; ADP approach/ principles, eg. leading problem solving • Integration into traditional budget process	• BU executive team *reinforcing* commitment to: personal change and development; ADP approach/ principles, eg. through the PDP process all leaders problem solving • Using strategy deployment	• Solving business problems at all levels – sand, people, rocks

Figure 3.5 The evolution of ADP. © 2016 GlaxoSmithKline group of companies

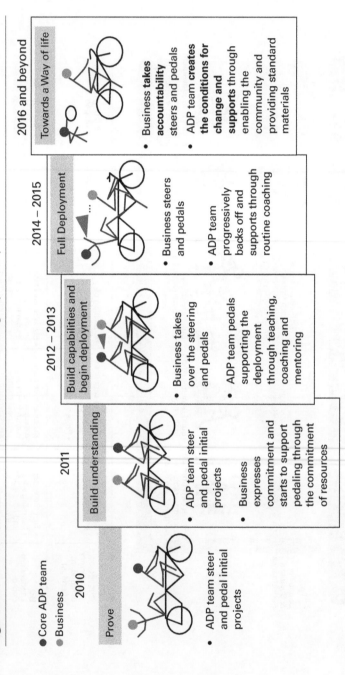

● Core ADP team
● Business

2010

Prove

• ADP team steer and pedal initial projects

2011

Build understanding

• ADP team steer and pedal initial projects
• Business expresses commitment and starts to support pedaling through the commitment of resources

2012 – 2013

Build capabilities and begin deployment

• Business takes over the steering and pedals
• ADP team pedals supporting the deployment through teaching, coaching and mentoring

2014 – 2015

Full Deployment

• Business steers and pedals
• ADP team progressively backs off and supports through routine coaching

2016 and beyond

Towards a Way of life

• Business takes **accountability** steers and pedals
• ADP team **creates the conditions for change and supports** through enabling the community and providing standard materials

the ADP team and the respective business unit leaders. In the final stage of the roadmap the business unit is considered self-sustaining in ADP and the 'transformation' is complete.

Phase 3

One of the keys to the success of ADP has been the strategy of building capability in GSK leaders with their teams and adopting a 'pull' not 'push' model where business units 'opt in' to the approach. 'Signing up' for ADP by business units was entirely voluntary; the CEO did not mandate ADP across GSK. Our experience was that there were always sufficiently curious 'early adopter' leaders who – once convinced that it worked – advocated its adoption and, in turn, convinced their colleagues. Once on board, participation in the ADP performance management system was mandatory. Each participating business unit self-set their performance targets against the ADP current year metrics and self-reported actual performance using a Policy Deployment Matrix (PDM) – based on the current year strategy house – at a weekly 30-minute global performance review meeting or Comms Cell. At the end of each year, all participating business units developed and agreed the content of the following year's strategy house – with its strategies and metrics – before again self-setting their own goals. Over time, this had the effect of business units becoming sufficiently self-sustaining in ADP that they required no further help from the ADP team. Figure 3.5 illustrates not only the effective evolution of the respective roles of the ADP team and business units but shows its application to GSK as a whole. This indicates that by 2016 the accountability for ADP is sitting entirely with business units and the ADP team has a minor supporting role.

What is the impact of ADP?

At a GSK level, ADP has established a common and systemic way to drive change and business improvement, and the benefits of applying ADP have been significant: enabling market share growth, increased sales, cost reduction and faster delivery of R&D medicines. What began as an experiment in 10 projects in 2009 has evolved to a widely adopted way of working across GSK, most notably in Manufacturing, Commercial, R&D, Vaccines and Core Business Services (CBS). Externally, ADP won the 'Excellence in OD award' from the European OD Network in 2014 and was runner-up in the 'Excellence in Performance Improvement' awarded by the Association of Business Psychology (ABP).

What about the global impact in terms of numbers?

- In 2011 and 2012 our internal research showed >£700 million of financial benefits. After that we stopped counting, as there was no longer any need to prove that it worked.

- Approximately 30,000 GSK staff are applying elements of ADP ways of working in their daily work.

- Approximately 80 per cent of GSK business units are participating in the ADP performance management system.

- Approximately 20 per cent of GSK business units did not 'opt in' to the ADP performance management system – these tended to be corporate functions rather than those involved in 'front-line' activities, but no further inference should be drawn. Participation in ADP was not a mandatory requirement.

- Teams led by leaders who are ADP practitioners are statistically significantly more empowered than comparable teams and demonstrate higher adaptability to change (evidenced by our global employee surveys).

- There are now >1,800 ADP practitioners globally and >65 ADP consultants in GSK.

- There are >700 mature performance management systems in use in GSK, with >4,000 assessed in the past two years; in 2014 our research showed that mature performance management systems deliver improved performance in our Vaccines, CBS and Commercial businesses.

- The ADP website is in the top three most visited websites internally in GSK and the acronym 'ADP' is in the top 20 most frequently searched terms in the company intranet.

Our research asked the same question – 'What is the impact of ADP?' – to the wider ADP community or 'users' of ADP. They reported not only 'hard' benefits in terms of cash benefits and accelerated project deliverables against timelines but also 'soft' benefits in terms of improved capability, increased discipline, focus and improved relationships with internal and external stakeholders. 'Users' commented specifically on an enhanced project management and planning capability, on an increased focus on continuous improvement and on the benefits of more effective and disciplined teamwork. They identified the ADP Fundamentals as strongly aligned to the desired ethos of their business units, and findings of accelerated project delivery 'through a structured disciplined approach' have been characterized as 'discipline, focus, standards, prioritization and simplification'. 'Users' also reported a set of benefits that linked to improved capabilities in 'diagnosis, root cause analysis and problem solving'. The action coaching that 'users' received was not only a core component of the experience but also one that was highly valued, and despite a focus on tools, most 'users' comment on the 'personal development' they have experienced – not only in terms of their own leadership capability but also their individual change journey.

Our research also asked this question to the CEO, who characterized the deployment of ADP as an example of how GSK had been able to drive itself, be more efficient, leaner and more focused. He described the benefits of the ADP ways of working as allowing more and more business units across GSK to do far more than they had ever done, more quickly and to a higher level of precision.

At this point it feels important that we're also honest about some of the challenges we faced in such a fast-evolving deployment and, looking back, there are some obvious things that we'd do differently:

1 The first 10 projects we experimented on were not all 'front-line' issues; some were programmes that had been running for a while and, while ADP had an impact on them all, when we switched to working at the 'front line' in 2010 (eg sales force, factory floor or medicine delivery teams), we found we had far greater relevance and impact.

2 In addition to this, we would also bring an earlier focus on developing advocacy through leaders: the shadow of leaders as role models had a big impact once we began to define what we needed leaders to do differently rather than what we wanted them to say about ADP.

3 A further learning is that we would spend more time, earlier on, creating an intranet presence to clearly position and communicate what ADP is and what it is not – and clarify the simple standard ways of working as a set.

4 Knowledge and successes were shared on a weekly basis and the ADP strategy was formally reviewed and adjusted at the end of every year. However, the programme evolved so fast and the learnings and adjustments were so profound that we would definitely be more intentional in capturing the routine learning history of our journey on a more regular basis.

We feel that ADP has now breached the elusive 'tipping point' of adoption in GSK, and business units are now taking accountability for driving the embedding of ADP as a set of 'ways of working'. Within this context, we continue to improve and simplify our standard approaches, develop regional ADP communities of practice and embed ADP into the 'DNA' of

GSK. Just as GSK continues to evolve, so does ADP, evolving to remain relevant, continually improve and maintain business impact.

The CEO has the final word of this story. He points out that ADP has meant that GSK is much more of an aligned organization. He argues that it doesn't have to be ADP, but in GSK it just happens to be ADP. If you go to any of the other global corporates, you will see other phrases, other technology and other techniques, but for GSK it is ADP.

Conclusions and key insights from ADP

These sets of reflections are based on those things that we would do all over again if we were starting tomorrow:

- *Build capability*: a core tenet of our work is 'teaching people to fish' versus 'fishing for them', so enabling them to solve their own problems. Applying ADP to 'real work' versus making it a training programme both delivered immediate benefits to participants and developed their own capability. At the heart of that strategy is building capability in GSK leaders with their teams: working with the team as a unit provided the best chance of reinforcing that capability and it becoming self-sustainable. The ADP team was repeatedly asked to provide training (with no follow-up coaching) to individuals or groups of specialists; in the small number of instances where we tried this, the return on investment was marginal at best. ADP is not a training course.

- *'Pull' is more sustainable than 'push'*: our adoption of a model where business units 'opted in' to the approach (ADP has never been a mandated way of working) was justified by showing that leaders who had 'opted in' promoted and used ADP with their teams. The more ADP was used, the greater the business benefits, and the link between ADP and business performance was reinforced in the minds not only of those leaders and their teams but also of those colleagues who were more sceptical. Our research showed that approximately two-thirds of people who came into contact with ADP embraced it by applying it and seeing the benefits both in themselves and in their daily work. The remaining one-third resisted applying ADP: they demanded proof that it worked, requested more 'training' in the tools or asked for clearer definitions of ADP.

- *Take our own medicine*: as a core team, the ADP team applied the principles of ADP to themselves, giving them credibility in the eyes of their customers by seeking to be a model of that change they wished to see.

The role of the ADP team was not to 'fix' problems but rather to consult, teach and coach leaders with intact teams to create a new habit for their work. This reduced dependency and a reliance on the ADP team in solving future challenges and problems. The ADP style of coaching is to observe, provide feedback and suggest improvements as they occur. By intervening 'in the moment', leaders and teams received immediate performance feedback on which they could act and improve. This 'action coaching' is one of the differentiators of ADP.

- *CEO sponsorship*: was unsurprisingly very important, as was the contribution of an active Steering Team made up of senior-level sponsors and representatives from those business units who had 'opted in' to the approach. While ADP always had a vision and goals (which changed over time), we constantly evolved the next best step to take versus following a grand 'master plan' – finding what was working and seeking to amplify that success. This was also characterized in terms of both a 'change approach' and 'leadership style'.

- *Create the vision*: the concept of a strategy house within a performance management system was used to create a single overarching framework and to set a clear strategic direction with a way of monitoring and tracking progress. This allowed people to make sense of the change and how their work related to it, while leaving space for adjustments along the way. Business units not only found the performance management system to be relevant but were also stimulated to improve their performance against the current year metrics. They saw their participation as part of the embedding process of ADP for their business unit, while the visual nature of the PDM allowed peer pressure to play a role if a business unit was in danger of missing its self-set targets.

- *The 'right' change approach*: building on the research of Rowland and Higgs (2009), ADP made a conscious decision to adopt an 'emergent' approach to change. This assumes that organizations are complex and cannot be directly controlled, and that leaders are only able to create the conditions for change by establishing a loose sense of direction for the change, by establishing a 'few hard rules' to govern what needs to happen, and then stepping back to encourage people around them to self-organize to do the rest. The required toolkits were developed by the people who would need to use them, and there was substantial investment in creating local sustainable capability while encouraging people to enjoy experimenting within some agreed boundaries and direction. The work of Rowland and Higgs indicated a positive relationship between these characteristics and successful change, especially high-magnitude and longer-term change.

- *Leading change*: the leaders of the ADP team also consciously adopted a 'framing/creating capacity' personal leadership style with the ADP team and in their engagement with internal and external stakeholders. This is very collaborative in nature: working with others to create a vision and direction while giving people space to do what needs to happen. It seeks to change 'how things get done' not just 'what gets done', by letting people know how they are doing and coaching them to improve while encouraging working across organizational boundaries and along key processes. The work of Rowland and Higgs (2009) also reported a strong relationship between 'framing/creating capacity' leadership and the success of high-magnitude, longer-term change.

Key questions

These sets of questions are intended to provoke conversations. They are based on our insights from the deployment of ADP and will be particularly relevant for those readers involved in high-magnitude, longer-term change:

- *The 'right' change approach*: what change approach have you adopted? Is it a 'directive' approach where the change is managed and controlled tightly by a small group at the top of the organization, with the 'what' and the 'how' being explicitly prescribed? Or is it an 'emergent' approach where the overall strategic direction is loosely set as well as a few big rules that create the conditions for change and allow it to be initiated anywhere in the organization?

- *Leading change*: what sort of a leader of change are you? Are you a 'shaper' who 'takes charge' and sets your agenda such that the change becomes leader-centric? Or are you a 'framer and creator of capacity' who creates the vision and then taps into the energy present in the system, allowing people space to make sense of the change and do what needs to be done?

- *CEO sponsorship*: is your CEO making the case for change and actively promoting the work that you're doing? Do you have a reactive Steering Team that contains only senior leaders? Or does your Steering Team proactively get involved in setting the overall direction and monitoring progress of the change? Does it contain representation from those teams who are involved in the change?

- *Building capability*: is your change team made up of experts applying sophisticated tools to other people's problems? Are you running training courses that apply advanced techniques to theoretical problems? Or are you coaching people in the application of simple techniques to their everyday business issues in order to build sustainable capability?

- *Take your own medicine*: is your change team an exemplar of the change? Are they living, breathing examples of the behaviours that you're seeking to embed? How would you rate them as 'influencers' versus being 'experts'? In their interactions with business leaders and teams, do they show up as expert teachers with the 'answers' or are they coaches who observe and provide in-the-moment feedback?

References

Checkland, P (1981) *Systems Thinking, Systems Practice*, John Wiley, New York

FranklinCovey (2014) [Accessed 15 June 2016] [Online] www.franklincovey.com/tc/public/images/books/tools/chapter1.pdf

Jolayemi, J (2008) Hoshin Kanri and Hoshin process: a review and literature survey. *Total Quality Management*, **19** (3), pp 295–320

Rowland, D and Higgs, M (2009) *Sustaining Change: Leadership that works*, John Wiley & Sons, Chichester

Shaping, scoping and designing a new total operating model

GILLIAN PERRY

Introduction

This chapter describes an organization design (OD) change to support a company strategy following a number of acquisitions. Specifically, it focuses on the early-stage processes of shaping, scoping and designing the new 'total operating model' (TOM). In describing the approach to the change and organizational design we'll look at what worked well, and where, with hindsight, what could have been done differently to avoid redesign.

This is a story of two parts. The first part comprised Project Marlborough as National Grid USA's first major review of its operating model following the acquisition of several companies in the United States. The second part looks at a major review of the total operating model created during Project Marlborough to identify whether it would be sustainable to ensure benefits to customers and returns to shareholders. This project became known as the Jurisdictional Evolution or JDx 2.0.

Background

A number of UK utility companies (specifically in gas, electricity, telecommunications and water) were privatized in the 1980s during a Conservative government programme which intended to promote wider share ownership by the British public. One of the aims was to drive down costs to consumers through a greater level of competition. Where it was not in the consumer's interest to have a competitive position, the monopoly position would be managed through a government-appointed regulator. In the gas and electricity market the primary aim of Ofgem, the UK regulator, is to protect the interests of Britain's gas and electricity consumers. This is accomplished in a variety of ways, including promoting competition and regulating monopoly network companies.

National Grid, originally the UK electricity transmission company, has grown through a number of mergers and acquisitions over the past 20 years. It was made up of the UK electricity transmission, natural gas transmission and the natural gas distribution companies. As soon as the electricity transmission company (National Grid) and the gas transmission and distribution companies merged in 2002, they were run as the UK business.

Between 2002 and 2007, National Grid acquired a number of companies in the United States, in Massachusetts and New York State, which were initially run as separate businesses with limited interventions from their UK parent. However, during the mid-2000s, following the acquisition of Keyspan Energy, a gas distributor and electricity producer in the Northeastern United States, the US business wanted to drive economies of scale to benefit both shareholders and consumers. The portfolio of companies was made up from a number of acquired businesses (Figure 4.1).

Figure 4.1   National Grid organization

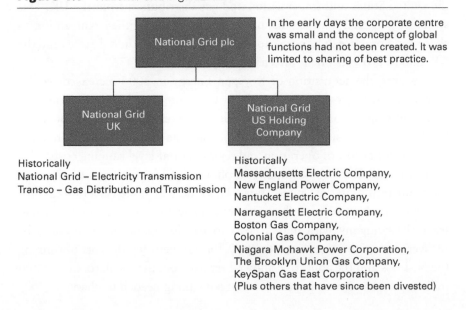

National Grid plc

In the early days the corporate centre was small and the concept of global functions had not been created. It was limited to sharing of best practice.

National Grid UK

National Grid US Holding Company

Historically
National Grid – Electricity Transmission
Transco – Gas Distribution and Transmission

Historically
Massachusetts Electric Company,
New England Power Company,
Nantucket Electric Company,
Narragansett Electric Company,
Boston Gas Company,
Colonial Gas Company,
Niagara Mohawk Power Corporation,
The Brooklyn Union Gas Company,
KeySpan Gas East Corporation
(Plus others that have since been divested)

There have been several iterations of the organization design with changes in the level of globalization and regionalization. This chapter will look at the most recent organization changes and reflect on some of the things that were highly successful and areas where lessons were learnt. We will focus on the changes in the National Grid organization in the United States, specifically on the initial processes of shaping, scoping and designing the new TOM. This change began in 2010 with Project Marlborough – the phase of work that set out to create the new US TOM. Since this time there has been an ongoing evolution towards a more state, or 'jurisdictional', focus.

Prior to the first major organization redesign, a review of the spans of control and the number of layers of employees was undertaken and compared to market best practice. The conclusion was that the organization spans of control were too narrow and the layers too deep, so that there would be significant benefits in reorganizing the US business to improve both organizational effectiveness and efficiency.

Project Marlborough

From 2006 and prior to Project Marlborough, a new Group CEO had been appointed. During this time, National Grid operated globally under three lines of business – electricity distribution & generation (ED&G), transmission (gas and electricity) and gas distribution. Each line of business was led by an operational board member, with the ED&G business led from the United States and transmission and gas distribution from the UK. This structure achieved many goals, not least the ability of the organization to share good practice in its core capabilities between the United States and the UK, and to grow its talent internationally.

However, the acquisition of Keyspan Energy in 2007 increased regulatory scrutiny. US regulators were keen to ensure that National Grid USA was delivering customer service and value for money at both a regional and local level. As a result, the regulator pressed the company to differentiate between global cost of operation and regional local-level running costs. This in turn would allow the company to obtain the appropriate rate of return for its operations in the United States. This would be done via a rate case for the regulators' approval; failure to gain approval from the regulator would leave the company with higher costs to run its operation than could be recovered from the customers. In 2010, the gap between the cost of running the business and the collective allowed return from the regulators was $200 million per year. It was imperative that something needed to change.

The first discussions that took place about the US TOM were simple: do we move away from a global-lines-of-business model and, if so, what replaces it? The US leadership team was given the responsibility for a resolution. They developed several high-level operating model options and a proposal was taken to the Executive Committee with a recommendation to move to a regional US–UK operating model. The Executive Committee endorsed the recommendation overwhelmingly. Work then began on how best to restructure the US business to address these cost pressures, and so Project Marlborough was born.

The organization review was to consider two key areas: first, where a global operating model should exist and where a US company level or a local jurisdictional-focused model should exist. The second key area was to review the spans of control in the organization and the number of layers of management. The review suggested that the company could run in a more efficient way if it reduced the number of layers and increased the span of control, that is, the number of direct reports each manager had. This would be a difficult project for those involved, as they would need to challenge some deep-seated beliefs. Many of them had worked for the utilities for many years and would have a belief that their operating model was the best approach; others would believe that a global line of business would satisfy the group board more than local control.

The approach taken was based on a mix of in-house practices and the range of research and thought-leaders available at the time. The works of Galbraith (2000), Gailoto *et al* (2006), Simons (2005), Stanford (2007) and Sy and D'Annunzio (2005) were of particular importance.

Organization design approach

Project Marlborough's design approach for National Grid USA aimed to ensure that the structure and associated roles would support the business strategy, enabling the company to:

- build a strong internal capability that would efficiently and effectively design and implement OD projects;
- consistently apply the banding framework and guidelines on managerial layers and span of control;
- become a more flexible organization, responsive to the changing environment;
- foster a global approach encouraging employee movement and development across geographies and functions.

Specifically, the approach used to design the TOM included the following components:

- structure design: layering and span of control;
- role design: role accountabilities, responsibilities and indicative metrics;
- capability requirements: skills and capabilities required to implement the design;
- resource requirements: number of roles aligned to the overall company strategy (shown as Full Time Equivalents or FTEs).

Core design principles

The approach used specified that *core design principles* were established for Project Marlborough. These were based on the specific requirements of the change and were able to translate the strategic objectives into tangible criteria against which the effectiveness and appropriateness of the proposed design options would be assessed.

These core design principles (Table 4.1) were created by a team of leaders in National Grid USA consisting of the US CEO, CFO, Group Strategy Director, Group HR Director and regional subject-matter experts from the HR organizational effectiveness centre of excellence part of the HR organization.

Four high-level design options were developed, most centring around a move to a jurisdictional model (ie New York, Massachusetts, Rhode Island, New Hampshire etc). Each option described the degree to which activities in the organization would be structured under such a model. These ranged from a *full jurisdictional model* (which would see each decentralization of core business operations into each jurisdiction) to a *light model* (which would see a thin layer of strategic and performance management capability under each 'jurisdictional president' but also maintain all operations under central functions). It was this latter model that was selected by the Project Steering Committee. This light model met the concerns that a decentralized model might create more inefficiency by duplicating operations and core services across each state, which would be in direct opposition to the requirement to deliver cost-competitive services.

Implementing the TOM

To ensure that the move towards this new organizational structure was successful, the transition had a change management team that provided support and guidance during the process and post-implementation. The

Table 4.1   Core design principles for Project Marlborough

Design Principle Focus	Key Design Questions (*to be used to test the strength of the design option*)
Stewardship	• Does it enable delivery of our commitments to external stakeholders? • Does it support our regional focus and strengthen our local involvement in the community? • Does it enhance relationships with key jurisdiction stakeholders and help them achieve their local economic and environmental goals? • Does it enable customer data and input to co-design the future?
Cost competitive services	• Does it align common practices and create efficient, effective processes? • Does it allow for transparent, accurate accounting and a clear P&L by jurisdiction? • Does it clarify cost drivers as articulated by functional and jurisdictional measures?
Customer responsiveness	• Does it simplify customer and regulator interactions? • Does it enable teams to meet customer satisfaction goals and provide timely, accurate and thorough regulatory support? • Does it support clear communications, contingency planning, and quick response during outages? • Does it facilitate customer input/feedback?
Safe and reliable operations	• Does it reinforce our focus on a safety culture, both personal and organizational? • Does it enhance our reliability and minimize our outage risk? • Does it support innovation?
People	• Does it support our culture of customer-focus, accountability and empowerment, shared mindset and execution? • Does it maximize employee capabilities and provide opportunities for development? • Does it clearly define roles and accountabilities in a way that enables innovation and teamwork?

approach also used a project management methodology with a number of stage gates and change considerations:

- Project initiation and scope sign-off: the change focus at this stage was ensuring that the *Opportunity* was understood.

- During the design principles development, the change focus was to create a clear *Vision*, including the 'what's in it for me'.

- This was followed by gaining senior support and plan sign-off.

- Developing the *detailed design*.

- *Implementation* of that design.

- Post-implementation review, including putting in place an approach to *sustain the change* to ensure that benefits were achieved.

After selecting and implementing the new organization design, a work stream called 'Build and Sustain' was launched. This had the responsibility to look across the US organization to identify what components would be needed to build a sustainable organization design, which included looking at the company culture, governance, employee development, metrics and leadership.

There was also significant concern across the company that without newly defined end-to-end processes, the resulting headcount reduction (1,200 jobs were eliminated through this process) could not be sustained in the long term and would add unbearable pressure to the remaining workforce. A focus was placed on understanding and improving the end-to-end processes in the organization, and that focus remains.

Post Project Marlborough reflections

There was a significant level of success achieved from the new organization. For the first time, there was one single way of operating across National Grid USA (NGUSA). Once the new organizational design was in place, further work was undertaken to drive a greater level of consistency. This included a single back-office instance of SAP that would handle the accounting in a standardized way across the US business. The new structure had created a matrix approach spanning different functions and which would ensure a common way of working. This had the benefit of driving common operations and purchasing the same components from the same suppliers, so driving operational efficiencies. The matrix structure had jurisdictional presidents responsible for working with regional regulators to ensure that the company had an approach to customers that fitted with local needs. Greater transparency to the regulators on the cost of running each jurisdiction and operating entity has greatly enhanced the relationship with regulators and the ease with which the company can engage them during a rate case filing.

All this success did not come without its issues. The organization had adopted a matrix structure. However, the organizational culture was not yet mature enough to work in these new ways to operate effectively and achieve all the benefits originally planned: many of the staff didn't truly understand how to work successfully in a matrix organization and continued to work with a silo mentality. This was a key reason why, by 2012, promised savings through headcount reductions had not been fully realized, and the use of external consultants continued. Project Marlborough had delivered around $100 million in savings – only 50 per cent of the overall cost reduction target. Further, the SAP implementation had not gone well and an internal review concluded that there was insufficient confidence in the quality of the data required in a rate case. This resulted in the company suspending rate case filings, which in turn would mean that it would not be able increase charges to customers and recover some of the losses being incurred.

The next chapter – Jurisdiction Model 2.0 (JDx 2.0)

In early 2015 it became clear that another organization change was needed. The US business was not functioning as well as expected. The company didn't want to react by making changes that would not continue the journey to a successful TOM delivering the company vision. The root causes of the problems weren't clear and it was decided to review the TOM to understand what was working well and what was stopping full achievement of the benefits. Was the root cause of the problems due to an organization design that didn't deliver the outcomes the business had expected, or was it due to ongoing challenges with a major back-office systems implementation impacting all of the people in the US business? Whichever it was, National Grid USA was ready to undertake a major review of its operating model and announced a new US CEO in December 2014.

At the same time, the New York regulator commissioned its own independent review through NorthStar Consulting Group. Their report confirmed and supported National Grid's corporate view that a new organization design was required, and so a new organization review got under way.

NorthStar report

NorthStar Consulting Group was engaged by the New York State (NYS) Public Service Commission (PSC), the state regulator for both gas and electricity, to conduct a comprehensive management and operations audit of NGUSA's three New York gas utilities. While NorthStar Consulting was carrying out the audit, NGUSA was facing two ongoing challenges:

- Issues arising from the implementation of a new SAP enterprise resource planning (ERP) system that went operational in early November 2012. The implementation of this new system had left some material weaknesses in its financial reporting.

- In the same year, the organization was impacted by Superstorm Sandy, which left the company with significant damage to the infrastructure as well as end consumers having lost homes.

As NGUSA faced these issues, it afforded NorthStar invaluable access to NGUSA's corporate governance and management decision-making processes, and led to the identification of opportunities for improvement across virtually every area of the audit.

In summary, the NorthStar report (2014) identified that NGUSA's New York gas operations performed well overall in providing gas service in a reliable manner. However, the generally strong New York gas operations were handicapped by a number of corporate management issues, including:

- a very small management team that did not provide sufficient management hierarchy for objective oversight;

- insufficient control or authority by the New York jurisdictional president over New York operations;

- administrative support functions that were focused almost exclusively on overall corporate financial performance, rather than providing information and analysis to support the utility operations which fundamentally drive that performance;

- an executive and senior management culture characterized by fraternal agreement, 'good news' management and a reluctance to speak out and to challenge the group;

- ineffective governance with little objectivity and minimal authority.

The report concluded that these management themes and their impacts were evidenced throughout the organization in every area reviewed as part of the audit. The US Foundations Programme (USFP), the name given to the implementation of a new SAP back-office system, had a number of systems and reporting challenges that the audit concluded were largely the result of these pervasive management issues.

Jurisdictional Model 2.0

The strategy had changed: there was a drive to get closer to the consumer and to gain support from the local jurisdictional regulators to ensure NGUSA was sufficiently remunerated for their operations. This led to a review of the organization design to create the next evolution of the TOM. This organization redesign became known as JDx 2.0.

A big part of this redesign would be to focus on the issue of accountability to ensure that at the highest level the US leadership team were clear on what they were accountable for and where they needed to consult with their colleagues. A strong focus was on governance and safety.

Finally, a decision was made to utilize the talented people in the organization to drive the design. This would create a greater understanding by the leadership team of how the new operating model would work; further, that they would be able to tell the story behind the design to their teams. The design team was selected to include people who had significant understanding of the existing model and people with a level of independence, as there would be limited change in their areas. This role would be in addition to their normal day-to-day work activities.

The biggest change in the organization design was a strategy to get closer to the customer, which in turn would ensure that the business catered for different state regulations. The team created from this a set of design principles that they would use to test every change they would make.

Organization design approach

The organization design approach used for Project Marlborough was also used for the JDx 2.0 organization review. The design principles for a jurisdictional-focused organization are shown in Table 4.2.

It was decided early in the project that this was not the time to make changes at every level of the organization structure. Instead, it was felt that accountability at the top of the organization was in need of review. At the next level down, this would mean that each of the reports to the senior vice-presidents would be impacted: some would retain the same reporting structure; some would now report to a jurisdictional president; a few would see their teams split and they

Table 4.2   Core design principles for JDx 2.0

Design Principle	Key Questions (*to be used to test the strength of the design option*)
The design will support our goal of operational excellence in our business	• Does the design keep process and performance excellence at the heart of everything that we do? • Does the design create more agility, innovation, speed and efficiency? • Does the design provide a clear and simple decision authority enabling us to meet our compliance obligations? • Does the design create a streamlined business planning cycle to effectively manage our business? • Does the design deliver clear accountability and eliminate ambiguity for all roles in the business? • Does the design enable improved management of all customer touch points? • Does the design enable us to gather and analyse data to make decisions that will enhance the customer experience?
The design will enable the four jurisdictional presidents to hold accountability of the P&L for running the operations while optimizing cash and ROE	• Does the design enable us to manage the natural tension between the needs of jurisdictions and central functions? • Does the design align operations jurisdictionally to the best extent possible but maintain central operations synergy? • Does the design allow the jurisdiction president to manage the P&L with accurate and timely reporting and analytics? • Does the design place accountability and decision authority at the right level in the organization? • Does the design provide agility to support ongoing rate case filings? • Does the design create and manage the necessary 'check and balance' between regulatory strategy and execution?
The design will support our growth strategy, creating long-term value creation for the company	• Does the design balance decisions that impact both jurisdictional earnings/regulatory strategy and operational performance? • Does the design enable trust and personal obligation for our collective achievement of business objectives? • Does the design consider near-term M&A activity for the company when building structure?

Figure 4.2 US total operating model post JDx 2.0

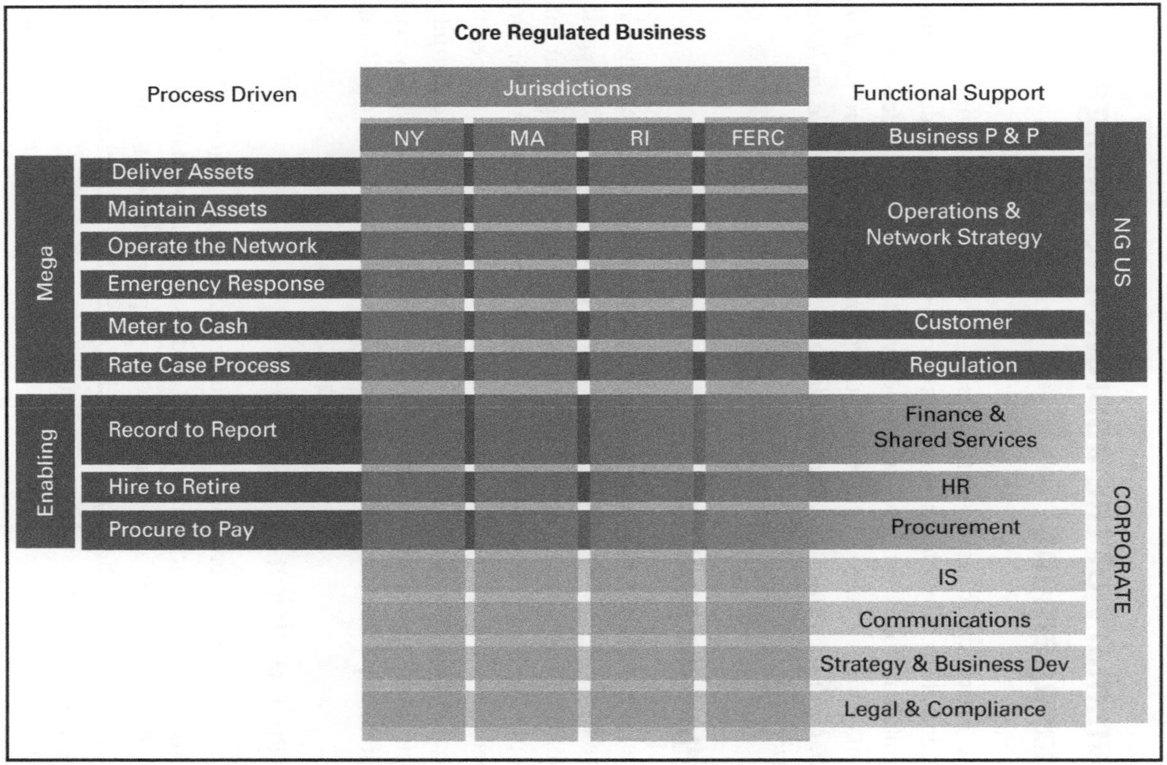

would see a more significant level of change. As the organization was reviewed, a change impact study was undertaken to identify the support required to embed to new design.

This resulted in the NGUSA TOM, as shown in Figure 4.2.

Summary of the approach to change management

The approach focused on the design to ensure an effective and efficient organization. Significant time was spent on getting the design right, and significant focus on how it would work to ensure success. The change management stream in the early stages focused on *why are we doing this*, *what will the future look like* and *how do we ensure people understand the vision*.

Define the opportunity

The key focus for the target operating model was to enable the organization to serve its customers effectively and to be viewed by the regulators as continually striving to serve customers, so in turn ensuring that rate cases would be filed, allowing the company to be compensated for supplying energy to consumers. There was a real opportunity to show the people in the organization that the leaders were building on successes and putting behind them the impacts of less effective organization structures, new computer system implementation challenges and the effect of Superstorm Sandy.

Create a vision

A clear vision was created for the future state organization, which would be shared across the organization. To understand individuals' commitment to the new design, an appreciative inquiry approach, with a number of focus groups, identified the *stop*, *start* and *continue* activities that would make the organization successful.

One of the key success factors in the design was to ensure that there were clear accountabilities and that the team engaged leaders in gaining understanding and support for this change. It was made very clear that this was not a wholesale change to people's roles; instead, it was driving change at the top of the organization. Most people would see a limited impact to what they did on a day-to-day basis and some, particularly customer-facing teams, would not even know a change had happened.

The vision for teams was to continue the safety compliance and performance excellence work, to deliver tangible value to customers as identified and measured by service level agreements, and to anticipate future customer needs and transform the customer experience. Effectively, to leverage the jurisdictional model and digital customer experience to ensure that the organization delivered effectively for its customers.

Conclusion

From our experiences of scoping, shaping and designing the new total operating models for National Grid USA through Project Marlborough and JDx 2.0, the lessons we would like to share are:

1 Choose the guiding team carefully. In the changes described, significant time was spent getting the right team in place, not just who was available at the time. The design team should comprise people with sufficient insight about what needs to change, incentivized to get the design right without significant impact that may lead to personal desires to grow their portfolio of activities to derive personal gains. A core design team was selected and they had the opportunity to test ideas with the key stakeholders. A governance structure was put in place to ensure that any design change decisions were taken at the right level in the organization and were tested against the design principles.

Project Marlborough had been the biggest change in the structure of the organization since the acquisitions began in 2002. The governance structure was made up of the program oversight committee, comprising executives from group strategy, group human resources, the US CEO and the US senior vice-president of HR. Plus, there were three project-level groups, one for the overall project plan, one group who would project manage the selection of people to the new organization, and the final group would look at integration into the new business model.

JDx 2.0 was a smaller group and again made of a subset of the US Leadership team.

2 Clear design principles created an anchor to test all changes against, ensuring that an optimal design would be achieved. They helped to focus effort and to ensure that any 'good ideas' raised were aligned with the changes.

3 Both TOM designs formulated for Project Marlborough and JDx 2.0 were appropriate in that they created the right tensions between local, regional needs and a one-company, one-way approach. However, the matrix structure drove complexity and the models failed to address how to handle and resolve conflicting priorities. The JDx 2.0 review was accompanied by a greater focus on accountabilities and a regular cadence review of performance metrics set up to monitor achieving results.

4 National Grid USA was clearly a learning organization. It was prepared to change when its leaders saw areas that were not working as designed. While it appears to have taken several years to derive the current structure, senior leaders were careful not to make changes quickly, which can often lead to a suboptimal design.

5 There was a need to challenge even some of the deep-seated assumptions. It would have been easy to accept that parts of the current model should be left alone and create a design around them. In the first instance the teams found it difficult to move away from a global-lines-of-business model that had been an established view of some senior people in the organization. Once the analysis had been completed and the case for change developed, there was a clear view that the global-lines-of-business model was not sustainable, and the strong business case made it clear that there was a need to move to a more regional (US) focus.

6 The matrix structure was the right decision for National Grid USA to drive the functional structure and gain economies. It also recognized that each jurisdiction had its own challenges in order to meet the needs of the customer locally. However, it became clear that the leadership team needed to help their personnel understand what it meant to work in a matrix structure effectively. People desire to have stable working relationships, and the conflicts created by the matrix structure can lead to psychological stress. One of the challenges which National Grid USA continues to face is that of a silo mentality. While the TOM design has addressed this, National Grid USA continues to review it on an ongoing basis.

7 Be brave about your own in-house capability. The skills and capabilities needed for JDx 2.0 were sourced internally without the need to involve large consultancies or other external organizations. The result is that National Grid USA now feels that it is in a good position to meet its future challenges using its own talent. Developing this capability around organization design and change can feel daunting. However, investing in internal capability can make the organization a more interesting place to work, provides clear development opportunities for individuals and ensures that any organization implementation can be more sustainable.

References

Galbraith, JR (2000) *Designing the Global Corporation*, Jossey-Bass, San Francisco

Gailoto, F *et al* (2006) *The Matrix Reloaded: The multi-axis organization as key to competitive advantage*, Booz Allen Hamilton, Washington, DC

NorthStar Consulting Group (2014) [Accessed 8 June 2016] *National Grid USA's New York Gas Companies: Case 13-G-0009* [Online] http://documents.dps.ny.gov/public/Common/ViewDoc.aspx?DocRefId={6F2D60D5-410C-49DE-994C-24D0FCABA134}

Simons, R (2005) *Levers of Organization Design: How managers use accountability systems for greater performance and commitment*, Harvard Business School Press, Boston, MA

Stanford, N (2007) *Guide to Organization Design: Creating high-performing and adaptable enterprises*, The Economist in Association with Profile Books, London

Sy, T and D'Annunzio, LS (2005) Challenges and strategies of matrix organizations: top-level and mid-level managers' perspectives. *Human Resource Planning*, 28 (1), p 39

The brain and adaptive change

05

PAUL BROWN AND KATE LANZ

Introduction

This chapter offers a particular angle of observation on change management. It comes from a new field of knowledge called applied neuroscience that uses 21st-century discoveries about how the brain works to rethink human behaviour.

It starts with the view that the two essential components of change – people and organization – are so poorly understood that it is not at all surprising that change management is so difficult. It questions the too easily used word 'change' and observes that resistance to change is a naturally occurring phenomenon that needs to be taken into account as a potential source of power, not to be fought against as something to be beaten down or conquered. And then it proposes that human energy as managed and directed (motivated) by brain processes is the key component that theoretical models of organizational behaviour and change practices have generally lacked. Having established these positions, it then considers what a whole-systems model of the organization might look like, and concludes with describing how applied neuroscience might contribute to altering the change conversation.

Getting a mindset going

Be a fly on the wall for a moment. At Oxford's Saïd Business School, 30 international senior project managers from one of the country's biggest energy companies are in the middle of a week-long executive development programme. On this day they are considering organizational change.

'Let's not worry about "change" for the moment', says the guest lecturer. 'Let's just work out how things are when they are at their best, because in any change process that would be a good outcome, wouldn't it, to have things at their best?'

There's no dissent. Interestingly, among a group of highly capable, exhausted and slightly cynical project managers, a spark of active interest seems apparent. Here's this supposed international expert on human behaviour come to talk about change and he says 'let's not'. That's surprising. Their attention goes up. 'Why not *not* talk about change – that's *thought-provoking.*'

'What I want you to do', says the speaker, 'is spend five minutes reflecting on the qualities of the boss you had when you knew you were doing your very best work ever in your professional career. And when you have got really in touch with who he or she was, distil in four words the qualities of that person.'

Five minutes later comes the speaker's request for those qualities to be shared in the group and captured on a whiteboard as they come. Without exception, the words that are used talk about the quality of relationship that existed, the personal satisfactions of working under such conditions, and the opportunities for professional challenge and growth that resulted.

'That's typically called soft stuff, isn't it?', says the speaker. 'But if that created the best, how much time and money is costed into complex project management protocols to create those conditions?'

'None', comes an immediate reply, with which no one disagrees.

'Isn't that curious?', says the speaker. 'What if it were not soft stuff after all, but hard science? Let me show you how it is.' And so he did.

A moment's reflection might occasion a little surprise that all change management happens, contextually, in the presence of two great unknowns. The first is in answer to the question: 'What is "a person"?' And the second is in answer to: 'What is "an organization"?'

Ask a group of mechanical engineers about the basic requirements for the design of a suspension bridge and there will quickly be agreement. If there is argument and disagreement, resolution can be had by reference to well-established principles. The same has not at any level been true for understanding people or organizations.

A little further reflection suggests that it is very curious that the enormous amount of teaching of both psychology and management that has taken place in the past 60 years or so, and in which psychology has laid claim to be the study of the science of human behaviour, has never systematically approached the fundamental question 'What is a "person"'? In other words, 'What is it that makes up the sense of Self that is the person who shows up at work every day?'

Now that 20th-century psychology can be seen in the context of 21st-century neuroscience, it is apparent that the so-called science of human behaviour has evolved as a *descriptive* rather than an *explanatory* body of knowledge: though in the absence of adequate explanatory models, description has often been taken as fact. In consequence, what has passed for apparent certainty proves only to have been assumption. This is not a sound basis upon which to develop predictive understandings in the realm of organizational behaviour.

So it becomes evident that the lack of an agreed understanding of 'the person' proves to be a serious limitation in devising change programmes when the agents or inhibitors of change are also those accumulated complex systems called 'people'. No wonder 'change management' is an expensive business fraught with uncertainty (Leeman, 2014). And that uncertainty is compounded by a parallel lack of any agreement as to what 'an organization' is. In the way that 20th-century psychology failed to agree any understanding of 'the person', so 20th-century management theory and its sub-specialty OD failed to agree 'an organization'. Brown, Kingsley and Paterson (2015) have explored this in some detail, arguing for an approach to a solution as first proposed some 30 years ago by Cousins (1986), which is presented in more detail below.

Relationship and change

Whether or not change is the only constant, let's first question 'change'. And also let's find out why resistance to change may not be such a bad thing after all.

In big concept terms, the brain can be described as the organ of relationship: the organ that makes sense for us and to others of how our senses see the world; the physical basis for creating a functioning mind; the chemical factory that determines all our behaviour; or the mainspring of all motivation. Each of those statements is true, yet elusively not the whole truth. What is certain about the brain is that each brain is unique to the individual who possesses (or is possessed by) any particular brain in question. In matured-brain individuals (aged 24+), the associative learning system that is the brain will have established pathways and patterns that, with a high level of reliability, continuously represent to the person and to the outside world a familiar pattern of thoughts, feelings and actions by which both the person and other individuals recognize a unique individual called 'my-Self".

The brain that continuously does this is an organ of habit. And although those habits may develop, alter or die under a wide variety of circumstances, they cannot be other than they are. They have been acquired by genetic endowment interlaced with experience in a highly individual mix of nature and especially nurture. Unlike the computers in a dealing room, all the individuals working those computers have different operating systems. It's surprising that human beings can be patched together at all. The fact that they can stems essentially from the brain working as the organ of relationship.

The brain each one of us has is the one that got each of us to where we are on any particular day in our life. Although we might have thought we directed our brain, from our experience it is the brain that directs us. What we have thought of as rational – our capacity to think and think about thinking – begins to look more and more like a *rationalizing* capacity. That is to say, our brain makes sense to us and for us *after* it has already started the course of action that we thought we were controlling. Consciousness, therefore, may be the illusion of control.

In consequence, whenever change is proposed there is an immediate threat to the brain. Not only is change demanding of effort and is itself resource intensive – think of setting out to learn Mandarin or an easier language you do not already know – but change especially requires an implied shift in 'me', in other words in 'myself'. So though cognitively it may be easy enough to appreciate the need for change, the emotional and neural *attachment* (remembering that the brain is the organ of relationship) to the proposed outcome may be an entirely different matter.

Organizationally, what is often referred to as 'buy-in' does not perhaps take sufficient cognizance of what 'attachment' means. The significance of attachment is that there is emotional bonding at a level that is deeper than 'buy-in' might imply. For if, as the later explanation of the workings of the brain shows, all our behaviour is controlled not by the way we *think* but by the way we *feel*, then only the emotions connected to attachment will create changes in behaviour. Thinking, feeling and behaving are the three irreducible components of being a functioning human being. They are mediated and managed by different systems, but they are all powered by the emotional system, not the thinking system.

One consequence of this is that what is often described as 'resistance' to change is not in itself resistance but simply an observation that the brain that is apparently resisting has not been moved (emotionally) yet to change. A heavy piece of furniture, needing moving, will be much easier to relocate if a well-designed set of small removers' wheels are placed underneath it through the careful use of a simple lifting lever rather than that the furniture is broken into small pieces. Yet metaphorically that second option is what many change programmes try to do when confronting 'resistance' and seeing it as something to be broken down. The more effective approach would be to ask and answer the question: 'How do we design the wheels and create the necessary lift?'

There is, however, a quite different way of considering change once it is accepted that wishing *not* to change is the generally preferred and more natural state. What human beings are especially good at is adapting both themselves and the external world in ways that are entirely beyond the capacities of all other animals, though some of the higher mammals – dogs, horses and elephants especially – have developed a not-insubstantial capacity to adapt to the requirements of human beings.

If the idea of adaptive capacity is used to replace the concept of change, then a different approach to creating future difference naturally occurs. Adaptation implies the possibility of benefit in a dynamic environment. More importantly, adaptation implies a starting point – 'from here' – rather than a goal – 'to there'. Adaptation has self-interest implied; change is imposed by someone else.

This distinction mobilizes different brain systems. One is habit. The other is goal-directed intention. If the habits that already exist can be attached to different goals, then that is most economical of effort. So with this perspective the task for change management becomes not how to convince people of the need for change. The task becomes how to explore the benefits of adaptation from 'here'. Once the benefits have been assimilated, the brain naturally gears up to create the outcomes. The outcomes will, of course, be a change from the previous state, but the means of getting there is not to push the requirement for change but the benefits of adaptation, even if, in some circumstances, the need to adapt is both very urgent and needs to take place in a very short time.

In a slightly different context, Sinek (2009) has explored the *Why* and the *How* and the *What* of inspiring behavioural action in any desired direction. He observes that most propositions underpinning the requirement for change are formulated from the vantage point of *What* needs to be done, which then backs up into *How* the *What* needs to be done. He makes a strong case, however, for the proposition that what really focuses behaviour is an attachment to the underlying *Why*. It is this that, in applied neuroscientific terms, becomes adaptation through attachment.

The emotional brain

The human brain is a complex and highly interconnected system that involves the heart and the gut as well as the four pounds of squidgy tissue that sits within the skull. For the sake of brevity and simplicity, this section deals mostly with what is happening inside the skull between the ears – what is commonly thought of as 'the brain', with its 86 billion nerve cells (neurons) each having the capacity for 10,000 associative connections to create the unique pathway architecture of the brain that makes each one of us unique and got each one of us 'here'.

The cortex is the observable outer surface of the brain, wrinkled into folds and not unlike a very large walnut in its preserved appearance. In humans the cortex has the job of making sense of what the brain is up to, putting all the stimuli from all the senses into order, and processing them through the power of speech *after* they have been attached to feelings. It's where decisions are made on the basis of feelings that give meaning. Without feelings there would be no capacity to make judgements. There would be a capacity to have reactions, for reptiles have those with remarkable agility. But on top of our retained capacity for instinctive reaction, like pulling a hand away from a sudden source of intense heat without a moment's thought, humans have the power to weigh alternatives. It is feelings that tip the balance and it is the outcome of that process that we call 'a decision'.

Feelings are themselves the compounds of emotions. In the way that all palette colours come from the three primary colours of red, blue and yellow, so all feelings come from eight basic emotions (Brown, Swart and Meyler, 2009; Brown and Brown, 2012). As the emotions are the basis for directing energy, they are key to an understanding of the motivational system.

Once the word emotion is hyphenated into e-motion (see Figure 5.1), that becomes obvious and, once obvious, it requires us to reconsider the whole question of what is rational and irrational. The Western fascination with the power of thinking that has dominated its cultures for four hundred years since Descartes coined his precept 'I think, therefore I am' may need changing into a more modern appreciation of 'I feel, therefore I can think I am'.

Of the eight basic emotions, five are concerned with survival. They are the ones that got us here. The escape/avoidance/survival emotions are *fear*, *anger*, *disgust*, *shame* and *sadness*. The energy they generate goes inwards to the protection of the individual, even if on some occasions, as in a protective fight, it appears to go outwards: but it only does so in support of the preservation of the individual.

Then there is one emotion that is a potentiator: it creates a state of preparedness. It is called *surprise* or *startle*. Some big companies like Disney run off a continuous capacity to generate surprise and some startle – though if the result is to trigger the escape/avoidance emotions then gate receipts will dive. What such organizations want to do is trigger the attachment emotions of *excitement/joy* and *trust/love*.

Figure 5.1   The eight basic emotions and the main neurochemistry that creates them. It is the infinite mixing of the basic emotions that creates feelings. Emotional patterning starts before birth, is the only effective means of communication for the first two years of life, and underpins all individual behaviour

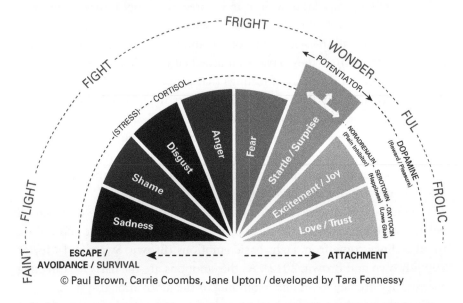

© Paul Brown, Carrie Coombs, Jane Upton / developed by Tara Fennessy

These then are the prime or basic emotions – the irreducible feelings, driven by the chemistry of the brain. We come into the world with the capacity to have them triggered by experience. They have evolved to ready us for responding to and making sense of what the world provides. The combinant emotions called feelings give colour to existence and underlie all decision making and judgement. What the world provides sets up the private and personal templates of our own emotional system that become the basis for shaping the individual Self, which, by the age of 24, will have established us as a fully functioning unique individual – though that individual will have been recognizably emerging for the whole of that period.

In any change process, is the preferred outcome one in which the organization thrives? Or just survives? If a person's brain is triggered to feel any of the survival emotions, they will experience a threat response and generate the associated neurochemistry. Such a neurochemical response will not readily enable adaptation of the brain in relation to the organizational change required. In fact, it will be quite the contrary. If, on the other hand, the neurochemistry of thrive is triggered – through trusting and supportive relationships perhaps – the brain is more ready to start adapting (see Figure 5.1).

Many organizations have a relatively crude concept of stick-and-carrot motivation. What applied neuroscience tells us is that what the brain remembers and what guides action is the stick. The carrot only keeps the beast alive waiting for the stick.

As human beings we are fundamentally a brain on two legs, receiving data from five senses, giving those data meaning through emotional loading, being able to develop the capacity to put those emotionally laden data into language and into thought, store them in fluid memory, and create from that a sense of 'me'. That is what change programmes want to change. Or, if more adaptively conceived, change programmes might choose to harness and direct that remarkable capacity in the service of the strategic and operational goals of the organization. The organization cannot change unless the individuals do. The case study below highlights how the application of neuroscience can support more effective change initiatives.

CASE STUDY CSC – Linking marketing activity to business results

A major division of a large well-known food business was facing major business transformation in order to build a company fit for the future. The company in question had never faced any change initiatives of such magnitude. Finance and IT teams were particularly implicated in the first phase of the transformation initiative, but duplications in roles across a wider range of departments also engaged in the transformation started to emerge as the process kicked off. This role confusion was breeding survival emotions in all divisions of the company. The atmosphere included all the primary survival emotions: fear, anger, sadness, disgust and shame. The environment was tense.

A key leader from one of the business change teams decided to adopt a brain-based approach to creating the transformation initiative. He took time to have detailed one-on-one conversations to understand the attachment emotion drivers and the survive emotion triggers with all members of his direct team. He did this with particular reference to the business transformation initiative. He was relatively new to the team as their line manager, although quite well known and liked across the division, but the care that he took with these conversations really cemented and increased the trust the team felt in him. The brain is the organ of relationship. Within an organization, sustainable change actually happens one relationship at a time through trust, and this was exactly what this leader had set about doing.

The second phase was to undertake a relationship 'heat map' to map out all the relationships that this team had across the division. The brain changes with relationships and it changes faster when 'thrive' emotions are activated. This detailed exercise enabled his affected team – who themselves were business transformation professionals – to understand the emotional landscape they were heading into as a result of the transformation changes they were trying to create, and hence how it would feel for them and their team members.

The leader also mapped, together with his team, the size and scope of the end-to-end business transformation process, using a change management framework. With their team members they jointly plotted where all relevant individuals across the business were currently 'playing' on the business transformation 'football pitch'.

They noticed that that there was more space on the pitch and more areas that needed focus than they were currently playing in. This opening up of space in people's minds allowed them to relax and see possibilities in the future contributions they could make. While people still harboured a good deal of uncertainty and therefore fear, he did a great job of accessing as much attachment emotion 'excitement' as possible at a difficult moment.

He then engaged other key departments in this process so that the conversation was both transparent and inclusive. This enabled all impacted parties to see where the 'plane of possibility' existed, without becoming too rigid or fixed in defending a particular view of the world.

At this point, with this emerging clarity about the scope of the transformation and having identified where gaps or duplications in the organizational system were making them less efficient than they needed to be, the leader played back the insights to key sponsors at the top of the organization.

The size and scope of the transformation also meant that there would have to be headcount reductions, which caused a strong 'threat' response across all levels within the organization as the likelihood of this became ever clearer.

The emerging challenge was now very much one of how to keep the change team motivated in the face of ongoing threat and uncertainty over their roles. This he achieved through two main activities. The first was to really get his team to think about 'what "great" would look like from their customers' point of view' in their business fit for the future. This reminds us of the visiting lecturer at Saïd Business School, working out how things are when they are 'at their best'. Second, in all their regular interactions he took care to contain the anxiety in the team through being open about the state of play, honest about the reality of what the changes could bring, empathic about the range of emotions this was arousing in people and continuously tapping into the vision of what a great future could look like. The connection and regularity of these team conversations helped people to support each other.

The whole way through, the leader had managed to create real brain-based adaptation, starting 'from here' rather than an imposed 'to there'. This meant that when the formal consultation process eventually started and people had to begin to implement the transformation agenda, resulting in the inevitable loss of roles, no one was surprised. All those impacted felt clear about 'Why' this was happening, felt that they had been heard during the course of the process and had contributed to the design of the transformation.

Attention to attachment/thrive emotion was the primary driver throughout. While there was sadness at some of the losses of both influence/power and actual jobs, people understood. This aspect of the process was handled in a grown-up way, with transparency, trust and supportive redundancy packages. People could see that a fair process had genuinely been applied.

The leader handled the frustration from head office at the speed of the process. He believed that a process driven from attachment emotions would provide a far more sustainable result in the longer term and that, once the business transformation was complete, the return to optimum productivity would be faster due to the relationship lens and attachment focus. People were genuinely excited at the change and what that meant for the company. They could also see his courage, and this increased the level of confidence and buy-in. Emotions can be viral, and the dominant emotions from the most senior people communicate the fastest. He was really walking the talk and people liked it.

From an organizational perspective, the leader had focused on relationship and attachment as the primary drivers of the change process, even if this meant taking some risk and heat from head office. This started to cause a conversation to run in the division that started to shift the culture from fearful to fear free. Many staff were connected to the process, so word got about. The initiative caused a lot of positive energy flow between the various organizational subsystems. He had costed the time and financial investment that it would take to cause change in this way. While the leader in question had to take some bruising moments at times during the process, when the pace picked up around the implementation his sponsors at head office started to understand better what he had been up to. It worked.

From brain to mind: how the human mind works

Five further factors about the brain need to be taken briefly into account. Together they lead to an operating conclusion about how the human mind works.

The first is that the brain consists of two halves. The second is that men's and women's brains may look the same but operate very differently. The third is that the brain works bottom to top, not top to bottom. The fourth is that there are two special regions of the brain, which together are called the amygdala, that manage the emotional system. And the fifth is that the brain operates by shunting around the available energy supply to where, within the complexity of its whole system, it is most needed. As the amygdala controls the emotions and hence energy flow, it is in the amygdala from where change is directed.

The brain consists of two halves

The brain is divided front-to-back into two halves, which are connected by a bridge of fibres between them called the corpus callosum. The left side of the brain deals with essentially what is known. The right side of the brain deals with the new and is on the lookout for the unknown or whatever might occasion surprise. This is clearly relevant to organizational change: the right hemisphere has a significant role, and organizations need to understand what their people's right hemispheres are noticing and how they are responding. The case study above is a good example of handling right-hemisphere responses effectively. When something unknown becomes known, it gets incorporated into the great store of the known on the left side. The right side is especially, though not exclusively, engaged with emotions. The left side is similarly engaged with language.

In a magisterial book on the differences between the left and right sides of the brain, McGilchrist (2010, 2011) has advanced the idea that Western civilization has become so enamoured of the capabilities of the left side of the brain that it has almost forgotten the great value of the right side. The left side, he suggests, is narrowly focused and sharpens attention to detail, while the right side operates a broad vigilant awareness.

The bridge of fibres that provides transport capability between the two halves may be up to four times larger in women than in men. There is still much discussion about what this might mean, but we suggest that the gender differences we see in the brain may have important implications for planning and managing change.

Men's and women's brains may look the same but operate very differently

Composite brain scans on one thousand men and women, boys and girls produced by the University of Pennsylvania (Grant, 2013) show that the way information flows in post-puberty male and female brains is remarkably different. The male brain appears to operate most characteristically in either half, with pathways being organized in a front-to-back-to-front fashion.

The female brain, on the other hand, has a multitude of interconnections between the two hemispheres, providing fast access between the right and left hemispheres. So despite the relative lack of *physical* differences between male and female brains, the way male and female brains *function* seems to be remarkably different. The full implications of these findings for the organization are not yet well understood.

The brain works bottom to top: the amygdala

Stimuli arriving through the senses are first of all directed in milliseconds to the amygdala, which has the function of assessing all incoming information for its emotional significance, the primary concern being danger. The amygdala then assigns the data to whichever cortical and subcortical pathways are the most appropriate. This assigning is *based upon all of that particular individual's previous experience*. There could be no other basis for any one person's brain being organized. In this process, all thoughts internally generated are treated by the brain as data to be continuously reassessed by the amygdala as if they were incoming data.

These processes happen very fast and below the threshold of conscious awareness. The brain may organize the body to respond within 80 milliseconds of a signal being received, but awareness of the reaction does not arise until 250+ milliseconds. This is why conscious agreement to something often results in no actual outcome behaviourally, as the pathways that have been activated are specific to the individual. The apparent agreement may only reflect, for instance, a pathway that does not wish for disagreement but is not an actual commitment to different outcomes.

So the practical question that arises is: if the amygdala controls behaviour through managing the e-motional processes, how can the amygdala be accessed in any working setting? The answer to that will become apparent later in the chapter.

The brain operates by shunting around the available energy supply

The brain works on about 25 watts of energy. The body as a whole runs on around 95 watts. Being only 4 per cent of total body mass, it can be seen that the brain is an energy-hungry system. However, when any one part of the brain needs a maximum supply of energy, the brain does not create more energy. It shunts the available supply around to where at any moment it is most needed. That is why, when driving a car and a sudden emergency occurs, the conversation that is simultaneously taking place does not register; or why it is dangerous to concentrate hard on an intensive mobile phone conversation and drive at the same time, hands-free or not. Energy in the brain operates on a demand-and-limited-supply basis as the mechanism underlying focus and attention (Godwin and Cham, 2012).

The energy supply is preferentially available to anything connected to the survival emotions. So whatever a person might wish to be concentrating on, anything else that is happening and that has survival emotions attached to it – worrying about a teenager acting impulsively and trying alcohol; a marital row; a presentation coming up that is generating doubt and anxiety rather than excitement – will take priority for use of the available energy.

One particular area of the right front side of the brain, the right ventrolateral prefrontal cortex (RVLPFC), seems to be especially involved with creative adaptive decision making. It is an area of the brain that is most useful to have fully powered up when complex decisions are being made and implemented and where continuous adaptation is required. But if someone leading a complex change project doubts the abilities of some key team members, knows there is going to be a major row later in the day with the client regarding cost and time over-runs, is troubled by end-of-year bonus doubts and has myriad similar issues demanding preferential energy supply, then the very part of the brain that would be most useful, the RVLPFC, will be starved of energy and so not functioning well at all.

Somewhere inside themselves, people know that they are not functioning well. That itself becomes another source of RVLPFC energy depletion. Conscientious people then push themselves harder. That increases the depletion further, interferes with sleep, raises stress hormone (cortisol) levels, creates early-hours ruminative waking, and generates increasingly tired people whose capacity to do their best goes on diminishing. It is like trying to drive a car with one foot on the accelerator and one on the brake. At some stage it shudders to a halt or something burns out. It is called executive stress.

In summary, what are the implications for change programmes?

What does this all this mean for change and for the management of change programmes? Some general propositions about change and change management can be drawn from the foregoing understanding of how the brain works. These are:

1 'Change' is itself a concept that is threatening to most people, who are self-regulating systems of great complexity because 'change' requires the acceptance of another brain's solutions. There are two ways of gaining that acceptance: abandon the concept of change in favour of something more appropriate to the way the brain works, which is about adaptation; and learn to use the attachment e-motions of excitement/joy, trust/love as the motivators. The case study is a good example of this.

2 Enabling the diversity of brains engaged in a change process to contribute will support a successful change. Of course, men and women function in very similar ways to a great extent, but there may be benefits gained from knowing how to use gender-defined strengths. There is much supporting research evidence demonstrating that gender-balanced teams produce superior business performance. Deszo and Ross (2012) look at the business impact of gender balance in key decision-making forums. Individuals will feel more part of creating the change and will *feel* more committed to facilitating it if a true diversity of brains has been involved in designing the change process.

3 The role of the leader is key, because it is from the leader that the key emotions flow into any hierarchical system. A leader who cannot create attachment emotions involving professional excitement, delight, satisfaction and, above all, trust is going to be wasting a huge amount of human energy both personally and in staff. Since it is only human energy that creates intended organizational outcomes – among which are profits – then having the knowledge and skill to manage that energy in the most productive manner is a leadership skill of great value.

4 Emotions can be viral. Humans pick up how others are feeling, especially when the emotions are strong. This transmits at a physiological level. Fear is the fastest emotion to transmit. Toxic emotions, say in relation to an unwelcome change, have destructive capabilities. As with the human immune system, stressed emotions transmitting between people can require a huge amount of energy to combat.

5 Human beings are remarkable self-regulating systems. The more the behaviour of good people is controlled, the less they will be able to give spontaneously. So, at the beginning of change programmes, identify how to access the knowledge, wisdom and self-regulating creative capacities of all the key individuals, including those who do not believe they are key. It will pay dividends, especially when the going gets tough.

6 Emotions are not soft stuff. There is hard science behind them. They are driven by the most complex neurochemistry which is itself the result of the way any of us 'see' any situation. In a relatively new science called epigenetics, it has become apparent that if the genes that control behaviour can express themselves in a huge variety of ways, then what tells the gene how to express itself in any particular circumstance is the neurochemistry created by individual experience that itself is triggered by individual perception. So the skill for creating change is getting perceptions lined up emotionally, not just intellectually, because it is the emotions that direct the genes that produce the desired behaviour and outcomes. And in this process the amygdala works out what the motivational significance of any perceptions is.

Change and the organization

It was observed at the beginning of this chapter that neither 'the individual' nor 'the organization' is a concept that has acquired a substantial shared, scientific understanding; in consequence, all change processes are operating on two aspects that are crucial to successful outcomes but which have no common underlying frame(s) of reference.

Brown (2010) and Brown *et al* (2015) have made reference to the relatively unknown work of Cousins (1986). Cousins, as a graduate student in the School of Education at Harvard under Chris Argyris, and starting from the stratified systems theory of Elliot Jaques (1961), derived experimentally a model of any organization which he called Spheres of Influence.

What he showed was that any effective organization, or any part of an organization, needs to have within it a system for:

- leadership;
- culture;
- the development of people, processes and products;
- staff;
- customers.

Together, these represent the essential spine of the organization. The spine is then supported internally by:

- strategy;
- operations;
- systems.

Figure 5.2   A dynamic whole systems model of any organization or any part of it, proposed by Cousins (1986) and demonstrated in use by Brown (2010). It is human energy that creates interconnectivity between the spheres, all of which are dependent on each other for a fully-functioning system. The model is an analogue of the human body and its eleven major systems

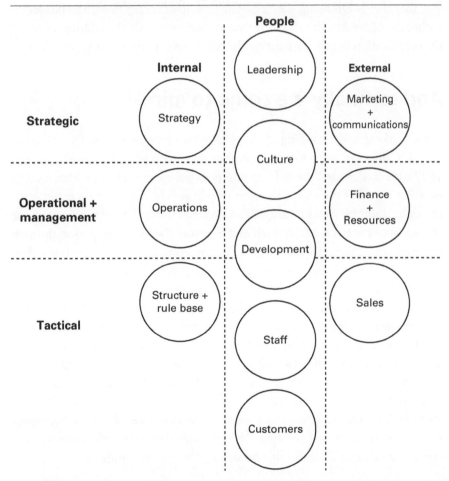

Externally the whole system then requires three more subsystems:

- marketing and communications;
- finance;
- sales.

Any one of the subsystems has all the 11 elements represented in it also, as is the case with each cell in the body and the presence of a complete replication of DNA. Each subsystem needs to be functioning in its own right – as with any system within the body such as respiration or the cardiovascular system; but to be doing so it will be interdependent with all other systems. It is thus a dynamic systemic model (Figure 5.2).

In organizations, what connects all subsystems together is the way energy is flowing between the subsystems. Before epigenetics had appeared as a science, Cousins demonstrated a methodology for showing how perception defines the way that energy is flowing. Consequently, a map of energy flows and blockages within the organization can be created, defining not only the relative health of the organization but also an approach to both managing and tracking change.

And so finally we come to mind

Some working understanding of 'mind' then becomes important. Dan Siegel of UCLA, California, is the foremost proponent of such an understanding (Siegel, 1999). He has created the field of interpersonal neurobiology, which focuses on what it is that transpires between people and how the brain creates itself through establishing relationships. This understanding of mind is important for change since the brain adapts itself and therefore the self of the person through relationships. If those relationships are engendering attachment emotions, then the minds (of which the brain is part) of the people affected by and effecting the change can begin to adapt. Siegel also proposed that what we see working as 'mind' is the capacity of the physical brain to organize itself around the continuous management of information, energy and relationships (Figure 5.3).

Moreover, the mind can function in one of three states. One state is of a restless energy that cannot keep focus, seeks continuous stimulation and produces an often infectious energy. Organizationally it creates a lot of excitement but little outcome, and organizationally is often called 'an awayday'. Clinically it becomes mania. The opposite of this is becoming over-focused, rigid, self-limiting through imposing rules and systems, and critical of others. Clinically this becomes obsessive-compulsive.

Figure 5.3   A representation of Siegel's (1999) proposal that the brain continuously organizes itself dynamically around the management of information, energy and relationship: and that in doing so it creates what we see operating as 'mind' which is not otherwise created by any specific physical structure

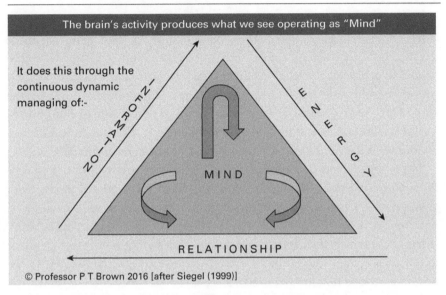

© Professor P T Brown 2016 [after Siegel (1999)]

In between these two states is a third state, which Siegel describes as 'the plane of possibilities'. It is where there is effective flow, where energy can be usefully and appropriately applied, and where the individual feels in focused self-regulating control. The practices of meditation and mindfulness can produce this state very effectively, but it is also an integrated mode of being acquired through a history of being in secure relationships. This has major implications for generating successful brain-based change initiatives: if leaders can generate a relationally based sense of emotional and psychological safety in their organizations, they will be generating this plane of possibility and their best chance of success.

Brain-based change in practice

As this chapter explains, the most effective fuel for generating sustainable change at pace is tapping into the attachment emotions of the individuals affected by the change. Without activating the attachment emotions, all an organization is achieving in any change initiative is compliance, *not* true buy-in. Productivity via compliance can only be suboptimal versus genuinely engaged excitement via attachment emotion activation.

Conclusion

What we seem to have done in the second half of the 20th century is focus organizations increasingly on quantities of information, ignored energy and produced protocols for relationships. Some significant parts of many organizations, notably HR, may have a vested interest in making that so, as Brown *et al* (2015) have described. Yet it seems inimical to the human condition if, as the evidence increasingly suggests, we thereby restrict the most effective operating of the minds that are the product of our extraordinary brains.

We suggest, from an applied neuroscience perspective, that it is time the whole concept of 'change' in organizations is reconsidered in favour of 'adaptation'. 'Change' programmes require a focus on what is to be done and how it is to be done. 'Adaptation' begs the essential question 'Why? What for?', which then focuses attention on the emotional bases of adaptation rather than the habits of action. As a result, the brain creates the adaptive actions that are required.

In order to develop a working model of adaptation there needs to be some agreed working model of the organization, so that the way energy is being applied in the system can be tracked. Figure 5.2 proposes such a model. Nineteenth-century medicine used science to work out the 11 main systems of the body, and goes on using science to refine its understanding at a molecular level so that all doctors trained in Western medicine use the same frame of reference, though all the patients that they see are individuals and unique. In the same way, organizational practice needs an approach to understanding the organization that really does systematically and scientifically describe a whole system that has dynamic capacity. We have described an approach to defining that model in this chapter.

References

Brown, PT, Swart, T and Meyler, J (2009) Emotional intelligence and the amygdala: towards the development of the concept of the limbic leader in executive coaching. *NeuroLeadership Journal*, Issue Two, pp 66–77

Brown, PT (2010) *Synergy in Buildings: Towards developing an understanding of the human interface*. Freiburg, Germany: Proceedings of the International Solar Energy Society, 23–24 June 2010, pp 149–54

Brown, PT and Brown, V (2012) *Neuropsychology for Coaches: Understanding the basics*, Open University Press/McGraw-Hill Education, Marlow, UK

Brown, PT, Kingsley, J and Paterson, S (2015) *The Fear-Free Organization: Vital insights from neuroscience to transform your business culture*, Kogan Page, London

Cousins, P (1986) *The Mapping Spheres of Influence: A visual typology of responses to rapid technological change in a large organization*, Harvard University Press, Cambridge, MA

Deszo, C and Ross, DG (2012) [Accessed 8 June 2016] Does female representation in top management improve firm performance? A panel data investigation [Online] www.onlinelibrary.wiley.com/doi/10.1002/smj.1955/abstract

Godwin, D and Cham, J (2012) [Accessed 8 September 2016] Your brain by the numbers [Online] www.scientificamerican.com/article/mind-in-pictures-your-brain-by-the-numbers/

Grant, B (2013) [Accessed 15 May 2016] Male and female brains wired differently, *The Scientist*, 4 December [Online] www.the-scientist.com/?articles.view/articleNo/38539/title/Male-and-Female-Brains-Wired-Differently

Jaques, E (1961) *Equitable Payment: A general theory of work, differential payment, and individual progress*, Heinemann, London

Leeman, R (2014) [Accessed 15 May 2016] 70% of change management initiatives fail – REALLY? LinkedIn, 14 September [Online] www.linkedin.com/pulse/20140914031708-7145156-70-of-change-management-initiatives-fail-really

McGilchrist, I (2010) *The Master and his Emissary: The divided brain and the making of the western world*, Yale University Press, New Haven, CT

McGilchrist, I (2011) [Accessed 15 May 2016] *The Divided Brain*, YouTube, October [Online] www.youtube.com/watch?v=dFs9WO2B8uI

Siegel, D (1999) *The Developing Mind: How relationships and the brain interact to shape who we are*, The Guilford Press, New York

Sinek, S (2009) [Accessed 15 May 2016] How great leaders inspire action, TED Talks, September [Online] www.ted.com/talks/simon_sinek_how_great_leaders_inspire_action

Working with resistance to change

06

**ROD WILLIS, ANTHONY BURROWS AND
SARAH COLEMAN**

Introduction

We all have heard the term 'resistance' to organizational change where people
within organizations don't embrace it with the anticipation, positivity or
commitment that we would have hoped. Having worked extensively with
organizational change during our careers, we recognize that this is an area
that continues to impact even the best designed and planned change initiatives.

The issue of resistance to change tends to move to the top of the agenda
during organizational transformation projects, since it works to hamper
delivery of change and so of benefits and value to the organization. Willis's
(2012) research project investigated resistance to change with current and
former change leaders, with combined experiences spanning more than 55
organizations operating across the oil and gas, professional and financial
services, and the public services sectors. He discovered that in the majority of
cases, leaders and managers do not have access to the necessary knowledge
and understanding to deal with many of the typical 'resistance to change'
symptoms identified within his research. This reflects Torbert's (2004) work,
which suggests that due to a lack of focus on people management, there is a
lack of recognition of the value of people-focused skills within management
development in general, which, instead, tends to concentrate on business-
related content such as accountancy, marketing and law.

We talk about 'resistance' as if it is a single and specific thing, but this is a
generic term covering a spectrum of ways in which ambivalence, focus and
energy diverted to other priorities, challenge, hostility and active opposition

to change manifests itself. People react to change in different ways given their own circumstances, ambitions and concerns, and it is not always help-ful to use a single term to cover such a range of seemingly negative responses. Kegan and Lahey (2001, 2013) take the view that resistance to change does not actually reflect opposition to change; instead, most people hold a 'sincere commitment to change' but at the same time spend most of their time, focus and energy on their daily operational roles, objectives and targets – all repre-senting possible hidden 'competing commitments'. They suggest that this results in what looks like resistance but is in fact a kind of personal 'immu-nity' to change. Finally, Thomas and Hardy (2011) have researched much of the literature on resistance to organizational change and have identified two dominant but contrasting approaches: the demonizing versus the celebrating of resistance to change. They recognize that organizations that are willing to build on challenges and resistance generate innovative change and knowl-edge; they also conclude that it is those individuals who are given the power to deliver change in organizations who in fact determine what is resistance to the change, and who have the choice of how to respond to that resistance.

In this chapter, we will share two case studies each relating to resistance to change from different industry sectors and different perspectives. The first describes the implementation of an enterprise information manage-ment system into a multinational organization and how, from an initial position of trust and collaboration, relationships across geographies dete-riorated into defensiveness and suspicion. The second describes turning around a European financial services institution and how resistance to change at the senior leadership level, distributed people leadership levels across the organization and at the individual employee level was addressed and resolved.

Enabling technology, virtual teams and resistance to change

CASE STUDY

This case study is an example of a major change initiative driven by the implementation of new enabling technology within the electronics manufacturing sector. An operations group decided to introduce a new enterprise system (ES) to track service level agreement (SLA) delivery. The objective was to enable greater transparency for enhanced operational efficiency. In addition, there was the desire to enhance the accuracy of forecasting of a broad range of resources required to meet the SLA while enabling the international virtual team to communicate and share information more effectively.

This team had a highly collaborative nature across all geographies. Some more than others wanted to enhance their ability to share information across all locations, as they could see future issues building. Others in the team were very content with what was already working well, one view being 'If it's not broken, don't fix it'. Different locations had very different views as to what 'problem' was being addressed by implementing the new system. The decision to make the investment and implement the new system was made centrally, with very little involvement from those in different locations. Part of the challenge for the central group was working with the virtual teams in different time-zones; getting everyone involved together physically would have been too costly. Given that the principal needs were seen to be the same for all, the central team pushed ahead, sharing updates along the way. Think of this as a broadcast rather than two-way communication.

Although the SLAs were quite similar, there were unique market requirements that were already covered by the existing system in place. It transpired that no one person actually had an overview of the total needs of the system. The various 'unique' requirements were not seen as unique within the region that supported them. When asked the question about any unique needs, the answer coming back was 'none'. For that region, the usage had effectively become a 'standard' offering.

When the new ES was being deployed, the issues started to appear. Not surprisingly, some functionality was missing, since any 'unique' requirements had not been highlighted. This resulted in frustration locally, compounded by an increase in workload: now two systems were in operation, the old and new in parallel. This workload increase was putting strain on the organization, and the more remote members of the virtual team stopped using the new system, or only used it when prompted. The situation was further exasperated because the internet was extremely fast and reliable in some regions and not so in others. The original ES was based on a local server structure, so internet bandwidth issues rarely came to the table. With the new ES, this became a major issue: in real terms, the new system was only half as responsive for some users when contrasted with the original system.

The last straw for the non-English-speaking regions was that the system did not support local languages. As all internal central communications had been in English, an assumption had crept into the overall requirements that a central system using English would be appropriate.

The central deployment team started to complain that the team members located in different parts of the globe would not adopt the new system, would not cooperate and would not comply with the central deployment team's instructions: effectively, they were resisting the change. However, when the central deployment team were asked to visit the other geographies to see the issues for themselves, they did not travel. They said there was no point; the other offices did not want the new solution because it had not been 'invented' by them.

What are the key lessons from this? Certainly adoption had become a major issue. It was clear that the new ES was not delivering at several levels. It was, however, doing what was wanted at central office. From their perspective, central office saw a 'successful solution'; any reports to the contrary created a defensive response and it became easier to point the finger at those who were struggling to adopt the new system, away in the non-English-speaking countries who were often not able to defend their position and bring the real data to the table. The architectural design of the new ES was actually part of the issue, but this was not an acceptable view. Instead, it became easier to agree to the often repeated mantra that *people are resistant to change* and to allow the change project to slide into obscurity over several years. When a fixation develops that others are resistant to change, we often fail to see the actual cause and focus only on the result, leading to a self-fulfilling prophecy that there are indeed many who actively seek to sabotage what we are trying to achieve.

How might this have been a handled differently to avoid this ending? In this case, one key missing aspect was the lack of involvement of the range of stakeholders across functions and geography: those who would be directly affected by the new ES, or who had an interest in its implementation and adoption. The central team's logic was that their involvement would have taken longer and delayed the project start; however, it would have enabled all the requirements to be explored in more detail, with far fewer assumptions informing the design. It would have also enabled people to discuss what form of training might be appropriate, any data migration requirements and how support for the new ES and communication infrastructure would be provided. Being a formal part of a change team tends to focus attention, discussions and decision making; being part of a virtual team where the lead is driven from another continent and where other team members are not visible often makes individuals and groups feel marginalized, with the result that their focus tends to be on the immediate daily operational challenges in front of them rather than on the bigger picture.

Owing to the poor scoping, shaping, designing, planning and implementation, two further challenges developed. The first was an excessive workload as a result of staff having to run both the old and new ES in parallel. Ultimately this had too high a personal 'cost' for several users, leading to a second challenge. The collaboration built across geographies within the organization over a number of years started to erode, and a *them and us* attitude began between central office and other geographic offices.

Transformation, employee engagement and resistance to change

CASE STUDY

This is a case study of a European financial services institution that, up until 2008, could pretty much do no wrong. It was an organization that was highly profitable in financial terms, where senior employees were regarded as pillars of the community and when people got a job there, their families were so proud they would throw a party.

Then along came the economic crash in 2008 and everything changed. This company would have gone out of business had it not been for a massive government bailout. While, on the one hand, it was great news that the government rescued this organization and threw it a vital lifeline, it also meant that the company become primarily state-owned and therefore not in complete control of its own destiny.

Fast forward to 2012 when the company had generated an annual loss of several billion euros and had a sky-high cost base. Staff morale had plummeted to an all-time low. Staff considered external newspapers and the radio to be the most effective communication channels for understanding what was happening, and the majority of people leaders were not leading their teams through change in an engaging and supportive way. One employee explained: 'One thing that would make a big difference to me is if my manager knew my name and something about the experience I have. When changes happen, they hide behind a crib sheet and are then nowhere to be seen.'

The immense pride people once felt about the company quickly turned to shame. Given the state of crisis in which the firm found itself, many difficult decisions were taken in order to try to get things back on an even keel. Sites were closed, headcount was halved from 24,000 employees, pay rises and bonuses were frozen, defined benefit pension schemes were removed. The media were not onside and the company hit the headlines on a daily basis for all the wrong reasons.

It was during this dark and challenging time that a new Group Head of Internal Communications and Engagement (GHIC&E) was recruited into the business, reporting into the Group Chief People Officer (GCPO).

Often in organizations, especially when things go wrong, there can be a tendency for HR departments to try to boil the ocean: to do lots of different initiatives to try to achieve the desired outcome, telling themselves that more is more. In his experience, the GHIC&E found that this often had the opposite effect: leaders and employees don't want to be bombarded by lots of disparate HR initiatives that can feel out of step with business priorities. Far better to do a few things successfully, and so it was decided to focus on two initiatives – *strategy alignment* and *employee engagement* – knowing that people leadership and great internal communication would need to underpin both.

First the GHIC&E wanted strategy alignment, where employees understood where the organization was headed and were clear about the contribution they could make. Then he wanted to unlock employee engagement, so that people's energy and motivation to deliver on the strategy could make a positive difference. He recognized that if both are right, it is possible to deliver strategy better and faster and ultimately to create sustainable competitive advantage. However, in 2012 most employees weren't really sure about where the business was going and didn't really care that much about it either. They had been through a lot and most were in shock and denial.

When the GHIC&E and GCPO took their plan to drive alignment and engagement through leadership and communication to the Executive Team, they met some initial resistance. Some executives thought that employees were clear about, and had bought into, the strategy already, because an e-mail had only recently come out about it; others said that engagement was only poor because of the negative public opinion towards the company and the damning tone of media coverage.

This was not a challenge they expected to hear, but they weren't going to give up. As a result of this conversation, they instigated a short employee survey to measure people's understanding of the company strategy, to see how well they thought their performance was being managed and to get a sense of their engagement. This was just a quick and dirty survey purely to provide a data point to prove whether there was in fact a need to continue. It included statements which staff were asked to rate, such as:

- I understand the strategic direction of this company.
- I can see a clear link between the strategy and my personal objectives.
- I value the time I spend with my leader discussing my performance.

This company hadn't done any employee surveys for over five years, so fresh data were needed to convince some of the more sceptical C-suite leaders. The survey results were horrendous, which was a gift. No one could argue with the painfully low scores and the shocking verbatim comments from employees. Overnight this gave the GHIC&E and GCPO full licence to execute their alignment and engagement plan.

So the first lesson about handling resistance to change is that data are always more powerful than just gut feeling and anecdotes when it comes to persuading executive teams to act.

As part of his plan to drive engagement, the company did the usual activities around choosing an engagement partner, running an annual survey and action planning on the results to drive improvements. For many companies that's all it is: 'transactional' engagement where you literally treat engagement as a process. The problem with this approach is that sooner or later people regard it as a task to be carried out mechanistically, a box to be ticked, rather than having any intrinsic value. The GHIC&E wanted much more than that; he wanted this to become the type of company that achieved 'transformational' engagement, a company that applied the principles of engagement – listening to people, asking for their input – and applying these principles to how they do business every day, not just once or twice a year when they run a survey. Companies that achieve this create a level of engagement that goes much deeper.

One example of transformational engagement at this company was when they created a new set of brand values in 2013. They took the usual steps of running focus groups with staff and talking to customers. They took this insight into a room and together came up with a set of values. And at that point, they had a decision to make: they could either go out and communicate these to staff, or they could take the opportunity to truly involve them.

They chose to involve them and ran an online 'jam' for 48 hours, where they put the draft brand values online and asked staff to provide feedback – to comment on which ones resonated and which ones didn't, to give examples of how they lived them and to talk about barriers that got in the way of being able to live them.

As a result of the feedback during the jam, the company changed two of their five brand values. When they communicated this decision to staff, their staff were shocked that not only had they been asked for their input but that it had been demonstrably listened to. This did wonders for improving trust and it also meant that the brand values had a greater ownership in the business as staff felt they had an opportunity to shape them.

So a second important lesson when handling organizational change is to involve people, since this drives their commitment to owning the change. Too often companies rely on broadcasting e-mails, on intranet articles and team briefings to drive commitment and behaviour change, often citing time as a reason for taking these short cuts. At best, these communication channels will achieve awareness and understanding of the changes. But to achieve buy-in and commitment it is necessary to involve people meaningfully. Involvement isn't a process or a tick-box exercise, it's a feeling and therefore needs to be handled authentically.

A further way the GHIC&E decided to drive transformational engagement was to help the company get better at the people side of business change. McKinsey's Global Survey (2014) reports that three-quarters of redesign efforts fail both to meet objectives and to improve company performance, a shocking statistic considering the time, effort and money being spent. Two key reasons why organizational change fails are poor leadership and poor communication, both related to the people aspect of business change which is recognized as being critically important to ensuring that change delivers the intended value.

Most organizations invest the majority of their change effort in the components of *change design* (getting the scope right, having the right business case) and *change implementation* (managing the delivery milestones and the risk logs). Few tend to prioritize *change psychology* – the bit that is about bringing people with you (Figure 6.1). This tends to be thought about quite late on and is often under-represented. And yet, remember the research findings that poor leadership and poor communication are two major reasons why three-quarters of business change fails to deliver its intended value, not to mention the psychological damage that can be done by handling the people side of change badly.

This is an area the GHIC&E cared passionately about, having been on the receiving end of badly handled business change himself and having seen a number of his friends and colleagues undergo similarly depressing experiences. One of the biggest things he did to help this company get better at the people side of business change was to invest time and effort with the people leader population. Too often, companies forget that people leaders are employees in their own right. They ask them to communicate changes to their teams when they haven't any grounding or training in leading and managing change for their own teams, and haven't had time to consider what the changes mean

Figure 6.1 Components of change effort. © Intelligent Emotion

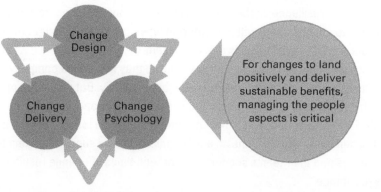

for themselves and their role. Taken together, this often leads to resistance and poorly communicated change from those same individuals on whom the company relies to motivate their teams and deliver change.

Upskilling workshops were offered to people leaders when they first became aware that changes would be impacting their business areas, with follow-up workshops run just before they had to announce changes to their teams. These occurred at all key locations, and around 500 people leaders attended over a 12-month period. The objectives were simple: to help leaders lead themselves through the change, to help them lead their teams through the change and to take control together. The workshops revealed the considerable gap between the leaders' perceptions of how they led their teams through change and their teams' views. That certainly got their attention. Then the leaders were expecting to get straight into capability building. However, the GHIC&E and his team turned the tables and instead gave them a platform to say how they really felt about the changes that were planned – to air their frustrations, concerns, hopes – and to do so in a safe environment without fear of judgement or consequences. This moment of catharsis was powerful: asking people leaders how they felt about change was not part of the DNA of this particular organization.

The next part of the workshop was to help them see change differently and to hold different assumptions about it. Typical responses to organizational announcements about change are frustration, stress or some form of subtle or not so subtle resistance because the experience of going through change can be particularly challenging. The leaders were asked to think about previous changes they had experienced at work and what the result was. In nearly all cases, they were able to say that they had learnt something really valuable from the experience and that they had come out the other side in a better position, whether in the same organization or in another one.

It was at this point that the energy of the leaders began to shift, moving from passive or even aggressive to more assertive, and they started to take control. The remainder of the workshop provided them with hints and tips on how to manage their resilience so that they could stay in control and energized, and how best to communicate with the different types of people in their team and maintain or even improve levels of engagement.

These sessions were incredibly powerful, as they helped the company implement a challenging change agenda more smoothly. But they were more than that: they were also an investment in developing people leaders. The GHIC&E's own experience had demonstrated that people leaders are the most trusted communication channel in any organization; that supporting them to lead themselves and their teams successfully through times of change resulted in less resistance.

A third important lesson, then, is to ensure that the upskilling of organizational people leaders starts with them first and how they feel. Their own resistance, concerns and uncertainties need to be addressed before they can start to think about their team. And to make a sustainable difference, upskilling should not just be about building capability, it should also be about moving mindsets and behaviours.

Shortly after the GHIC&E joined the company, he was informed that employees had recently lost a key benefit as part of a number of measures to cut costs and make the business viable again. This benefit entitled them to a preferential rate of interest when they saved money. The GHIC&E learnt that employees had been informed of this loss of benefit by letter – a rather cold letter that offered little explanation for the change and even less empathy. As a result, a large number of employees had taken the decision to withdraw their savings and place them elsewhere. This in turn worsened the company's financial position. The GHIC&E was asked to run an internal marketing campaign to showcase to employees the great savings products the company had on offer in an attempt to persuade them to move their money back. This was a classic case of management misjudging their audience: employees were feeling anger and resentment over the way they had been treated and were not amenable to this internal marketing campaign. The GHIC&E suggested that a different approach was needed, and recommended inviting employees together in large groups, engaging them face to face to explain why their preferential savings rate had been removed and how it formed part of a broader suite of changes which also affected customers. He suggested that the company needed to show empathy because the change was unpleasant and would have impacted their staff's financial wellbeing. He suggested they needed to acknowledge that their employees, working in the financial services sector, were financially savvy people and that the company would fully expect them to shop around and do their research. Then, and only then, would it be appropriate to point out a number of intangible benefits that employees could expect if they saved their money with the company. Above all, the GHIC&E suggested that the company's employees needed to be treated like adults.

He won the argument and the briefings went ahead. Sure enough, employees started to shift funds back in a way they definitely would not have done if they had been the recipients of an upbeat marketing campaign.

So a fourth important lesson is to appreciate your audience when communicating organizational change, particularly to recognize their level of understanding about the rationale of the change, how it will unfold and affect them and where they are along the 'change curve' (Kubler-Ross, 2009). Often when organizational leaders communicate new initiatives, they wonder why people aren't as excited as they are. Typically this is because these leaders have thought about it and worked with it for some time, progressively moving to the top right of the change curve ('acceptance' and 'commitment'). Conversely, their employees, especially in turbulent times, are likely to be behind them on the change curve, still in the early stages of shock, denial, anger or resignation. The gap here between employees and organizational leaders is large, making the latter look out of step with the heartbeat of the organization.

A final lesson is that when resistance does occur, it should not necessarily be regarded as negative. Resistance shouts out that something is wrong and therefore it's important to take time to find out what the issues are through careful exploration rather than by trying to overcome it automatically through repeatedly explaining the rationale and benefits.

And the outcome of involvement of the GHIC&E? He left the company after three and a quarter years and, in that time, they had delivered one of the biggest two-year increases in employee engagement of any company based in Europe. The company also won three prestigious engagement awards in under a year. Customer opinion had started to turn around and the business went from posting a €3.6 billion pre-tax loss in 2012 to a €1.1 billion profit in 2015. It now has a positive energy about it, a bright future ahead, and its ambition is to return to private ownership.

Conclusion

What are the ideas and learning we can draw from the two case studies above? First, that 'resistance' can manifest itself in a number of ways and that it is a generic term covering a range of responses, from uninterest to active sabotage. So, resistance from whose perspective and how do you decide how to respond?

Data from benchmarking exercises can help to prove the requirement in a particular area (in the second case study, the need for good employee communication and engagement). Both case studies also heavily underline the need for involvement from all affected parties regardless of geography. Virtual teams are a particular challenge, but dismissing their concerns or marginalizing their issues because of different location, time-zone, culture or language will only decrease change adoption and so erode value and benefit to the organization.

Few organizations take the time and opportunity to develop their people leaders and managers in change. Inadequate support and development of people leaders, as well as poor communication during times of change, are often cited as the two most important aspects to the success of organizational change. Organizations typically recognize that involvement and engagement of stakeholders and personnel are central to building awareness, understanding and support for change, but continue to broadcast messages, believing that they have presented the information and accomplished communication.

Key questions

- How does your organization typically view and respond to resistance to change?
- How does this resistance manifest itself?
- Whose perspective is used when determining resistance to change?
- What are the typical reasons for your organization's staff resisting change initiatives?
- How do you decide how to respond to resistance in each case?
- What are the successful ways in which you and your organization have responded to resistance?

References

Kegan, R and Lahey, LL (2001) [Accessed 4 August 2016] The real reason people won't change [Online] www.hbr.org/2001/11/the-real-reason-people-wont-change/ar/1

Kegan, R and Lahey, LL (2013) *Immunity to Change: How to overcome it and unlock the potential in yourself and your organization*, Harvard Business Review Press, Boston, MA

Kubler-Ross, E (2009) *On Death and Dying*, Routledge, London

McKinsey Global Survey (2014) [Accessed 5 August 2016] The secrets of successful organizational redesigns [Online] www.mckinsey.com/business-functions/organization/our-insights/the-secrets-of-successful-organizational-redesigns-mckinsey-global-survey-results

Thomas, R and Hardy, C (2011) Reframing resistance to organizational change. *Scandinavian Journal of Management*, 27, pp 322–31

Torbert, WR (2004) *Action Inquiry: The secret of timely and transforming leadership*, Berrett-Koehler, Oakland, CA

Willis, R (2012) [Accessed 4 August 2016] What drives resistance to change? A leader's perspective [Online] www.academia.edu/8024819/What_Drives_Resistance_to_Change_A_Leader_s_Perspective

Creating the resilient organization

07

TIANNE CROSHAW

Introduction

What if your people embraced change positively as a normal part of working life? Our constantly changing business environment and world are here to stay. The old ways of archetypal leadership are not as effective as they were in the past. It is going to take an inclusive style of leadership driven by a more human-dimensional approach to sustain business and propel it forwards and upwards.

As everyone involved in driving change through an organization knows, one of the most critical steps is the buy-in, emotional engagement and support of the people involved. But even the most effective engagement plan can still catch employees unprepared and can cause individuals to suffer personal stress and anxiety, and result in the initiative being perceived negatively. If this feeling spreads and reaches an influential level, it becomes a tipping point, which creates a significant risk to success. The solution is to develop your people so they are prepared for change, can manage their own emotional response to it and are more capable of supporting themselves through the process.

This necessary capability is 'resilience', and one very significant bonus to increased resilience is that employees will be more capable of dealing with those unplanned surprises and challenging situations that are part of their working life and cause stress.

Using case studies to share my experience of taking individuals and organizations through programmes focused on improving resilience, and introducing some specific tools, this chapter will help you understand organizational and individual resilience, with specific focus on how personal resilience supports change.

Introduction to resilience

There are many ways to demonstrate resilience as an individual. The main three traits that I come across are:

- Personal control: A resilient person will focus on what they do have control of or can influence rather than what they can't. To them, worrying about uncontrollable events on which they have zero impact is a waste of valuable and productive energy.

- Problems are seen as challenges: When a person with resilience makes a mistake or fails, they are able to have the awareness of what went wrong, acknowledge what they need to do differently and take appropriate action, all without damaging their self-esteem. This person will see 'failure' as feedback and as a learning opportunity.

- Commitment: They are not afraid to dedicate themselves to the things they find important. This could be their career, relationship, friendships or anything else they value.

Resilient people have learnt their skills through challenging experiences to bounce back from situations without too much self-damage. They have the ability to adapt to the new circumstances and recover quickly. Imagine running or being part of an organization where these kinds of resilient characteristic are the norm: where individuals work together around change initiatives as they recognize that the only certainty in life *is* change and that by adapting to it they can become even more resilient and be part of a more successful business. The key to the success of any organizational change is to understand your people and how they can better adapt to change.

CASE STUDY 1

This case study describes one of our pharmaceutical clients who went through our Resilience Programme. As a direct result, not one person across the rapidly growing site went off work with stress or anxiety for the full three years the programme ran.

The business context:

- rapidly expanding site, from 250 headcount in 2011 to 450 in 2015;
- increase in product volume and Food and Drug Administration (FDA) inspections, as well as over-the-counter launches;

- increased work-stress-related absence levels (8 per cent) among the senior leadership team (SLT) and the extended leadership team (ELT), which was in excess of the industry average for manufacturing.

The brief:

- To identify an intervention to address key performance indicators (KPIs) relating to sickness absence.
- To support key employees throughout uncertainty, change and growth.
- To encourage supportive, cross-departmental knowledge sharing.
- To develop leaders who can inspire, engage and motivate their teams.

The outcome:

- cultural shift – widespread use of 'the language of resilience', tools and techniques deeply embedded into the values of the site;
- zero sickness absence due to work-related stress for three consecutive years since implementation of the programme, with a cost saving of £87,000;
- increased referrals to Occupational Health to proactively seek support, revealing greater awareness of early warning signs of stress;
- enhanced personal development, health and engagement, reduced presenteeism (people who are at work physically though not as present mentally).

How we did it:

- profiling with SLT members to understand specific organizational challenges;
- workshops to teach psychological tools of resilience for SLT/ELT;
- pre- and post-workshop one-to-one coaching to further embed tools and techniques;
- shared the importance and power of using positive language, which helped to change perceptions during communications and provided one common language;
- self-support resilience groups to share challenges, cross-department knowledge, peer support and to celebrate success;
- wellbeing programmes for the employee population.

Having worked for a number of years with a variety of industry sectors helping to increase resilience, it's certainly our experience that organizations that don't take their people into consideration or train their workforce to be resilient are likely to experience lower engagement, higher presenteeism (physically present but mentally elsewhere) and increased levels of stress and anxiety in their people. From a wellbeing aspect this is not healthy physically, mentally or emotionally. And at a bottom-line level, this has a huge impact financially. The Health and Safety Executive (HSE) has identified six factors that can lead to work-related stress if they are not managed properly. These are job demands, control, support, relationships, roles and change. The Chartered Institute of Personal Development (CIPD) research (2008) also identifies workload and management style as the top two causes of work-related stress.

Leaders who know how to inspire and create vision can take a team forwards even through the most challenging situations if they have the tools, techniques and language of resilience and lead by example. Typically, this means first developing their own mental and emotional resilience and then sharing their learnings to help create a long-term culture of resilience and adaptability to change. Reducing stress opens up space for creativity, which can enable the business to stay in touch with a rapidly changing marketplace and respond quickly to the need for change.

Training individuals and teams in resilience tools helps people embrace change positively. The six human needs below is one such tool that proved hugely successful for the organization in the case study above. You are invited to use it to assess yourself and your direct reports.

Assessing resilience levels: the six human needs

During the first workshop, we introduced Tony Robbins' model, Six human needs that make us tick (Table 7.1), to help managers gain further understanding of individual drivers and motivators. This model is based on Maslow's hierarchy of needs but is more relevant for business use. The analysis started with the individuals themselves, and then moved on to their team members. The focus was how to bring out the best in people during a time of rapid change by working with their main drivers. This was further developed during the follow-up coaching sessions so that we could work with the managers, their real-time examples and challenges.

Table 7.1 Six basic needs that make us tick. Adapted from Robbins (2014)

Need	Description
Certainty	Familiar, secure, safe, equilibrium
Variety	Stimulating, new challenges, invigorating, exciting
Significance	Feeling heard, valued, recognized and respected
Connection	Part of a team, supported, sharing challenge, not alone
Growth	Learning, evolving, discovering, interesting
Contribution	Making a difference, giving, thinking outside of own needs

Later we will map these to show how they might influence someone's handling of change initiatives and provide examples of how to decide what areas to develop and how this is achieved, but here we present the theory.

We all have these six human needs regardless of our background, culture or race. The more needs we meet positively in our workplace or personal life, the stronger and more fulfilled we feel. One of the most important keys to help people embrace change rather than resist it is to involve them earlier on in the process and frame your communications around the six needs.

Certainty

All humans seek out some form of security and familiarity. It is demonstrated by the same routine we follow as we get ready for work, our usual tea or coffee brand or coffee house, e-mailing and calls at a set time or catching up on the news at the end of the day. Our habitual habits meet this need. We feel more comfortable if we have regular income coming in, so a big change such as a threat of redundancy can wreak havoc with our mindset and efficiency. When something interferes with our 'usual way of doing things' it can disturb our equilibrium, causing stress or anxiety, particularly for those people in the organization who are driven more strongly by this need for certainty.

Variety

The irony is that too much certainty leads to boredom and a feeling of 'same old same old'. We thrive with some variety in our lives since monotony can be detrimental to our wellbeing. In your communications with those who embrace variety, sow seeds early around the opportunities your initiative can bring, which can help create interest rather than fear of the unknown.

Get these people's input and thoughts around the possibilities and challenges the change may bring and where each person might contribute positively to help this process run more smoothly.

Significance

There is nothing like the boost to self-esteem and self-image we get when we feel valued and listened to. Individuals who have this as their main driver can be invaluable to you in the change process if you make them a significant part of that process from the onset. It is important to remember that a pat on the back, or a word of appreciation in the ear, is equally as valuable as a letter from the C-suite, a financial bonus or a company announcement. It depends on the personality of the individual.

Connection

Humans are tribal by nature and benefit by belonging to a group. It is programmed into our brains that our survival depends on being accepted by our group. Those driven strongly in this area tend to have large networks of contacts and are influential in their own right. As such, they are a great asset if you get their buy-in early, since they can be your champions encouraging others to engage and see the ultimate benefits of the change programme.

Growth

Of course, the organization's new change initiative has the potential to meet the fifth need for growth if it can be perceived and demonstrated as a chance for improvement and reward once the goal has been achieved. Setting the context around this initiative can present the change as an opportunity to expand people's minds, knowledge and experience. Escaping stagnation or 'being in a rut' will bring these growth-driven people on board easily if you deliver this promise.

Contribution

The final need of contribution can be activated when we see the bigger picture, so how you paint the outcome is critical. By demonstrating that the changes are going to make a real difference to more than just an individual, a stakeholder or a small section of the business, people can feel they are making a difference.

Let's take a look at entrepreneur Sir Richard Branson. He is a good example of how our two main driving psychological needs show up in our behaviours, choices and ultimately how we work and live.

Branson clearly enjoys variety, as over the years he has been involved in many areas of business, such as record shops, recording studios, trains, holidays, retail, finance, airways and space tourism to mention a few. Having met Branson at a business convention, I would guess that his strongest two drivers are connection and contribution. People are clearly important to him, so much so that if someone was significantly under-performing in one of his organizations after the usual support and discussions, he would move them to a different area of the business rather than terminate their contract. After a legal dispute with British Airways in the early 1990s, Virgin was awarded over £600,000, which was distributed among the employees.

It is also strongly apparent how much of a difference the successful entrepreneur wants to make in the world, which is driven by his need to contribute. Among his humanitarian endeavours are the establishment of The Elders, to which the late Nelson Mandela belonged. The aim of the organization is to solve difficult global conflicts without any personal gain. Branson also supports many charities, such as exploited children, global warming and the energy crisis to name a few (Bower, 2014).

During resilience training we guide each participant through a deep analysis of their needs. Here's how we worked with Mike and Ann around their main drivers.

CASE STUDY 2

Mike (not his real name) sat in the coaching session frustrated with some of his direct reports. 'I don't get why some of my team embrace change, seeing it as a refreshing new challenge, and others dig their heels in, becoming more negative and resisting every step of the way even though it is going to be more helpful to them in the long run!'

As the Senior Leader of an automobile organization, Mike couldn't understand why some of his team were kicking against a particular change initiative. Since it was non-negotiable, his perception was that they should accept that the change was inevitable and just get on with it.

It was particularly challenging for Mike as he had come from a military background and was conditioned to receive or give orders – no questions asked. Preferences and emotions aren't relevant in a battle situation and could seriously risk lives. The shift that was needed here was that although change for some people triggered uncertainty and discomfort, it didn't have to feel like a battle zone. If handled correctly, those 'resisters' could become the next champions if they felt listened to and understood. By listening to Mike and understanding that he had a strong need for certainty, we worked with him and his team to understand each team member's psychological needs and what would motivate them to support the project to its conclusion.

CASE STUDY 3

Ann (not her real name) was clearly annoyed that yet another change was being announced in her organization that would directly affect her and her team's way of working. She was particularly irritated as her team had not completed the previous change initiative yet, despite being on target. 'The corporate management come in, have these great ideas, shake everything up and then will complain if we get behind schedule. I am fed up of being set targets and before I complete them, the goal posts get moved.'

I asked Ann if she got pleasure from ticking off completed tasks. 'Absolutely,' she said, 'which I am not getting the chance to do.' The rest of the coaching session was used to increase Ann's resilient thinking skills rather than vent her frustration and anger on her line manager. In Ann's one-to-one with him she was able to express her concerns and offer solutions. It was agreed that as Ann's two strong drivers were certainty and significance, she would be involved much earlier on in the change process rather than feel that things were being 'sprung' on her at the last minute. In her line manager's session with me, he shared how he now understood Ann's need for completing tasks, how that impacted her perception of the organizational change, and how his own driver of variety meant that changing part way through something was stimulating for him.

The shadow side of our needs

It is important to consider how people's behaviours can be affected negatively where their driver is not being met in the working environment. There is a shadow side to these needs, which can magnify when a person without the appropriate resilience or emotional skills is feeling under extreme stress:

- Certainty: A person may become excessively rigid and/or inflexible. Details and specifics become even more important as the person seeks a sense of control.

- Variety: If there is a lack of stimulation over a prolonged period of time, people with this strong need can become bored, unable to focus and disengaged, even unconsciously disruptive.

- Significance: These people can demonstrate demanding and overbearing behaviours or, by contrast, become withdrawn and moody when they feel unappreciated or not recognized for their contribution and efforts.

- Love and Connection: If this type of person feels disconnected or isolated in their role, they can be prone to sharing their negative feelings with the relationships they have formed at work or with their line manager. In turn, this can impact others' energy levels and attitude for the worse.

- Growth: Those that thrive on learning and development can become bored or find a monotonous project or role very challenging when they feel they are stagnating.

- Contribution: For those whose main driver is contribution and making a difference, they can lose their sense of their purpose if they feel that the role they are doing isn't amounting to a bigger picture or helping others.

Thinking back to some of the negative reactions you may have experienced from people during a change initiative, how could you communicate more effectively by recognizing their main psychological driver and how the shadow side might have been demonstrated in that reaction?

Exercise

To assess your own six human needs, take a look at the simple exercise below. It will help you determine which need is dominant, which need is a secondary or sub-driver, and which might be areas for exploration. You can also refer to Table 7.1 (Six human needs that make us tick). It's useful to observe how much your driver is determining your behaviours and habits. Later we will map these to show how they might influence someone's handling of change initiatives and provide examples of how to decide what areas to develop and how this is achieved.

Step 1

Below is a list of specific statements. Please tick if you 'Broadly Agree' or mark with an x if you 'Broadly Disagree' with them. Leave blank for 'Neither' statements. Keep hold of your exercise results since you will need them in the next section.

Certainty:

- You like to know your schedule in advance.
- You are organized and generally punctual.
- You need to know changes in good time so you can plan effectively.

Variety:

- You get bored of routine easily.
- When fast-paced change is required of you, you feel excited and generally adapt easily to reasonable change.
- You thrive on multi-tasking on various tasks you find interesting.

Significance:

- Where your skill base is relevant you prefer to be an integral influencer at the onset of a change initiative.
- It is important that your views and ideas are listened to and acknowledged even if they are not agreed with.
- Respect for and recognition of your hard work and efforts are important to you.

Connection:

- Working with others with whom you get on well is highly important to you.
- You are quick to support others if you feel they are in need.
- You find your mood and mind state can be influenced by the work relationships around you.

Growth:

- You are at your most efficient and content when you are learning new skills or adding to your knowledge.

- You'll make changes swiftly if you feel stagnant or 'stuck' in your role.
- You embrace change if you can clearly see the growth opportunity for the organization.

Contribution:

- You get great pleasure when you know your role is making a real difference.
- You tend to see the bigger picture rather than get stuck in detail.
- You can be prone to working longer hours than others and find it difficult to say 'no' to others' requests for support.

Step 2

Choose two influential stakeholders connected to your change initiative, ideally two people who have not been cooperative or have been openly hostile. Identify both people's main driver by considering their negative behaviour and seeing how it fits with the descriptions in Table 7.1 and the shadow behaviours.

An example might be:

- Behaviours: Objecting, challenging, negative, putting up obstacles
- Main psychological driver: Significance
- Sub/secondary driver: Connection.

Questions:

- How valuable would it be to have this person onside?
- Is it possible that they feel less than significant/listened to/respected in this situation?
- Could you have involved this person in earlier discussions, valuing their input and using their knowledge of how the people they represent might feel?
- When you are communicating to this person about the change, how can you positively link it to the benefits for individuals and teams?

We have found the six human needs model to be a powerful tool helping link specific needs of individuals to specific behaviours. Taking the time to understand motivators at the individual level can help develop resilience within individuals, teams and across the organization. We typically encourage the development and use of the language of resilience within organizations by means of workshops, in-house communications such as magazines and intranets, action learning groups, seminars and roadshows as well as one-to-one coaching. Resilience language is positive, backed with realism and facts: it talks of challenges instead of problems and lessons instead of failures. It is honest, open and respectful between communicator and recipient and enhances an environment where authenticity is encouraged. Work is not a place to complain but to discuss and communicate confidently even during difficult conversations. This conscious culture can be taught and created with the critical support of the senior and middle management teams.

How people respond to change

The four As of major change (Figure 7.1) describes the journey of emotion and mind state in four steps:

- Step 1, Announcement: The big change occurs and the first impact is that the status quo has been rocked. The psychological reaction can be that of shock or denial.

- Step 2, Anxiety: The person feels a real sense of disruption, possibly reacting with fear, anger or paralysis to what the organization is trying to implement,

- Step 3, Acclimatization: In time, this turns into acceptance and a willingness to explore the new way of doing things,

- Step 4, Adoption: Finally, the person becomes committed and can rebuild their way of embracing the change into their everyday working life.

Whether they are particularly successful or unsuccessful at handling change, everyone follows the same steps. What varies between individuals is where they get stuck in the process and potentially suffer stress as a result. It is the role of management to support their employees skilfully in moving towards adoption. However, resilience training provides development support to individuals by analysing how well each of their six needs is satisfied within

Figure 7.1   The four As of major change. ©Tianne Croshaw

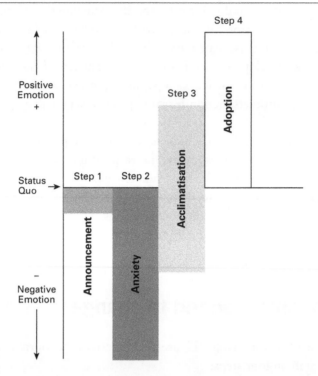

the context and implementation of change, and how that might impact each stage of the change process. This provides employees with the skills to better support themselves through the process and prevent some of the classic negative reactions to change.

How resilience training can help people embrace change

Table 7.2 shows how resilience training can help employees be better prepared for change during each of the four steps. In practice, this would be conducted in a variety of group and one-to-one sessions as needed, and requires some skill and experience.

Using your answers from the exercise above, pick the column in the table that most closely fits your answers. If your answers were inconclusive, both columns apply.

Table 7.2 How resilience training can help individuals move through the four As of major change

Need	How Resilience Training Can Help	
	Broadly agree	**Broadly disagree**
Certainty	Learning coping skills and tools to handle the high levels of uncertainty. *(Helps move past Steps 1 and 2)*	Learning the skills to provide peer support during times of change. *(Helps move past Steps 1 and 2)*
Variety	Learning to take the time to discover what new opportunities might be available as a result of the change. *(Supports transition to Step 3)*	As there will be little interest in the upside of change, learning to seek and understand the business reason for change and learning to accept the decisions of management. *(Supports transition to Step 3)*
Significance	Learning to ask for a role in the change process; for example, if colleague's feedback isn't being sought, take the initiative and offer to gather, collate and present it. *(Assists in early move to Step 4)*	As there is little need for being heard, there is still the danger of feeling disenfranchised. Learning to notice when negative feelings of not being heard occur and learning to appreciate the value of self-recognition will help. Then techniques to communicate feelings and concerns will also help. *(Helps prevent stalling at Step 1)*
Connection	Share the importance of them taking time away from the desk to support others and listen to their concerns. *(Assists in early move to Step 4)*	There is a danger of social distance or silo-mentality due to the low need for collaboration and connection. Encourage participation and engaging with other people to experience the rewards of helping others. *(Helps those who reach Step 3 quickly but then resist fully committing)*

(continued)

Table 7.2   *(Continued)*

Need	How Resilience Training Can Help	
	Broadly agree	**Broadly disagree**
Growth	Changes that are a threat to growth will be seen as negative. So encouragement to take ownership, to seek opportunities for growth within the change that is invariably there, and ways to minimize the negative impact on growth, or find alternative methods to fulfil personal growth needs. *(Helps transition from Step 2 to 3)*	Change initiatives may force growth on those who have little need for it, which can cause resentment. Teach acceptance that change often means learning new things, but also the empowerment to request appropriate training, which fits individual learning styles and at a suitable pace. *(Helps transition from Step 2 to 3)*
Contribution	Learning to seek out greater involvement in the change can generate even higher levels of meaning. *(Helps avoid Step 1 and 2 and to quickly commit to change)*	Encouragement to ask management to explain the bigger picture and commercial benefits of the change will provide a sense of meaningful impact. *(Helps quickly move through Step 1 and 2)*

Key roles for organizational resilience programmes

This chapter has described how the organization can help its people develop the skills to make them more capable of embracing organizational change initiatives. Each of the following typical change roles has its own objectives for resilience and ways to achieve these.

The role of the change manager with the resilience programme

Resilience relies on satisfying six core human needs, so employee engagement communication needs to address this through use of language, channels etc. To do this effectively you will be resilient yourself and be able to share the tools and language that helped you. Sharing this knowledge and toolkit widely will support the development of a culture of resilience during times of significant change.

The role of the first-line managers with the resilience programme

To duplicate the resilience tools, techniques and language with your direct reports and also to use a coaching/mentoring type of approach to assist people through a time of uncertainty. Regular reviews will keep your finger on the pulse of how individuals are managing in the current environment of change, as will checking in with employees to see how well they have been using the resilience tools and techniques. Regular feedback and check-ins between you and your change manager is vital at this stage of great growth.

The role of Human Resources/Occupational Health with the resilience programme

Your role is also an extremely valuable one as it is highly likely that you see first-hand what type of effect a change programme is having on the workforce, be it positive or negative. You will undoubtedly also be aware of just how damaging stress can be to individuals, teams and organizations. Reducing stress and increasing resilience is critical. When discussing resilience coaching and training with key stakeholders, our recommendation is to investigate your organization's stress and anxiety absenteeism figures, and to look at the human cost, company reputation and the financial costs. Management and leadership are generally open to these kinds of discussion. The resilient tools we share are transferable so that your trainers can be trained to pass them on, contributing to culture change.

Conclusion

I opened this chapter with the following question: *What if your people embraced change positively as a normal part of working life?* I hope you will agree that this aim has significant impact and worth, but most importantly is achievable for organizations regardless of size or sector.

Through theory, case studies and exercises we hope you can recognize the following:

- If employees are resilient, they can support any change that might occur, whether it's planned or an unexpected event.

- A resilience mindset can be taught to your people and learnt by using specific psychological tools.

- People can learn to support themselves through change long-term by repeatedly adopting what they've learnt to become automatic responses.

- Understanding an individual's personal challenge is essential to helping them become more resilient.

- The six human needs model is a great tool to help identify specific areas for development.

- There are qualified resilience consultants who can help provide a company-wide programme to ensure you achieve your own change objectives.

We know that a change journey isn't always comfortable for everyone. However, when an organization values its people, their needs and individuality and promotes a culture of embracing change, locking arms, getting through the uncomfortable stages and on to thriving, there is a high chance of success for everyone. It only actually takes a few successes to be shared and openly recognized for the word and positive energy to spread through the organization. If you can create an environment that does this openly and authentically, your resilience profile will increase dramatically. We strongly believe that people can embrace change positively as a normal part of working life!

Key questions

The following questions will help open a discussion about your own organization's resilience:

- What does a resilient organization look like?

- On a scale of 1—10, how close are we to that vision? (1 having a very low level of resilience; 10 being highly resilient)

- What behaviours do we as leaders and managers have that encourage or inhibit resilience thinking?

- How well do we know our teams' specific drivers, using the six human needs?

- In relation to our change programme, where are we in respect of the four As of major change?

- How good are we at using the language of resilience? (For example, are we proactive and solution focused, or prone to blame and considering ourselves as victims?)

- What can individuals do to take responsibility for their own mental and emotional resilience?

- What does the organization need to do to meet the resilience training needs of its employees?

References

Bower, T (2014) *Branson: Behind the mask*, Faber & Faber, London

CIPD (2008) [Accessed 4 April 2016] Building the business case for managing stress in the workplace [Online] www.cipd.co.uk/hr-resources/guides/building-business-case-managing-stress-workplace.aspx

Health and Safety Executive (nd) [Accessed 4 April 2016] Causes of stress [Online] www.hse.gov.uk/stress/

Robbins, T (2014) [Accessed 10 November 2016] Six psychological needs that make us tick. Entrepreneur [Online] https://www.entrepreneur.com/article/240441

Leading change in a not-for-profit organization

08

JACQUELINE MITCHELL

Introduction

After more than 100 years, a well-respected and financially strong not-for-profit (NFP) organization was at a pivotal point in its history. A new leadership team was on board, keen to shake off some of the bruising legacy of recent internal discontent and disharmony. There was a thirst for change coming from influential trustee stakeholders too, recognizing that change was necessary, although what the change would be was as yet unclear. Nevertheless, two key drivers stood out as the initial impetus for driving the need for change.

First, the most significant proportion of the NFP's commercially derived income was subject to an established business model. This was under threat by external influences disrupting the way the marketplace operated, affecting not just this NFP but also its commercial competitors. As a result, the NFP needed to reduce the cost per unit of its core commercial product to fit the new business model being forced on the wider industry. To achieve this, it needed to substantially realign its internal operation, create greater financial efficiencies through a different operating model, and grow the volume of its commercial business. If unable to do this, the commercial strength of the NFP would be severely undermined and its continued viability would be in question.

The second key driver for change was its staff and their performance. Employing 350 or so staff, recent years had seen the organization fracture into silos, creating divisions between departments and the two main UK locations. People tended to pull apart rather than pull together, senior deci-sion makers had pursued their own goals and substandard performance often went unchallenged. Enforced change at the executive level had removed the core obstacles, but still there was the job of winning over the hearts and minds of those wedded to the 'old' ways, as well as bringing clarity to a shared collaborative purpose where high performance standards were clear and expected.

The new leadership team recognized that they had the personal will and the opportunity to challenge and repurpose the organization in order to future-proof it: making it not just sustainable in the face of its commercial challenges, but become more agile and grow in terms of organizational size and financial strength, improve the reach and credibility of its commercial enterprise, and hone and deliver well its broader charitable objectives. This became the start of an initial three-year journey for determining, shaping and embedding lasting root-and-branch change within the NFP.

Clarity of purpose – gaining buy-in

The first step for the CEO and executive team was to determine what they wanted the future to be for the NFP. To do this, they went back to the original purpose for which the NFP was founded: they challenged its vision, strategic objectives, internal structure, culture, operations and engagement of stakeholders; examined whether opportunities were being maximized, and whether the threats and risks could be better managed. Opening up the conversation about the future and potential for widespread change forced the executive team to examine every aspect of what, how and why the NFP did what it did, what was working and what was not.

The team recognized that central to meeting the challenges and achieving the change it consequently set itself would be building strong relationships with key stakeholders, understanding that their resistance to change would likely feature as a prominent issue.

The Trustee Board played a crucial part in enabling the organiza-tional change to happen, since ultimately they had the ability to veto or endorse significant change proposals. Having been given the challenge to make change happen, the CEO and executive team headed multiple early workshops and discussions with Trustees to start to steer the conversation towards what change might look like. Enabling these stakeholders to intro-duce their own ideas was important to gaining their ultimate buy-in to an ambitious and far-reaching vision.

The support of the Trustee President and Treasurer as senior trustees helped the CEO meet the inevitable challenges along the way. Both the President and Treasurer shared strong values and ethics, both personally in their approach to decision making, but also in terms of the purpose of this NFP. They were respected and trusted by the majority of their peers and demonstrated a pragmatic and realistic business-like approach to decision making, which was important to a commercially led NFP. They clearly supported the CEO as the visible leader of the change programme and dealt with resistance when it arose by soundly backing the direction of travel otherwise endorsed by the Trustees.

Winning over the more sceptical Trustees wasn't necessarily straightforward. While the concept of change was accepted, the reality of implementing change revealed some resistance along the way. The impact of change on some staff and their roles, and on the NFP activities that were to cease or substantially change, caused some Trustees to reverse their earlier support, often purely on emotional grounds. Dealing with this emotional response, as opposed to logical reasoning, was particularly difficult; it required the CEO, executive team and the senior Trustees to negotiate some small concessions to process, while re-enforcing the clarity of vision. For the team, too, this required them to maintain a shared conviction and consensus in what was happening and why, and to demonstrate tenacity throughout some very difficult conversations.

Internally, and aside from the engagement of the Trustee stakeholders, there was significant operational change to deliver. Here each director had a key part to play (Figure 8.1). For example, the finance director was responsible for realigning business planning, financial management and budgeting

Figure 8.1 NFP hierarchy and formal organizational communication flow

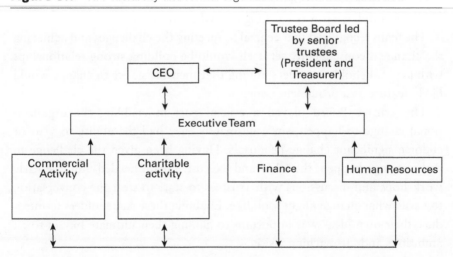

activities. This activity was driven and managed from within the finance team yet introduced a closer partnering approach to working with budget holders across the NFP. The commercial director took the lead on redefining the commercial operation to address the identified external challenges. Here the director championed and built belief in big product-led challenges and devolved ownership to his teams to work on discrete projects that taken together tackled different aspects of the commercial change. The director responsible for much of the charitable activities set about reviewing what and how things were done; this required firm but sensitive collaboration and brokering of expectation from staff and Trustee stakeholders in order to challenge and repurpose activities. And the HR director took the lead on the people-focused behavioural change programme, which, as a group-wide activity, required engaging and empowering staff beyond the HR function to contribute, while also having a clear framework of needed deliverables.

Together the executive team recognized that engaging staff and delivering a transformational and successful programme of change would not be achieved if the buy-in, impetus and drive to succeed were attempted on the back of negative reasons for change. Instead, it was imperative to build a vision for a future built around opportunity and a sense of excitement and challenge. Regular full staff presentations, most often led by the CEO, departmental briefings, workshops with staff to explore, inform and 'round out' the strategic picture and discussions with staff and union representatives all contributed to openly sharing, updating, informing and reinforcing key messages throughout. This was linked to encouraging excitement and participation in picturing the achievement of a big challenge – 'What will we do differently?', 'How will we get ahead of our competitors?', 'What will we do that is more relevant to delivering our strategic aims?', 'What too will this do for us?'

The NFP also recognized that not all staff would engage in the same way with change. Having come out of a difficult period of very visibly fraught senior-level discord, it was apparent that there were three distinct groups within the organization:

- staff who remained wedded to the old ways under former senior executives, distrustful and resistant to anything that would set out to change their loyalties;

- staff who had a natural aversion to change because it had the potential to be frightening, unsettling and different, but who could be more easily supported to move forward;

- staff who to a greater or lesser extent were open-minded, interested by or even excited to engage with the challenges and opportunities being proposed.

These groups were scattered across the organization with no clear pattern within functional areas or hierarchy. Therefore, harnessing the broad engagement of staff – and being flexible to meet the challenges and needs of these groups – influenced how the internal change would be led and managed across the NFP.

The executive team had a clear sense of the strategic framework needed and many of the big operational changes necessary. They understood that there needed to be clarity and openness in order to break down distrust and to broach misperceptions and assumptions. Also, the executive team needed to invite challenge, ideas and questions, and to delegate ownership for not only making change happen but also what change would look like. Actively communicating with, facilitating and enabling staff to contribute, share ideas and help shape the changes to even quite a strategic level was fundamental to what happened throughout.

Nevertheless, this could not all be led from the executive level. Identifying key influencers among the staff where the trust of peers was greatest was a key step to accelerating buy-in and building trust both organizationally and at an individual level for the executive team. This buy-in was particularly relevant to support the associated behavioural change programme, which would seek to question and challenge existing performance and behaviours at all levels and across all staff.

Behavioural change programme

Identifying the new, challenging strategic objectives was only part of the overall programme of change this NFP was undertaking. Achieving those big goals required people to behave, act and even think differently in order to be high performing individually, in teams and organizationally.

The training manager had a key role in influencing how behavioural change might be achieved. She became pivotal as a key influencer outside the executive team for her insight into the practical steps and operational framework that would form the structure for determining and implementing the behavioural change needed, uniquely bridging the perceptions of the executive team and those of the rest of the staff.

Underpinning the behavioural-led change was the need to identify and understand the values of the organization, and what resonance the stated values really had for how the NFP did and should operate internally. The training manager devised a series of workshops bringing a wide swathe of people together, enabling values to be explored conceptually, and then applying the values concept to the NFP to identify what the NFP really stood for, as seen from the bottom up, and from which the behavioural change could be drawn.

At this point the executive team could have delegated much of the behavioural change activity to the middle managers. However, from the start it was decided that ensuring behavioural change across all staff needed drive and buy-in at all levels, and that this was best achieved by engaging peers to help effect that change. As a result, a working group was established with staff drawn from all parts of the organization, regardless of hierarchy, to help shape the design and delivery of activities needed for behavioural change to happen (Figure 8.2). Group members took on change responsibilities in addition to their operational roles and were carefully chosen: some were particularly looked up to and trusted by their peers and colleagues – those that others naturally gravitate towards; others were sceptics and challengers but not unreasonable blockers to change; some were insightful, skilled knowledge owners – realists and visionaries; and finally, there were those staff who were enthusiastic and volunteered for a change agent role. All were people

Figure 8.2   NFP change activity influencers and primary information flow

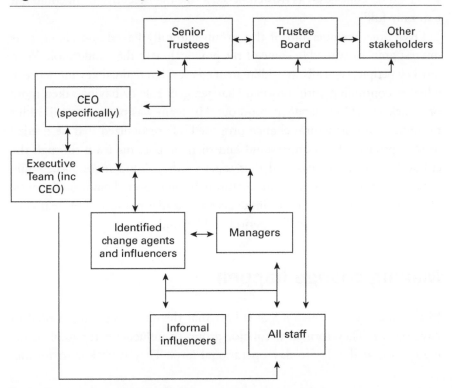

who stood out from among their colleagues, regardless of hierarchy or seniority. They were chosen for their openness, their willingness to contribute and desire to make a difference, for their ability to challenge well and be challenged. Importantly, the executive team knew that staff would listen to them and respect their judgements.

This working group reported to the training manager and under her guidance was influential in shaping what much of the behavioural change would look like once operational. Initially they took the outputs from the organizational values workshops and helped interpret and shape this understanding into clearly valued associated behaviours that could be embedded throughout the NFP. This created a clear and fundamental link between *what* the organizational goals were and *how* people would behave to achieve them, regardless of role or hierarchy. The working group went on to influence many of the associated practices, tools, standards and rewards needed to support the new culture. They became pivotal in reaching, engaging and translating to colleagues what was happening and why, and how it would impact them and what they did within the organization. They acted as a voice for their colleagues within the organization, and were instrumental in supporting communication flow formally and informally. They were seen by their colleagues as trusted peers, a role the executive team could not naturally fulfil.

Over time, membership of this group naturally flexed and changed as interest grew or waned in some of the practical tasks they undertook. Yet a few key people, typically at middle manager level, remained key influencers, whether continuing with a formal change agent role or having taken more of a back seat. One manager stood out. His team was particularly hard hit by some of the structural change proposed. He recognized that he needed to seek proactively to understand and then support his team through the cultural change. He reasoned that together they could more successfully anticipate and manage the journey through the expected emotional stages. He continued to be a valuable influencer and leader not just of his team but more broadly throughout this period and beyond.

Making change happen

Middle managers formed a key cohort that the executive team needed to have onside. They formed the major group of influencers for implementing change at the day-to-day operational level. They were key to turning strategic objectives into operational activities, for modelling and driving the behavioural change within their teams, and for encouraging and supporting those staff inherently less comfortable with change.

However, not all managers were on board or capable of making the changes being sought by the NFP. Some had strong allegiances to the former senior executives and felt threatened by anything that might suggest they needed to do things differently. Yet all had a level of influence across their colleagues and operational teams, so all had the capability to be leaders and influencers of positive or negative change – promoting acceptance and support, or objection and resistance. Therefore, in order that the role of the managers could be a positive and enabling one, it was important to broker and build trust, and identify shared responsibility between the executive team and these middle managers.

Given the importance of and sensitivity to building that relationship, the executive team recognized that this might not be something they could initially broker themselves. They recognized that discussions needed to be open, honest and challenging, and that this would require a level of independence and neutrality to help facilitate it. External facilitators were hired to help create an open environment, setting aside formal hierarchical barriers in order to allow the two groups to come together to uncover, explore and identify where there was discontent and concerns as a means to identifying where trust was weak. For the executive team, most important was tacitly acknowledging, accepting and working on the barriers identified to enable those managers who had a will to be part of the change to move forward collaboratively. And for those managers who were sceptical, to have been given every opportunity to become enablers and advocates of the change process. This was one of very few occasions when the NFP engaged external support.

Throughout the programme of change, a shared will and need to change continued, initially driven from the executive team and then increasingly taken up by middle managers, change agents and influencers who could see the positive changes take effect. Inevitably there were key messages that needed to be accepted by all staff. These included the different activity the NFP would focus on in the future, the behaviours expected from staff and changing commercial priorities. The executive team encouraged input and feedback, backed up by change agents and managers across the organization who provided support, tools, training and development to help staff 'step up'. However, there was also another consequence to the changes.

Not all staff wanted, or were able, to make the changes the NFP asked of them. Some decided that this new world was not for them and left the organization. The NFP needed to manage others out. But for the most part, staff understood this to be a new era for the NFP, with opportunities for those who wanted them. In time, the phrase 'high performing' became naturally embedded in everyday language as people talked about and questioned what they did and how they did it with this ideal in mind.

Communication from the top down led by a visible CEO ensured that people were kept in the loop and had regular opportunities to have a voice in what was happening, how and why. 'All-staff presentations' were a useful forum for sharing important updates; newsletters and team briefings supplemented this regularly at a local level; workshops explored and honed detail; staff surveys measured impact and employee engagement, and enabled resulting action to clearly link back to their input, ensuring the staff really were involved and being listened to.

At the strategic level, regular board meetings with, or separate from, those with Trustees, and routine collaboration across the executive team and CEO were absolutely key to holding it all together. Being able to talk, discuss, listen and challenge was important within the team and yet not always easy to do objectively. While the executive team shared a common vision, there were the inevitable tensions regarding interpretation, particularly at a local level. Ensuring that adequate time and attention were paid to addressing these tensions was important. The CEO's role was to ensure that he brokered these discussions where needed, and gave direction and clarity where necessary.

Outcomes

The NFP had set itself a medium-term plan of five years to make significant headway towards achieving a substantial proportion of key organizational goals. It recognized that bringing about root-and-branch change could neither be achieved in the short term, nor could it be attempted half-heartedly. As a result, it remained a core item on the strategic agenda throughout. It was therefore significant to find that over the intense initial three-year period of change, the NFP's staffing grew by over 50 per cent; it broadened its international footprint by opening overseas offices across Asia, the Far East and the United States; it acquired key businesses to provide a coveted USP; it formed strong bonds with key influencers in the UK and abroad; and it broke into new international markets ahead of competitors.

Its commercial arm went from strength to strength. Not only did it meet the financial challenges seen previously to threaten its future, but it outperformed targets with its range of commercial products. As a result, it became the global number-one provider in its field for many of its products and more than doubled its market share, advancing beyond many of its commercial rivals owing to its significant brand quality as well as efficiency of operation.

The NFP's charitable activities became more focused on what it was really good at, while innovation, agility and efficiency meant that it was often ahead of the curve in developing and delivering new areas of activity or product.

Externally validated engagement levels among staff improved and were climbing steadily; managers were equipped with the tools, knowledge and confidence to be better managers, and underperformance was being robustly managed.

Most notable was that all this was achieved through one of the deepest recessions in recent times; in comparison, many similar NFPs were downsizing, having been unable to remain competitive and relevant to their own markets.

Conclusion

This NFP not only wanted to change, but needed to. The need to change, beyond the mere desire to, provided significant and necessary impetus and drive to focus on what it was doing and why.

While the initial drivers for change were to overcome negative issues, this NFP recognized that this needed to be expressed in positive ways to enthuse and engage all stakeholders. Nevertheless, having that clarity and keeping those issues at the core of the change process meant that it was something that the executive team could revisit and re-examine with staff. This ensured that the direction of travel remained as expected and that momentum continued, as well as providing evidence of improved organizational performance to the board.

Key to first identifying and then achieving the changes envisaged was the consensus and shared vision among the senior trustees, CEO and executive team. This scale of change simply could not have been achieved otherwise. Equally, each director had a distinct role to play but, importantly, none stood alone; they each required and needed the support and collaboration of their colleagues to achieve the challenging goals.

This NFP recognized, importantly, that not all change is led from the top. Key influencers who will naturally act to lead, support or hinder change are apparent throughout an organization; harnessing this leadership capacity wherever it sits enriches the organization and its capacity to achieve its goals.

More broadly, the NFP recognized that the buy-in of stakeholders and staff was necessary to making change happen well, and to make it sustainable. It recognized that not everyone would readily buy in to the same vision or support the plan for achieving it, so that communication and the request to staff at all levels to contribute was a key part of the strategy. All staff were informed and included in what was happening when and why, and given every opportunity to contribute and question. Importantly, different people at different levels of the organization had different roles to play. The CEO was focused on engaging key stakeholders and the strategic influencers who had the potential to be significant resisters and disrupters. Directors, middle managers and internal change agents were empowered and enabled to ensure that relevant change happened on the ground, breaking through silos in functions and offices.

The changes identified, designed and implemented across the NFP were evolutionary. The organization didn't knowingly follow any recognized change model; instead, it led and delivered change almost totally through internal effort, exploiting the knowledge, experience, capability and often 'gut feel' of those involved.

The significant investment in developing people – their competence, behaviours and performance – over a long-term and in-depth programme was an unusually comprehensive and high-profile approach to pulling the whole organizational change activity together. This was pivotal to enabling people achieve and in some cases exceed the challenging strategic, operational and financial changes being sought by the NFP.

Key questions

Think about a change programme your organization is planning or implementing:

1 Is there clarity at the organizational level and at the individual level as to the reasons and need for change? Are these compelling enough?

2 Can your organization embrace the potential for your change initiative to be led and/or influenced irrespective of traditional hierarchical or role expertise boundaries? How might you encourage this?

3 How will you ensure that in leading your change you are most likely to be successful in taking people with you on the journey?

4 What measures of success can you identify for your change initiative such that acknowledging their potential for achievement will engage those it affects?

5 Do you have consensus and buy-in at the top of your organization if the change initiative has not been initiated there? How might you need to influence this team to ensure that they visibly support the change?

6 Can you readily identify who else within your organization might be resisters or agents of change, and how you might utilize this knowledge?

Employee communication and engagement during change

09

Insights from neuroscience

HILARY SCARLETT

Introduction

Research from neuroscience has provided new insights into communication and employee engagement. The first part of the chapter provides a brief overview of neuroscience and its relevance to organizations. The chapter then touches on how our brains respond to storytelling, emotions, sense of purpose, language and visuals. This is followed by a case study from TUI UK and Ireland, illustrating how these elements can successfully engage employees. The final section sets out a practical and science-based framework to build motivation and employee engagement for your own organizational change initiative.

Reports such as David MacLeod and Nita Clarke's *Engage for Success* (2009) show the difference that engaged employees make to an organization's success. Despite this, during organizational change, communicating with employees is often an after-thought. The direction is decided, strategies and plans created, and, only as a final step, leadership teams consider what needs to be communicated, how and when. This is in spite of the many research reports showing that change initiatives often fail owing to lack of employee commitment to the change.

People's responses to change, both rational and emotional, are seen as problematic and unpredictable. Leaders may feel more comfortable dealing with areas they can better predict and control. Yet by shying away from this 'difficult' area, leaders often scupper the successful implementation of their desired change.

To this day, one CEO I worked with stands out for his commitment to communicating with employees through a transformation programme. He said this commitment stemmed from being involved in much organizational change and that where employee communication had been neglected, employees were less committed to the changes and change was slow to happen. He believed that a day in head office was a day wasted: he wanted to be out at the sites, talking with employees face to face. His energy and commitment acted as a great role model to other leaders in the company. Perhaps not surprisingly, the transformation programme under his stewardship was a success, and this CEO was declared the 'turnaround king' by the *Financial Times*. He knew that until employees understand the changes and feel able and willing to implement them, very little will change in the organization. Significant, sustainable change cannot happen without employees' support.

Insights from neuroscience

Communication and employee engagement have been seen as 'soft' areas of business, but this is changing. Research, such as that produced by the Engage for Success movement, is helping change attitudes; as are the findings of neuroscience. Neuroscience – the study of the nervous system, including the brain – can help us to understand why communication and employee engagement make a significant difference to our brains and to our ability to focus and perform well during change. This section takes a look at some of the key points we need to understand about the brain and how it reacts to organizational change.

Our brains' need to predict

The overarching goal for our brains is survival, and to achieve this end they want to perform several key tasks. One of these is to be able to predict. Out on the savannah, predicting that a rustle in the undergrowth might be a snake, has obvious benefits over the absence of this ability. The brain that cannot predict or make sense or meaning out of what is going on around it is unlikely to respond optimally. As part of this drive for survival, our brains are 'prediction machines', constantly trying to work out what might happen next. In the 21st-century workplace, our brains might not be on the lookout for snakes but they are constantly, subconsciously, trying to look after us, and to do this they want to predict what might happen. This is especially true during change.

Threat and reward states in the brain

As part of its goal to protect us, the brain wants to seek out 'rewards' and avoid 'threats'. Of the two, its desire to avoid threat is by far the stronger. We can forego shelter, food and even water for some time, but if a threat in the shape of a predator got us, it would be 'game over'. Threats and rewards in the 21st-century workplace might look quite different from those our ancestors faced, but they are very much there. For our snake on the savannah read the difficult boss, the aggressive colleague, conflicting deadlines, unpredictable requests for our input, not knowing whether we will get a desk to work at, feeling excluded. The threat and reward responses are constantly triggered in our brains each day at work, and people are much more sensitive to negative messages than positive ones. Our brains' drive for survival means that we set more store by the negative/threatening than we do to what is positive/rewarding: the threat response kicks in faster and is stronger than the reward response, and the feelings stay with us for longer.

As a simple example, in the workshops that I run I ask people to think about an unpleasant, personally critical e-mail they have received and then compare how receiving this e-mail felt with receiving one that was complimentary about their work. Memories of the negative e-mail in particular tend to come flooding back. In our brains, when we receive the negative e-mail, levels of stress hormones rise, and dopamine, a neurotransmitter which – in the right balance – enables us to feel positive and to learn, decreases. Stress hormones have their uses – they help us to respond quickly to an immediate threat. One problem with 21st-century work is that this threat response is constantly being triggered. We need to bear this in mind when communicating with employees through change. The SPACES model at the end of the chapter looks at six specific factors that can send our brains into a threat state or into a reward state.

Why does all this matter in a chapter on employee engagement during change? Figure 9.1 sets out the impact of the threat state and the reward state on our brains' ability to think. A brain in a threat state is a brain that cannot function at its best in terms of thinking and staying calm. A brain in

Figure 9.1 The impact of threat and reward states on our brains and on our ability to think and perform

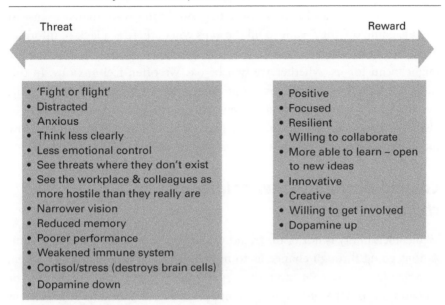

Threat   Reward

- 'Fight or flight'
- Distracted
- Anxious
- Think less clearly
- Less emotional control
- See threats where they don't exist
- See the workplace & colleagues as more hostile than they really are
- Narrower vision
- Reduced memory
- Poorer performance
- Weakened immune system
- Cortisol/stress (destroys brain cells)
- Dopamine down

- Positive
- Focused
- Resilient
- Willing to collaborate
- More able to learn – open to new ideas
- Innovative
- Creative
- Willing to get involved
- Dopamine up

a reward state, on the other hand, is a brain that is focused, collaborative and engaged. There are many different definitions of employee engagement but, quite simply, a person on the right-hand side of the chart in Figure 9.1 is one who can perform at their best. Organizations need to stay aware of what impact their communication and interventions will have on employees' ability to feel positive and perform.

The impact of organizational change on our brains

Change means that we cannot predict what is going to happen, and not being able to predict is uncomfortable for our brains. Both change and ambiguity cause an 'error alert' in our brains that something is wrong, sending them into a 'threat state', which in turn elicits the familiar 'fight or flight' response (see Figure 9.1). In this state, blood flows away from the prefrontal cortex (PFC) – the part of our brains behind our foreheads where we do our considered thinking and planning, and where we control our emotions. Instead, blood flows to those parts of our brains that prepare us to deal with the threat: to fight or run away. When we are in this state, we exaggerate threats or see them where they don't exist. The brain's uncertainty distorts what we see and hear. We think we see reality but in fact we just see a view of the world as interpreted by our brains, and when our brains are in this threat state caused by organizational change they tend to see the workplace as much more hostile than it really is.

This threat state is also very distracting: our brains want to make sense of what is going on; they want to fill the gaps where there is a lack of information. Instead of focusing on our work, we speculate as to what the changes might mean for us, whether we will be ok. We often feel anxious. In this state, we have less control over our emotions: we become more volatile, quicker to feel emotional, and less empathetic towards others. Our field of vision narrows and we become less perceptive of our surroundings. How much of an asset to an organization is an individual/team in this state?

Communicating sooner or later during change – a dilemma

While uncertainty is not brain-friendly, there remains a dilemma for organizations going through change as to how much to communicate and when. Communicate too soon and the organization might have to retract or amend some of what it has said. We put pressure on leaders to be consistent and not to take U-turns, so communicating when much is still unknown is uncomfortable for them. However, if leaders wait to communicate until they have more of the detail, there is a communication gap or void. This registers as an error alert in employees' brains, and they are distracted and less focused on work until the gap is filled. Our brains crave information. This is in part why the rumour mill goes into overdrive as employees speculate and gossip about what might happen as a consequence of the changes. Our brains want to fill the gap. There is no right or wrong answer to this dilemma, but neuroscience would suggest that it is better to communicate early so that employees are less distracted. Even if there is not much information to communicate, at least telling employees what the communication process will be gives them some certainty to cling onto.

Past experience and expectations shape what we perceive

We have all had that experience where we have gone to a meeting with a colleague, discussed it afterwards and have both heard different messages. Why is this? Why do leaders think they have communicated clear messages about upcoming change, and yet some employees say they have not heard them? Past experience, current context, personality, expectations and biases, all have an impact on how we perceive the world and what we take in. For organizations, where communicating a consistent message and alignment in understanding are important, this can be a challenge.

Subconsciously, our brains are constantly comparing the current situation with past experience. Different past experiences mean that people process the same information differently. An employee who has had a negative experience of change in the past is more likely to have those negative feelings reawakened; one who has had a previous positive experience of change is more likely to relish change. In addition, 'confirmation bias' means that we look for information that supports what we already believe and ignore evidence that contradicts our views. Expectations also have an impact on what we experience. Research shows that if we expect an experience to be painful, it is more likely to be so. This explains in part why people's reactions to change can be so varied. What each of us thinks is reality can be highly subjective. In change, we need to be ready for these different reactions: just because someone's reading of a situation is different from ours does not necessarily mean they are being deliberately perverse or stupid.

This is one of the reasons why managers play a pivotal communication role during change – they are better placed to see what each team member understands and how they are reacting to the changes. Managers are best placed to know more about the past experience of the team member and can deal with each person individually. The impact of past experience and expectation on what we take in also reinforces the need for organizations to keep repeating messages and to follow up face-to-face meetings with recordings or notes so that employees can check what they have understood.

The role of storytelling in change

There is a lot of talk in organizations about storytelling, with leaders and managers being asked to tell more stories. Many are slightly puzzled as to why they are being asked to do this. Neuroscience brings insights as to why storytelling works and why it can be a very useful method of communication during change.

Our brains can't help themselves: they love to hear and tell stories. Take a look at Heider and Simmel's 1944 short animation of two triangles, a small circle and a 'box'. They are just geometrical shapes being moved around. This is not a story, or is it? Our brains, with their hunger for a narrative, can't help turning the movements of the shapes into a story. We give meaning and intentions to the shapes. We feel moved by the emotions we project onto them. This short film is a great example of how our brains just can't help themselves: they want to make meaning and tell stories.

Why have our brains evolved to like stories? What purpose do they serve? Much of what drives our brain is social: a need to be able to get on with others. Again this goes back to survival: we were much more likely to survive if we were part of a tribe than on our own. To be able to get on with other people, we need to be able to understand them and what they might be thinking and feeling. Stories allow us to look at the world from others' perspective and so potentially to understand them better. Stories also give us the opportunity to explore simulations and different scenarios safely and to get better at predicting outcomes. This helps us to prepare for changes that we have not personally experienced. The benefits of this during organizational change are obvious.

Why are stories persuasive?

When we make a presentation, we tend to fill our slides with words, bullet points, facts and figures. These activate certain parts of the brain involved in processing language and analysis. This means that as we listen to the presentation, we are likely to critique what we hear and question whether we believe it. We remain somewhat distant and questioning. Do I agree with this? Does this sound true to me? Storytelling, however, activates not just language networks but additional parts of the brain: for instance, if we hear about someone kicking a ball, the part of our brain that is activated when we *actually* kick a ball, the motor cortex, is stimulated too. When we hear a story our brains fire up as though we are *in* the story; neurologically we experience the sensations and emotions that the subjects of the story are experiencing. Told in the right way, a story is a much less threatening way of planting an idea in someone's head than telling someone that they need to change. We experience and identify with the protagonist in a story, whereas we filter and analyse a presentation. The more engaged people feel in the story and the more vividly they experience it, the more they adapt their beliefs. In particular, if we empathize with the character and that character changes their beliefs, we are more likely to change our minds. This was used with great effect by the head of sales in the merger of two pharmaceutical firms. Members of the salesforce of one of the two merging companies were unhappy about the merger. The leader told a very personal story about the emotions that he had experienced, sadness about 'losing' the former company, but he then went onto explain why he had decided to stay and said that he hoped others would too, but that it was their decision. The fact that he told a story about himself and what had led him to make his decision was less threatening and more persuasive than telling people that they should stay.

Stories also have the benefit of being more memorable: they are easier for us to remember than lists of points because they have a beginning, a middle and an end. There are causes and effects, that is, a pattern to them, and our brains like patterns. Often there is a novelty element to stories, and our brains also like novelty: it catches our attention. Stories also allow us to reach our own insights. Insights are rewarding to the brain and help build commitment to an idea.

The role of emotion in communication

One of the other reasons why telling a story about change can be more effective than using a series of slides and bullet points is that stories tend to use emotions. The leader mentioned above talked to the salesforce about his emotions about the merger. One of the reasons we have emotions is that it is the brain's way of making note that we should remember this event. If something has stirred strong emotions in us, it is more likely that the event is significant to us, be that a positive or a negative emotion. Emotions help us to remember. We can remember the moving story much better than a list of rational facts.

Sense of purpose

There is an increasing body of research that underpins how important having a sense of purpose is to us. Dan Pink sets this out in his book *Drive* (2009). When people have a sense of purpose, of doing something meaningful, this has a positive impact on the brain. When communicating change, people also need to be given a sense of purpose. Too often, organizations tend to focus on the facts and the numbers. Providing a sense of purpose needs to come first, and, to be more precise, this sense of purpose needs to be about the positive impact the organization and the change will have on other people. We are social beings, and understanding how what we are doing will positively impact others is rewarding to the brain and puts the brain into a more positive and resilient place.

Language

Elizabeth Loftus and John Palmer (1974) conducted a fascinating piece of research that demonstrates the influence words have on what we see and what we remember. Participants were asked at about what speed they thought two vehicles were travelling when they 'smashed/collided/bumped/hit/contacted'. The word 'smashed' led to higher estimates of speed. Not only that, but one week later, those participants who had heard the word 'smashed' were more likely to answer positively when asked if they had seen broken glass in the film, even though there was no broken glass. This demonstrates the importance of choosing our words carefully when communicating – the very words we choose and the questions we pose will influence people's perceptions and memories.

Just as with timing, there is a fine balance to be found in the use of language when going through change. If the language is too positive and does not ring true to people, it will trigger an 'error alert' in the brain because the language does not fit with what people are experiencing. That said, people need a positive narrative to latch onto. People need hope and a reason to work towards the changes. It's important to remember that the brain is much more sensitive to negative messages or 'threats', so these need to be counterbalanced. In a letter to employees, just after the banking crisis, a bank set out honestly the challenges the bank was facing and why cuts were needed. At the same time, he reminded employees of the strengths of the bank and put the cuts into context: the short term would be difficult, but there were many positives that meant that the bank would be successful in the longer term. He needed to give hope to those who would be staying.

Positive messages needed to be repeated but at the appropriate time. One public sector organization insisted on putting lots of positive messages into a document that then went on to talk about site closures and redundancies. Employees skipped the positive messages and went straight to the section that would throw light on whether they might have a job in future or not. Most employees were not yet in a place where they could hear the positive messages.

As the Loftus and Palmer research shows, we need to think carefully about the words that we choose. Research conducted by Carr and Walton (2014) at Stanford University showed that just the use of the word 'together' increased employees' willingness to stick at a task and to try harder. Inclusive language reminds us that we belong, and this is important to the brain.

Visual communication

Vision has evolved over millions of years and is a more efficient way of storing and remembering information than words. Stop reading for a moment and look around you. You will be able to retain that picture far more easily than if I asked you to read a written description of it. In short, we remember visuals better than words. In an article by Andrew Carton in *Harvard Business Review* (2015), he suggests that when leaders talk about the future and want to convey a vision that people can really see and latch onto, they need to use images. Colleagues and he argue (2014) that clear images are particularly useful when talking about the future, because the future is full of so much uncertainty. Images are more concrete than abstract concepts and values. Images give people something that they can imagine, envisage and work towards.

Case study: TUI UK & Ireland: storytelling, involvement and visual communication

One approach to communicating that combines both visuals and storytelling is the use of 'big pictures' or 'rich pictures', also known as 'learning maps'. TUI UK & Ireland is one company that has used big pictures with great success. This is their story.

CASE STUDY

Context

TUI UK & Ireland is part of a leading global leisure travel company, flying more than 5.5 million customers each year. Employee research showed that awareness of the company's goals was very weak: 80 per cent of employees could not name even one of the goals; and one in three could not name any of the three goals or four strategic imperatives. In addition, nearly one-third of employees said they could not openly express their opinions. If TUI UK & Ireland was going to achieve its goals, everyone in the business needed to understand them and see how they could contribute to them.

Objectives

The overarching goal was to build 'line of sight' between the activities of individuals and teams and TUI UK&I's strategic goals. We wanted a process that would enable people to 'get it': 'I see how I fit and what I can do to help'. To achieve this, we needed team-based conversations focused on business strategy. We wanted a unifying approach to reflect the fact that every employee contributes to the customer's experience, but we also wanted people to have local conversations that were meaningful to them.

The big conversation

We needed a process that generated a high level of ownership of the solution among leaders. This would not only secure commitment to support the process but would also ensure that the picture reflected the priorities across the functions. Co-creation of the picture was as important as the final image. With this in mind, we held sessions with each functional team and with the CEO and his colleagues. During this conversation, we found the team making key decisions about the future prompted by the emerging picture – the picture itself was compelling the leaders to be clear and unified about future direction.

Once the picture was agreed, we facilitated a session where the CEO talked through the big picture with 70 leaders. Each function developed its plans to conduct *the big conversation*. Every manager would be a participant in a conversation before being a facilitator. Meanwhile, we finalized the managers' pack, including a short video from the CEO positioning the work and talking about what the picture meant to him. Images from the picture are now being used in other internal media to act as a reminder of key messages.

The picture was co-created by the business, and the key deliverables were hundreds of conversations about vision and strategy. The process was designed to maximize ownership throughout line management and to ensure that people understood we were aiming not for one-way presentations but for a dialogue leading to understanding and action.

Measurement and evaluation of outcomes

The key metrics against objectives are:

1 87 per cent said *the big conversation* brought to life the goals and helped them understand the strategy;

2 95 per cent said they now understood how they and their team contributed to the business strategy;

3 90 per cent said they were encouraged to express their views during their big conversation;

4 90 per cent of managers said the big picture had been an effective tool for communicating strategies and goals to their team.

In addition, following *the big conversation* more than one in two people could name all three strategic goals. Sixty-two per cent of these people got the exact numerical target for each goal (compared with earlier research where just one in five people could name one business goal, and one in three could not name any). The project was so successful that the approach has been repeated in UK&I and adopted at Group level, involving over **50,000** employees spread across the world. This is a great example of involving employees, using visuals, conversations and storytelling to make the future vision meaningful and real to employees.

Employee engagement during change – SPACES (©Hilary Scarlett)

SPACES (Scarlett, 2016) is a practical model for planning communication and employee engagement during change. It sets out six factors that have the ability either to put our brains into a threat state, with its attendant negative effects as shown in Figure 9.1, or into a reward state – see the right-hand side of that same diagram – where employees are engaged. SPACES stands for Self-esteem, Purpose, Autonomy, Certainty, Equity and Social connection.

Look at SPACES with Figure 9.1 in front of you as it sets out the impact of threat and reward states on people's brains. Below is a brief description of each of the six factors:

- Self-esteem: this is about our need to feel respected. In part, our sense of self-esteem comes from feeling important relative to others, doing better than others, but it is also about learning and developing, self-development, mastering a skill, having a sense of achievement, and feeling valued. During change, where are the opportunities to enable people to learn and develop?

- Purpose: employees need to have a sense that they are contributing to something, that what they do makes a difference. This factor also touches on the fact that cooperating and helping others is rewarding to the brain. How can you remind people of the difference they make at work?

- Autonomy: having choice, a perception of having some control over events or our environment, is hugely important to us. Being able to influence decisions, even small ones, makes a big difference to our levels of engagement. No one wants to be micro-managed. Where can you let go and give some decision making, even very small, to employees?

- Certainty: not knowing what is going to happen is hugely distracting to our brains. Our brains crave information. What more can you tell people?

- Equity: feeling that we are being fairly treated is especially important during change. We want transparency and for the process to be fair. Are the processes fair? Could they be more transparent?

- Social connection: as mammals, we are born depending on someone who cares about us. This carries on throughout life. We need to feel accepted and connected to other people and to feel part of an 'ingroup'. Feeling rejected reduces our speed and capacity for decision making, our IQ and resilience. How can leaders and managers connect better with employees?

SPACES is a useful planning tool for change: the aim is to move people to the right-hand side of Figure 9.1 where they feel they have at least some of these six factors. Feeling positive against the factors activates the reward system in our brains and creates a climate where employees can focus, collaborate and facilitate rather than impede change.

Reflecting on the TUI UK&I case study, the approach included each of the six factors. *Self-esteem* would have been boosted because employees were not being told what they needed to do but were being asked questions and were part of a conversation about how to achieve the goals. The picture overall gave a clear sense of direction and *purpose*. *Autonomy* was provided through co-creation of the picture with employees and then later by allowing leaders to decide what the focus of their conversations would be. In addition, leaders didn't tell the team what they had to do; the emphasis was on asking the team questions, and collectively agreeing their role. The picture provided *certainty* as the vision and goals were clearly set out. As we know, depicting the future helps people to envisage it. Each employee would feel that they were being dealt with equally – every employee right across the company was involved in a conversation. The very fact of spending time together, discussing the issues and what to do, improved *social connection*.

The model has been used by communications teams to identify how they can craft their messages so that employees are more likely to be in a positive state of mind as a consequence. An intranet team used it to identify why they might be meeting resistance from people using a new part of the intranet. One leader who had some difficult one-to-one conversations used it to plan how to hold those conversations so that employees left the meeting in a 'toward' mindset. One government department is using it widely as they plan difficult messages about downsizing: they are using it to identify what they can do to help keep people as engaged as they can be in a very uncertain world.

Conclusion

Communication has historically been one of the more neglected areas of managing change. Neuroscience helps us understand what people really need in terms of communication and involvement in order for them to stay focused, resilient and constructive.

As part of the brain's drive for survival, it craves information and wants to be able to predict what will happen to us. The human brain is very sensitive to any potential threats: uncertainty and a lack of information cause a threat response in the brain. This means that the brain is uncomfortable with the uncertainty that organizational change brings. A threat state means that we cannot perform at our best – we are distracted, anxious and have less emotional control. Organizations need to plan change and communication with this in mind.

Storytelling can be a very effective means of communication during change because it presents ideas in a non-confrontational way. We experience a story with the storyteller, whereas we are far more analytical and wary when presented with facts and figures. Stories are memorable in part because they use emotion, and the brain remembers emotional experiences. As we saw in the TUI UK&I case study, pictures, stories and discussion are a very powerful combination.

Key questions

- Brains crave information and certainty: what can you do to provide more certainty for people during the change? Are people clear about how and when you will communicate?

- The brain is much more sensitive to threat than to reward: how balanced is your communication in terms of negatives and positives?

- Lack of communication leads to rumours and distracted brains: has communication planning been built into your change planning process? How well informed do employees feel?

- Past experience and expectations shape what we take in. What is employees' past experience of change in the organization? What past experiences will be subconsciously reawakened by this change? How will this affect what people hear this time?

- Storytelling can be a very persuasive communication technique. Do your leaders and managers know why it works? How skilled and confident are they at using stories to communicate? What stories are there that will help to convey the key messages?

- The brain remembers emotions: to what extent do you use emotions in your communication? What will touch people's emotions? Are your leaders comfortable talking about emotions?

- Having a sense of purpose, particularly a sense of purpose about helping others, is rewarding to the brain. In what ways will the proposed changes help others? Are employees aware of the benefits? How strongly have you emphasized a sense of purpose? How committed are employees to that purpose?

- The words that we choose shape people's understanding, emotions and memories: have you reviewed the language that is being used about the change? Are leaders and managers aware of the importance of words? How can you make sure you are choosing words with care?

- We remember visuals better than words: have you used images in your communication? What images do you need to convey the future?

- Where can you use the SPACES model to plan change in the organization? Which of the six factors would you say employees have at the moment? What can you do to give people more of those six factors and so create a more engaged group of people?

References

Carr, PB and Walton, GM (2014) Cues of working together fuel intrinsic motivation. *Journal of Experimental Social Psychology*, 53, pp 169–94

Carton, AM (2015) [Accessed 19 October 2016] People remember what you say when you paint a picture, *Harvard Business Review*, 12 June [Online] https://hbr.org/2015/06/employees-perform-better-when-they-can-literally-see-what-youre-saying

Carton, AM, Murphy, C and Clark, JR (2014) A (blurry) vision of the future: how leader rhetoric about ultimate goals influences performance. *Academy of Management Journal*, **57** (6), pp 1544–1570

Loftus, EF and Palmer, JC (1974) Reconstruction of automobile destruction: an example of the interaction between language and memory. *Journal of Verbal Learning and Verbal Behaviour*, **13** (95), pp 585–89

MacLeod, D and Clarke, N (2009) *Engaging for Success: Enhancing performance through employee engagement*, Department for Business Innovation and Skills, London

Pink, D (2009) *Drive: The surprising truth about what motivates us*, Canongate Books, Edinburgh

Scarlett, HF (2016) *Neuroscience for Organizational Change: An evidence-based practical guide to managing change*, Kogan Page, London

Project Carpe Diem

10

The systematic journey of
a multi-locational and multicultural
transformational change programme
in a large telecoms company

VIREN LALL

Introduction

This chapter explores the journey, leadership challenges and insights gained from a multi-locational and multicultural transformational change programme within the service delivery function of the Global Services Division at one of Europe's largest telecoms groups. The Global Services Division incurred significant trading losses, which in turn led to a turnaround programme, changes of CEOs and a series of market unit reorganizations that left service delivery to customers in shambles. This resulted in poor service delivery records, inconsistent customer experience depending on which location you were being served from, and extremely high costs to fulfil customer orders. Low levels of customer satisfaction had a further knock-on effect, resulting in fewer customer contracts and lost contract deals. This chapter is the story of how and why that happened, the programme the corporation put in place to deal with the problem, and what we can all learn from the experience. The company name, project name and all actors have been anonymized.

Its name was Project Carpe Diem (PCD) – Latin for 'sieze the day' – which, when you've just written down £1.2 billion a few years earlier, isn't that hard to see. The programme's aim was to rationalize the organization structure, standardize the customer order fulfilment process and, in turn, reduce costs and improve customer service. The impacted teams were from different geographies, cultures and functions. The programme had the potential for huge savings from reduction of duplication and hand-offs, and to provide the agility to launch a new series of services that was previously impossible. It would impact over 3,200 people, bringing in teams from seven different geographically dispersed units based in seven countries to work together on a common platform. Not all of these teams were telecom corporation employees, nor did they all do the same job in the different regions.

Background

The Global Services Division (the 'Division') was set up in 2004 from the merger of a number of existing and disparate telecom businesses. Globally, it supplied managed networked IT services to multinational corporations, domestic businesses and national and local government organizations. Its strategy was to develop international markets by leveraging its profitable position and product portfolio in the UK.

The Division had three core processes (see Figure 10.1):

- to win business and deliver contracted services to the customer, usually called 'lead to cash' (the focus of this chapter) or provisioning (performed in part by service delivery teams);
- to maintain these services in operation during the contracted period, called 'trouble to resolve' and handled in part by service assurance teams;
- to design and introduce new products and services into the market, called 'concept to market', which was handled by the product portfolio and service design teams.

The service delivery function, however, was dispersed across market units, service design teams, a global customer service organization and third-party suppliers, all of which were located across seven countries. This meant that the core lead to cash process lacked governance and overall accountability, and that its operations were far from efficient.

Figure 10.1   Three core processes of the Division

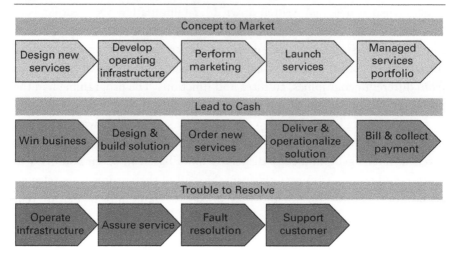

The first problem and the turnaround programme

From its inception, the Division expanded rapidly. Revenues of £6 billion in financial year (FY) 2005 rose to over £9 billion in FY 2009. The aggressive expansion via mergers and acquisition resulted in a far-flung multifaceted global organization. Operations were hampered by insufficient integration of acquisitions, poor portfolio management, little reuse of solutions and a lack of an industrialized delivery capability. The Division's constituent businesses were not working together efficiently, which led to poor execution on many large contracts, loss of revenue, increase in costs and a decline in profits. In the FY 2008–09 the Division wrote down £1.2 billion in losses and a new CEO was appointed to turn the company around.

From 2008, therefore, the Division went through a series of reorganizations and adjustments to its corporate strategy. The first in a series of massive leadership changes resulted in a turnaround programme that continued for a couple of years, with the result that the Division managed to stem its cash losses, by reorganizing its market-facing units.

The Division's internal and external causes for decline were quite typical of those found in a company: these included large projects, complex organization structure, ineffective acquisitions, inadequate financial tracking and poor working capital management. The turnaround programme was designed to focus its corporate strategy and implement a new operating model. Stringent cost controls were implemented rapidly so that management could gain control of the cash outflow. The focus changed from a geographical orientation to a global market alignment.

The Division's performance improved over the next few quarters, but this was due to the stringent controls and cost reduction measures that were immediately put in place as part of the turnaround programme. It was too early to say if this was sustainable.

The second problem and the remedial programme

While the market units were organized to respond better to client requirements, the service delivery units had been largely ignored. From the customers' viewpoint (corroborated by customer satisfaction surveys), service delivery was rated as one of the biggest causes of customer dissatisfaction. Depending in which geography the services were located, the multiple processes and hand-offs between teams of different cultures and attitudes resulted in an inconsistent customer experience, unacceptable delays in delivery and often failure to deliver the service the first time around. Some global connectivity products would take more than 250 days to install and commission, way below the industry expectation. From 2010 onwards, the Division's revenues continued to decline from the £9 billion that they had been at its peak, adding management pressure on containing costs.

The telecoms group engaged its London head-office-based group cost transformation team (a unit made of consultants and programme managers) to carry out an audit of the service delivery practices and propose changes.

The core business

For a complex service delivery requirement for a large customer there is typically a myriad of service delivery components, including LAN, WAN, ICT, telephony, desktop services, help desks and project and service delivery management for the customer. Multinational customers would outsource the upgrade and future operations of its multi-location network and IT services to the telecoms group for a fixed contract period of seven years. Upon signing, the Division would transition the existing network service operations and, over a period of, on average, two years, replace the infrastructure with new technology and operate it over the contracted period. Customers benefited from state-of-the-art technology and services and the Division would be able to reduce operating costs. This required large-scale provision of new services, sometimes in the region of £100 million. Teams of project managers coordinated the delivery of all the components so that they could be installed and tested, and then operated as a managed service. A component across many orders was the Division's flagship product – the global connectivity product based on multi-protocol layer switching technology (MPLS) that would allow multinational corporations to build point-to-point connectivity using a secure cloud. The Division had the largest outreach across the globe, with points of presence in 170 countries.

Orders of MPLS would take too long to deliver and were often incorrectly configured. There were nine separately managed teams reporting to different units, responsible for carrying out everything from order intake to final delivery. Teams in the order processing chain would constantly verify order details captured upstream, yet inaccurate order capture resulted in delivery failure for more than half of the orders. Faulty processes pushed back the order to the very initial stages of its fulfilment journey, and start again. This would add significant time delays for the customer and considerable rework within the Division. There was no single accountability or joined-up leadership.

Part of the problem was unclear roles and responsibilities among the Division's market units, contract delivery commercial units, the service design, service delivery teams and customer service organization responsible for smooth operations. The other part was cultural. These teams were split into multiple locations in different geographies. Further, some of these teams belonged to partner organizations, which brought in their own organizational culture, work practices, incentivization schemes and performance indicators. This led to inefficiencies and duplication. Some of this non-standardization was due to legacy arrangements when the services had been acquired and merged. The lack of ownership at each stage of the lead to cash process resulted from a task-oriented operational model, which led to the necessity to create additional layers of delivery management. The Division had created a multifaceted cottage industry of delivery management capabilities across its service design unit, market-facing unit and customer service organization, resulting in costly manual progress-updating mechanisms and order chasing. There was limited 'end-to-end' accountability for service delivery success, and although there were a number of teams responsible, no one could be held as accountable.

A new organization design and a target operating model (TOM), to bring all the service delivery units under one roof, were put in place. The TOM (Figure 10.2) was designed by the head-office-based group cost transformation team in consultation with the senior management of the service design units. On paper, the design did not face any cultural challenges at this point because it had not been implemented. The consultants had taken a simplistic view of rationalizing the service delivery function and had not appreciated the different cultural working practices in each of the

Figure 10.2 New Division target operating model

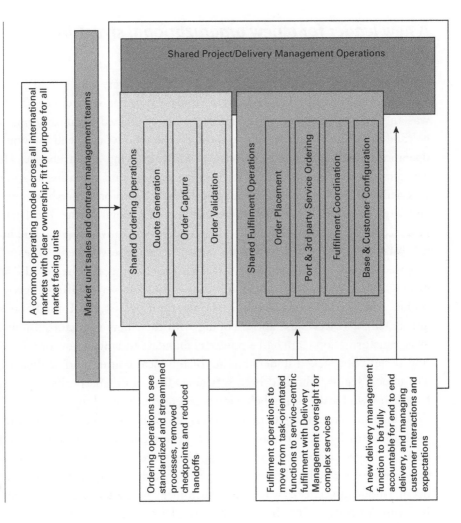

A common operating model across all international markets with clear ownership; fit for purpose for all market facing units

Market unit sales and contract management teams

Shared Project/Delivery Management Operations

Shared Ordering Operations

Quote Generation

Order Capture

Order Validation

Shared Fulfilment Operations

Order Placement

Port & 3rd party Service Ordering

Fulfilment Coordination

Base & Customer Configuration

Ordering operations to see standardized and streamlined processes, removed checkpoints and reduced handoffs

Fulfilment operations to move from task-orientated functions to service-centric fulfilment with Delivery Management oversight for complex services

A new delivery management function to be fully accountable for end to end delivery, and managing customer interactions and expectations geographies in order to make this happen successfully. A key part of the operating model was to bring all the delivery managers from the various business units into one centre of excellence and expand their role to provide end-to-end accountability. In Europe, there were service delivery teams that were cross-functional: members of a team did delivery management, order taking and fulfilment activities. In other countries, large teams performed a single specialized function. It was a classic cell-based operation.

A new leader for a new organizational structure and culture

A new vice-president of the newly created Service Delivery Unit (VP-SD) was appointed, reporting to the President of Global Customer Service. The VP-SD was an active and visible leader, and in the newly created organization unit he carefully went about identifying those people who would head the unit's operational functions and those who would help bring about change. He brought in a mix of inspiration, energy, engagement and empathy, and this was demonstrated in how he conducted himself in senior leadership events and large collaborative hothouse workshops. The design of the TOM had preceded his appointment, so he had inherited a prescriptive proposal and his role was to enable the change and to lead and manage service delivery teams.

Based on analysis of the group cost transformation team, the new TOM brought in service delivery and fulfilment teams from seven different geographies (the UK, Hungary, India, Malaysia, the Far East, the United States and Brazil) that were just about coping with their new reorganized units. This transformation team had a powerful mandate to build a new organization design, but lacked understanding of the local culture and challenges. These local teams, who had been servicing clients in their specific regions, had their own local culture, behaviours and norms of working.

As an example, in the Japanese markets the local teams viewed validation of customer orders as a customer-intimate process, one by which they would develop deeper customer relationships. They were driven by an extraordinary sense of servicing the customer need, checking every aspect of order detail. Duplicating checks was seen as customer care rather than inefficiency. In Latin America, teams built process workarounds to service customer needs, while still maintaining good customer relationships. In Hungary, the professionalism meant that people built informal networks across the functional teams to call upon each other to clarify ordering issues.

In India, some of these order processing and order fulfilment functions had been outsourced to third parties that were driven by key performance indicators (KPIs) on task completion time and volume. They carried out the minimum possible activity that met their performance indicators and moved the order on: a failed delivery or dissatisfied customer was not their fault.

A common theme was lack of trust in the quality of work in upstream functions carried out by other teams. Little trust led to lots more redundant checks and rework, which resulted in delay and costs.

A transformation mechanism: hothouses to mobilize multi-locational, multicultural change

The new organization design needed new working practices, consistent processes and standardized systems to put it into practice. The targets set by the head office were challenging and needed mobilization at all levels. Three hothouses focused on mobilizing the teams in order to create a joint vision and plans for the new TOM. These hothouses were two- to three-day collaborative interventions that allowed geographically dispersed, multi-functional teams to come together to create, own and commit to implementing a shared vision. Opportunities had to be found to turn around the factors that were crippling delivery. Bringing people together was seen as the best way forward from across the globe so that all would own the solutions. The hothouses included people from the three core service delivery functions, including delivery management, order management and fulfilment. A separate business transformation team would design and run these hothouses.

With people busy in their day-to-day operations, normal requirements capture mechanisms often fail to create the inspiration, urgency and buy-in to commit to a transformational programme. For this particular situation, a hothouse event was the mechanism chosen to make it happen. Not only were the stakeholders in this case geographically dispersed, but some belonged to other organizations. In addition to the operating teams who would be impacted, the Division needed to bring together all the other stakeholders who would design and deliver the change. This included designers, architects, business analysts, programme managers, the sponsoring unit and the business transformation team.

Hothouses allowed the building of relationships and informal networks beyond the event and helped all to understand stakeholder concerns and constraints. Another reason for choosing the hothouse mechanism was to bring a reality check on whether the 'ask' was doable: it allowed for mobilization and the building of momentum in a short period.

Challenges in setting up the hothouses

The hothouses were located close to London so that people travelling from abroad or within the UK could easily reach the venue. They allowed for theatre-style seating and four major breakout areas in one hall, with conference and presentation equipment for each breakout. To create the right quorum of participants for the hothouse, the business transformation team set out to canvass operational and technical teams to nominate candidates. Difficulties arose for people having to travel from India, the United States and Latin America, as the organization had stringent travel policies in place that allowed business travel only for client-facing projects. The VP-SD had to arrange special dispensation for travel and budgets.

Candidates who were also busy in their day jobs had to be continued. People resisted attending: 'What is the hot house about? Why do I need to be there?' This led to a series of programme briefing global conference calls where the current business challenges and programme of work required was introduced by the VP-SD, followed by Q&A and closed with the 'ask' of sending representatives to the event. UK line managers for people who were travelling from abroad were coaxed into arranging team meetings. In the six weeks leading up to this event, invitations were sent out by the business transformation team and people were called individually to get confirmation. For people too busy to attend, their line managers were canvassed to create the headroom for travel and attendance.

For UK-based candidates, the challenges were around availability: 'I can't attend; I am really busy as I am deeply involved in project delivery at the moment.' The conversations to influence key members varied between the cause ('Why this programme of work is crucial') to the individual ('Why you are the best person to contribute to make it happen'). Everyone who was invited to attend needed to see the bigger purpose and feel the importance of his or her attendance. Sometimes conversations were escalated. Negotiations and horse-trading on priority projects to enable key members to attend continued until the last day before the hothouse event.

Running the hothouse

Seventy to eighty people attended these hothouses. A group of technical experts were identified to join. They included a team of technology platform architects, end-to-end designers working together with business analysts to help provide the new business solutions and ground the requirements in reality. This group were the doers and they were referred to as the 'Rainmakers' – a team of incubators and innovators who make things happen. Giving this cross-functional team a new identity for the purposes of the transformation programme brought in a sense of purpose, ownership and pride.

Each of the three days had a different community of stakeholders driving the event. On Day 1, the sponsoring unit and operational business units would vision and specify the business challenges. Towards the end the first day and following on to the second day, the business analysts would convert these business challenges to concrete requirements and go through a process of clarifying, detailing and challenging the benefits. As requirements became clear enough to action, these would be passed on to the Rainmaker team to action and create projects around them on Day 3. Their responsibility came towards the end, when they had to make sure that the proposals were feasible and affordable. They were also responsible for realistic timeline scheduling and rough cost estimates. Having taken part in the three days would mean that they understood the business drivers. The responsibility and accountability shifted subtly across the three days from business owners to analysts to the Rainmakers, who were then required to make a public commitment to their colleagues about requirements and timelines for what had been confirmed at the end of Day 3.

Hothouses had strict rules of engagement and participation. These were designed to hit big goals, empower contribution from any level in the organization, and build consensus. It also broke through formal authority and chains of command. A junior business analyst had the space to challenge proposals made by senior vice-presidents. Formal authority was not allowed to overrule; decisions were made by consensus and not majority rules. During the hothouse the rules allowed people to consult others – including those who were not present. Every hothouse started with a seed list of business demands that had already been agreed.

The outcome of the hothouses was a set of 25 disparate business requirements and their impact on the internal or external customers. These included a broad understanding of technology and process changes that would be required to be able to deliver successfully. The biggest impact would come from industrializing the quote-to-fulfilment order journey for the Division's MPLS technology-based product. It had large volumes, highest order value by revenue and also the biggest delays. It impacted almost all the service delivery functional units. In the closure session, virtual teams were created to come up with broad programme plans based on the hothouse results.

Detailed programme plans were developed over the following two months, with architects, who were a part of the Rainmaker team, detailing what new platforms and systems needed to be developed and how these would be integrated with the legacy systems. For incremental changes to existing systems, the risks were handled as a part of the software release process. The in-life operational teams, who would be impacted, nominated customer experience champions to understand the changes that would happen downstream on a future delivery date.

The greater challenge was moving away from legacy environments to completely new processes. These required significant investment to develop and deliver, and each initiative formed an investment case. The impact of this cutover and change for the operational team would come much later in the process, once the funding had been approved, as the new environment was created, tested and made ready for deployment.

Checking progress

In parallel, a joint project management office (PMO) function comprising group transformation, business transformation and service delivery unit heads was set up to monitor and enable this transformation. It would report monthly to an executive board. PMOs generally plan, monitor and report against the project deliverables, outcomes and benefits. Workstream owners were chosen for their seniority in their communities and for their ability to understand the vision and translate it into realistic projects.

The programme plans were developed into investment cases and then put to the PMO and the investment committee for funding. Funding was released in tranches, with the business sponsors prioritizing which projects needed to be delivered first. This was typically based on impact, delivery of quick wins and the size of business benefit. The series of capability-enablement tranches were each tied to releasing measureable benefits that would hit both their cost efficiency and timely delivery targets.

The PMO became deeply involved during the deployment stage since in-life business-as-usual teams would need to make a significant shift to their typical way of working. As a result, the PMO started engaging with operational managers and heads of delivery units to prepare them for the changes.

Making change stick

Once ready for deployment, a change management team was set up within the operational units to mobilize and help staff adopt the change. The TOM organization redesign had been under way for a while and soon supporting systems and processes were brought online. The biggest example of this was the roll-out of the new global MPLS ordering system. Presidents of the various regions were informed about the big changes through the Division's CEO forum. They were then required to get their market-facing teams across the regions (Europe, Middle East and Africa, Asia Pacific, Latin America) ready to move to new ways of working.

All in all, the process from diagnosis to implementation took 18 months. However, there was severe resistance to the changes from the operational teams, for three reasons. First, the operational teams had already provided local solutions to some of the problems, and they did not see the value of implementing a new strategy from head office. Second, they were entrenched in the status quo and actively looked to find defects in the new systems to justify their continuing to work on older systems. Last, with customer orders already processed (some of these would take 6–9 months to deliver) it was hard for them to support dual ways of working with a transition to the new environment. After months of tracking new orders and checking if the new process was being applied, the sponsoring team and VP-SD found that adoption had not happened with the speed expected and that the business was failing to realize the benefits of using the new streamlined approaches. Although the delivery had succeeded from a programme standpoint, it had struggled to create a permanent change in user behaviour.

The resulting challenges and lessons learnt

Project Carpe Diem was originally designed to bring operational efficiency within the Division but fell short. As the programme proceeded, teams learnt that every stage unravelled a layer of complexity that had not been anticipated, and the programme began to stall.

Reason 1 – lack of urgency at the implementation level

While there was a lot of urgency and commitment at the top levels of leadership, the same sense had not cascaded down to the development, implementation and operation teams on the ground. Not all levels of leadership had bought into the new system and not all levels of leadership shared the same vision. As a result, they failed to mobilize and motivate their teams, including aligning incentives and rewarding behaviours that would make true adoption a success. Embedding the changes that followed new team formations required a lot more effort and care. A programmatic approach to pushing change would only get the Division this far. For busy operational teams, their ability to absorb changes was limited and this change was ill thought through. The Division had to revisit and review how it led, promoted and embedded change. Each stage of this transformation journey and each level of the hierarchy required leadership capabilities. The Division should and could have used this as an opportunity to develop change champions and future leaders.

Reason 2 – poor handling of exceptions

The new organization design, with its process and systems changes, was not equipped to handle exceptions. When operational teams were placing complex orders for customers, the system did not allow for customized requests. In essence the system had been designed as 'one size fits all'. As a result, operational teams retained work practices that followed routines rooted in history of how things had always been done, so that they could continue to meet the needs of their customers. This affected performance targets.

Why did this happen? When they proposed their new TOM, the group transformation teams had not done enough groundwork to understand how complex orders were made up and the full spectrum of needs a customer may have. They had been working from a small sample from a 'happy path' – the ideal journey for an order, if everything went according to plan – in order to drive ambitious targets. They were also not incentivized to do more detailed work, only being focused on identifying large-scale transformation opportunities driven by cost reduction motives. Team members often went on to other projects, leaving the change programme to sort itself out. In the end, front-line agents and staff had not been empowered to contribute and recommend changes within the new system.

Reason 3 – internally focused transformation, customer impact ignored

The change programme ultimately went wrong when cuts in the name of efficiency went so deep that the Division ended up dropping KPIs related to customer satisfaction. They continued to lose future orders, and in order to get out of the death spiral they had to hire more staff. The urgency to drive change overlooked validating the edict, evaluating options, and identifying what could go wrong. Was the solution biased by the sponsoring units' own personal preferences? Yes. Were any techniques used to validate prescription? No. What is well known in management literature (Kahneman, 2011, 2012; Ariely, 2008) is that there are two main causes of poor decision making: lack of motivation and cognitive biases. The Division's senior leadership team had a bias for action; it was not lacking in motivation at that level. The problem here was not the lack of 'communication' or the 'sense of urgency' that is typical of a change process. It was the combination of a bias for action, overconfidence by managers, and confirmation bias brought about by a number of transformation teams only seeking out evidence that confirmed their original plans.

This led to prescriptive solutions handed down from the head office to operational centres around the world. It happened at the cost of looking for alternatives to evaluate that would meet the same outcomes. This was not entirely the fault of the head office: UK managers were pushing to get things done quickly, overconfident in their estimations and confident of a positive outcome without any regard for possible bottlenecks, mistakes or challenges.

Project Carpe Diem 2.0

It became apparent that initial optimism, and the scale of transformation deemed achievable, had to be readjusted. The VP-SD recognized this and drove the formulation of the next phase of the transformation. He had inherited a prescriptive proposal when he was appointed into his new role and had seen customer service drop as the original plans unravelled; this had severely impacted the morale of his operational teams. He promised to reshape the next phase of the programme. PCD had provided solid momentum and visibility but needed to reinvent itself. It moved from being solely cost focused to being customer focused and was called PCD 2.0.

PCD 2.0 was targeted to deliver a significant reduction in cycle time ('the 100-day challenge'), something that had not been taken into account in the original programme. PCD had expected that a reduction in costs would automatically impact cycle time, simply by eliminating duplication and making the system more efficient. Cost efficiencies were delayed and customer satisfaction became worse. PCD 2.0 allowed for bottom-up transformation idea generation and these came from the service desk field staff.

To deliver this ambition, two additional work programmes were started. The first worked with continuous service improvement and operational teams to identify non-technology requirements that would have a positive impact on cycle time, beyond reducing rewinds of orders and duplication efforts. Examples of this were reduction in spurious tasks that had no impact on the order (eg filling out forms) and getting customers to do certain validations themselves. The second programme (operational excellence) was designed to identify changes to the way the Division worked, and looked for incremental improvements, based on experimentation and innovation, in processes and systems. Small changes in systems reduced 12-hour waits and resulted in a better process to handle changes in orders that were already under way. Rapid experimentation was promoted. Beyond system developments, new tactical tools (called Heatmaps) were rapidly prototyped to drive performance. These tools were used to identify bottlenecks and provide intelligence to pinpoint where the improvement efforts needed to be focused. This included the reduction of ageing orders, improving delivery stage throughput and end-to-end (E2E) reporting capability.

The bottom-up initiatives were not just limited to the operational teams; the development teams were also encouraged to share their views.

When asked about their biggest difficulties on delivering the organizational challenges, the Indian partners mentioned lack of influence and voice, and wrong drivers. A typical quote was: 'Based on my individual understanding of the business complexity and business benefits, I have shared feedback to re-prioritize the demands in a certain sequence and consider alternates.... I felt, from the position where I am able to contribute, my feedback has not reached [the] right level and was unable to make the right impact... at senior management level.'

The VP-SD set this right by co-locating development and operational teams in various geographies to suggest value creation opportunities.

The benefits to customers included orders delivered right first time, massive reduction in cycle time, timely and accurate customer updates and, lastly, reduction in downtime when orders were modified. The Division also accrued benefits as a result of these changes. The staff were motivated as their working conditions improved and non-value-added work was reduced. Above all, there was a significant improvement on the delivery timescales to customers, keeping delivery promises and meeting industry benchmarks.

The VP-SD brought an outside-in focus to the transformation. Whereas he had inherited prescriptive solutions defined by head office for the original PCD, he was able to refocus PCD 2.0 using a customer perspective. As such, first-line service delivery agents were empowered to identify process bottlenecks in service delivery and then to suggest solutions and create champions for successful delivery. This was a mindset shift on how the transformation could be owned and delivered. Cost efficiency benefits were a natural outcome of this process, rather than a driver to the process.

The VP-SD developed new leaders, promoted their new responsibilities relentlessly and gave them autonomy to start influencing their communities. He ensured that their line managers recognized the new responsibilities their team members would hold. The VP-SD also actively took time out to coach them and develop their influencing skills across the organization.

Champions were installed in various regions and operational centres. Training was provided to the leadership teams in operations centres on system thinking, statistics, and simple tools for identification of change opportunities.

What happened next?

The continuation of the PCD programme and its successful pilot was a result of visible sponsorship by the VP-SD, who demonstrated vision and a coaching style of leadership right through the process. He promoted innovation and experimentation. He developed his transformation team and allowed for grassroots emergence of leadership from team members, even if they were several levels below. PCD 2.0 used a much more collaborative and bottom-up approach to opportunity identification for incremental and radical transformations.

In 2015, the VP-SD was voted the top person from the Division's 20,000 employees and was recognized by the telecom group's CEO for exceptional achievement. In December 2015, the Division publicly claimed: 'We put our customers at the heart of our decision-making and have made progress in improving customer service. By increasing the speed of delivery of our main products, we improved our Right First Time measure by 8.6 per cent.' It reflected the momentum set out by PCD and the renewed efforts and direction of PCD 2.0.

Conclusion

PCD had set out all the characteristics of a well-planned and well-mobilized transformation programme, but had lacked critical engagement at deeper levels of the organization. Change process models have abounded since the 1990s, but leading strategic change is more than following an eight-step process (Kotter, 1996). Instead, it is a combination of leadership goodwill, decision-making skills that overcome common biases that result in poor outcomes, change that makes sense overall, and change savvy-ness. Leadership is a critical transformational skill, not just at the level of the sponsor but also cascaded down levels of organization where change happens at the coalface.

Some of the more generalized learnings from both PCD and PCD 2.0 are:

- Mobilizing large change requires hothouse-type events, with visible sponsorship, bringing different communities to join in on a single purpose. It allows for building relationships, understanding constraints and stakeholder concerns, and a joined-up building of execution plans. New team identities and the informal networks persist beyond the event and help inspire and improve cooperation. Arranging these events needs a number of individual bridging and persuading conversations.

- Hothouses may create the necessary conditions for mobilization but are not sufficient to make transformation stick; the latter requires continuous levels of cascading leadership. A sense of urgency and commitment at the top levels of leadership does not automatically filter down to the development, implementation and operation teams on the ground.

- In the role of sponsoring leadership, it is not sufficient simply to communicate the vision; it is also important to empower the new leaders, coach them in influencing skills and visibly promote their new responsibilities.

- A top-down cost efficiency programme combined with an outside-in customer satisfaction improvement approach is a powerful framework. The outside-in approach focuses on the removal of non-value-added work, duplication and delays, thus improving both efficiency and customer satisfaction. In contrast, cost transformation by itself can severely impact customer service; an outside-in bottom-up approach by itself can miss big structural improvements.

- For complex transformation, bottom-up engagement is also crucial: line staff and operational teams have a worm's-eye view of complexity and exceptions, and also good ideas about how to resolve them. It is not just operational teams that need to be empowered, but also the development teams on what could be improved and make the biggest difference.

References

Ariely, D (2008) *Predictably Irrational: The hidden forces that shape our decisions*, Harper Collins, London

Kahneman, D (2011) Before you make that big decision. *Harvard Business Review*, June

Kahneman, D (2012) *Thinking, Fast and Slow*, Penguin Random House, Harmondsworth

Kotter, J (1996) *Leading Change*, Harvard Business Review Press, Boston, MA

Operational readiness for change

11

ROD WILLIS, JOHN McLELLAND, KEVIN PARRY
AND SARAH COLEMAN

Introduction

This chapter looks at how organizations make themselves operationally ready for change, using diverse case studies drawn from an airport cargo terminal construction in Southeast Asia, an ICT outsourcing deal, new product introduction and its implications for the supply chain in an aerospace manufacturer, and a merger and acquisition in the electronic manufacturing sector.

Delivering change in terms of operational readiness can be quite a challenge, not least because it is something that is seldom given sufficient focus. Readiness for change – whether this is at the organizational level, operational level, team level or indeed at the individual level – can be a nebulous concept, tends to be thought about quite late on and is often under-represented within the change process. At one level we seek simple instructions or pre-defined process steps, so it is easy to ensure that the most visible aspects of change – process, structure and procedure – are ready; but it is a little more complex than this. The operational requirements around process, structure and procedure need to be complemented by other people-focused components such as mindsets, values and skills. These latter aspects are about the human side of change and how prepared organizational personnel are: we can be aware at a rational level of the need for change but be unprepared at the emotional and behavioural level to embrace change personally (Balogun and Hope Hailey, 2004). A further dimension is that there will be various levels of readiness across the organization, especially around awareness and commitment.

Much of the effort in organizations is focused on doing change rather than on early-stage designing and planning or later-stage landing, performance evaluation and sustaining. Deloitte (2012, 2013) identified that up to 30 per cent of the value of a capital programme can be destroyed owing to operational readiness failures, and again recognized that it is often the 'people' side of change delivery that presents the greatest challenge and is the least predictable part of change.

So far within in the book we've looked at early-stage shaping, scoping and designing change; we've focused on particular aspects of change such as leadership, building resilience, employee communication and engagement; we've also provided narrative and insights around how organizations and industries have made their change. Now we'll focus on the later stages of change: how organizations prepare for change delivery and how change lands.

Getting operations ready for change

Operational 'readiness' is an ambiguous concept. Time spent defining what 'ready' looks like, identifying readiness activities and integrating these into the change plan are often under-represented. As Lord Sebastian Coe, Chair of the London Organising Committee of the Olympic and Paralympic Games, commented for the 2012 London Olympics, 'As an athlete, you never want to perform something in the final that you haven't spent thousands of hours preparing for...' and the same sentiment can be applied to organizational change.

This preparation may sound relatively straightforward, but it usually isn't. For example, operational readiness must consider possible causes of failure, whether internally caused or due to external factors, and in both cases how the operation will recover. It is particularly important to consider resilience at this stage, as either inexperienced staff or the use of a new facility will tend to make automatic recovery from setbacks that much harder.

To do this, we need to consider the critical points in the value chain, which could represent 'pinch points' for the throughput of the business. In a call centre, for example, this could be the first-line handling of inbound calls or the way that automated call management software handles volumes that exceed the maximum predicted. If every subsequent stage depends on the first point of contact, then both the technology and the people at that first point should be the most tested and the most prepared by means of scenario planning, simulation and rehearsal.

The people factors include some quite mundane things: access to site and car parking, security passes, the distance to the next nearest working toilets if the planned ones are out of action, peak working temperatures and the way that breaks are planned. Preparations should also include the way that the work itself is carried out when things go wrong, such as equipment breaking down or software glitches. It is also important to consider how such risks will be prioritized and managed. If the biggest risk is a security breach, for example, then the same principle applies, with the operational planning team putting themselves 'into the shoes' of the would-be intruders, imagining multiple failures of the primary security measures and then finding the gaps and blind spots well before the operational design is completed.

CASE STUDY

Lessons from Denver International Airport, Heathrow Terminal 5 and the move from Kai Tak airport to a new airport at Chek Lap Kok all underlined the importance of operational readiness to the successful delivery of a new airport terminal in Southeast Asia. These previous examples demonstrated that operational readiness needed to be planned separately from the project scope of technical and building completion; it needed visibility and reporting lines directly into senior management so that issues could be quickly resolved and so that progress was always visible and shared.

The programme used a single integrated project plan for operational readiness based on the milestones from the complex construction project plans from the contractors, technology suppliers and legal obligations under the Franchise Agreement, as well as operational objectives from the parent company. The consultant in charge of this aspect used a 'reverse-engineering' approach to plan the opening of the new airport cargo terminal, working from the full opening to the present time and identifying critical success factors, risks and milestones. This provided a single source of reference for the programme team and for the client who would operate the terminal once opened.

From this plan, the programme team identified dependencies, contingencies and inconsistencies through to personnel hiring requirements and subcontracting of services, certificates and licences required to legally occupy, operate and open the terminal on 'Day 1', the first day of live operations with real customers. The plan was reviewed on a weekly basis with internal and external project managers whose work represented key dependencies for operational readiness. This was an unfamiliar way of working for the older cargo hands, who were used to relying on their own experience to prepare for operation; the weekly review was regarded as unnecessary or bureaucratic, and often highlighted uncomfortable truths about workload, progress or risks.

Other airport terminals had fallen foul of a 'big-bang' opening, so the decision was taken to cut over to the new cargo processing centre in stages. Identifying the critical path for each stage required detailed planning by the suppliers, contractors and cargo terminal operator as well as reverse-engineering the organization's requirements in terms of skills availability and volume of staff required. These were constantly revised on a two-weekly cycle, with detailed analysis behind each revision. Despite this apparent science, the team had to test their readiness in simulations, and it was only from this trial and error experience of what worked and what didn't that plans could be verified. Each transition stage involved an operational readiness test, which timed and checked the people, equipment, facilities and IT systems in a simulation of peak and mixed cargo handling. Plans for the transition stages were very detailed and in the final 72 hours were defined hour by hour.

At the cutover to a new transition stage, the cargo terminal had 48 hours during which they could revert back to the older shared facility previously used. This enabled the company to mitigate the most serious risks involved as much as possible. Typically cutovers took place at 3 am during the quietest time for cargo aircraft arrivals, again to mitigate as much as possible any risk involved in the actual switch from one terminal to another. As part of the planned activities for each stage cutover, a crisis management team was assembled at midnight together with the management of the previous terminal from which the cargo processing was being transferred, who were included as advisers.

All these preparations and rehearsals helped to ensure that the transition for each stage went smoothly. In particular, the people taking on the work for the first time felt confident in their ability to work as a team and meet the targets set, most importantly protecting the organization against the reputational risk and revenue impact of a high-profile failure. In the first 12 months after opening, three other airlines opted to use the terminal for their critical global cargo needs.

CASE STUDY

One of the global telecoms companies negotiated and signed up a UK client for an ICT outsourcing contract worth tens of millions of pounds sterling. Working under a heavily proscriptive service level agreement, the outsourcing contract required the telecoms company to cover hardware and software maintenance and upgrades, asset management, help desk facilities, project management office (PMO), telephony, security and firewalls. The contract also required the movement of over 50 IT infrastructure, development and maintenance personnel under the UK Transfer of Undertakings (Protection of Employment) Regulations (TUPE). This should have meant that as part of the preparations and operational readiness for the transition, the telecoms company provided an extensive induction process, welcome and introduction to their company and to their way of doing things, as they would normally do for new starters. However, the original planning with the Bid Team and Sales Team and the original negotiations with the client had focused purely on process and technology change from the UK client to the telecoms company; HR had not been invited to the table during the early discussion and design stages of the transition opportunity and, as a result, declined to get involved because no budget had been allocated for this activity.

The outcome? The process-driven aspects of the outsourcing contract proved relatively straightforward, albeit lengthy. Asset registers were established and populated, third-party supplier contracts were renegotiated over to the telecoms company, a new telephony system was installed, data migrations were completed, and users were kept abreast of what was happening, when and why.

However, the real issue focused on personnel. Although these 50 IT personnel now relied on pay, development and promotion from the telecoms company, in reality they were still sited in their original offices, with their original equipment, having lunch and going out socially with their original colleagues. No formal demarcation of offices or personnel was established: with no office or environment change and no formal induction or welcome process, these personnel continued to work as they had done while directly employed by the UK client.

What this meant in practice was that the performance of the contract was flagged 'at risk'. Because the IT personnel felt closer to their old colleagues and because allegiance to their new employer had not been sufficiently established, colleagues of the TUPE'd IT personnel would continue to walk down the corridor to ask them 'please would you...', and of course they were happy to be as helpful as they had always been. As a result, none of this 'please would you' work was documented, planned or recorded which, in turn, had a direct impact on resource availability and the bottom line of the outsourcing contract.

The outsourcing contract transition director decided to spend a great deal more of her time on site to try to understand what was happening. Once she had the opportunity to sit in the open office with the TUPE'd personnel, noticing everything that was happening and listening to the conversations around her, she understood the problem and took steps to resolve the issue. The key learning for the transition director was to force her involvement in the early stages of an outsource opportunity with the bid and sales teams, which she could now do with leadership team's blessing, using this contract as an example of how it could all go horribly wrong. In doing this, she ensured that all process, structure and people aspects of any outsource contract would be given proper consideration.

CASE STUDY

This case study describes how a mature high-technology aerospace company, employing over 20,000 people, globally focused on new product introduction. At the time, annual spend on R&D and new products was over £1 billion and the company's operation covered the complete product lifecycle from engineering creation through production and long-term customer support. The Head of Product Introduction (HPI) was tasked with preparing the internal supply chain organization for the launch and introduction of a major new product.

The company was organized into several customer business units (CBUs) trading with a separate internal supply chain organization (see Figure 11.1). This organization had the task of managing a range of manufacturing facilities, suppliers, joint ventures and partners across the world. The supply chain organization comprised supply chain operating units (SCOUs) organized around specific commodities and containing all the skills necessary to design, buy and manufacture component parts or subsystems for delivery to the final assembly line. Their operation was supported by several functional teams encompassing engineering, manufacturing engineering, quality, planning and control, purchasing, finance and HR:

- The Supply Chain Development (SCD) team, working with the SCOUs, was accountable for the strategic supply chain design and structure. Its role was critical during the product concept phase to ensure that the technology and business requirements of the product were aligned with the supply chain design and its capabilities.

- The New Product Introduction (NPI) team, as part of a cross-functional supply chain operations team, was accountable for the integration of the supply chain status across the full product bill of materials for all SCOUs. This included ensuring robust planning, commitment acceptance and expediting during the development phase and importantly also oversight of the smooth introduction of the product into the production systems of the SCOUs later.

The CBUs managed the relationship with the customers and worked alongside the future products team to develop and offer new products to meet their needs.

Figure 11.1 High-level supply chain organization model

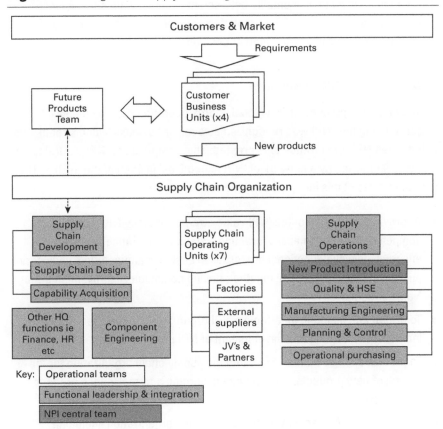

The challenge of New Product Introduction (NPI)

As always, the customer requirement was demanding in timescale. The product specification required not only new design technologies, but also the development of their associated manufacturing processes and a step-change in the supply chain cost base. In addition, this all had to be achieved while the organization was already engaged with the development of several other major products that were straining resources and capital.

By their nature, every new product will have its own story and specific set of challenges, but however unique, they all share some common themes, and this case study shares four particular areas that proved critical to success. These were:

1 developing an NPI organization and making it a core competence;

2 having a formal launch process into the supply chain for new products;

3 building a robust bottom-up plan *jointly* with the project leaders in the business units;

4 creating a *single team* mentality between the supply chain and business/ product teams around a 'burning platform'; in this case, the necessity of recapturing a key client and market position.

1 *Developing an NPI organization*

Introducing new products into a global, matrix operation can be complex. Understanding this, NPI was recognized as a major business 'value stream' and a dedicated NPI organization was created. This comprised an NPI central team that was supported by a network of 'NPI executives' in each of the SCOUs. The joint objectives of this integrated team were:

- To provide leadership of the 'NPI value stream'; to make NPI a core competence for the company; creating a standard operating model and ensuring individual functional processes in design, manufacturing, engineering, purchasing etc worked well together; driving continuous improvement through 'value stream eyes'.

- To create and maintain an effective NPI organization in the operating units, including the training and development of NPI professionals.

- To provide a single point of entry into the supply chain organization for the launch of new products; creating and governing a formal launch process (see below).

- To integrate all NPI activity in the supply chain organization, including programme, resource and budget planning, supporting IT, performance metrics, reporting, escalation process etc.

- To lead and govern the execution of NPI programmes in the supply chain using a gated maturity process for product and production readiness.

The NPI executives also had their own dedicated resources, which included programme managers aligned to support specific product lines in the CBUs and a small team of logistics personnel specifically skilled in introducing new products into a running operation. There were two additional aspects that made this structure effective:

- The central NPI team reported to the Executive Vice-President (EVP) of Supply Chain Operations and had the necessary *organizational power* to govern NPI activity across all SCOUs and CBUs. This helped in creating a standard operating model and in driving a consistent approach when dealing with strong personalities in a matrix organization.
- The HPI had *personal credibility* with both the SCOUs and the CBUs. The value of this should not be underestimated, and it proved critical to the successful performance of this role.

2 *Formal launch process*

With an NPI organization in place, the next step was to establish a formal launch process. Experience had shown during earlier new product launches that there could be poor synchronization in planning and often confusion in the organization as to whether a new product had actually been approved. This was addressed by introducing a formal gated launch process within the supply chain organization. This in itself did not authorize the product launch (which was typically a board decision), but it did authorize supply chain personnel to engage with the business units to prepare a detailed plan, approve it and then launch the product into the supply chain in a robust way.

A simple three-gated process was introduced for all new products:

- Gate 1 raised awareness of the product, its requirements and its strategic importance as well as highlighting new challenges and key risks. The gate output was agreement for supply chain resources to engage in a 4- to 6-week joint 'work book' study to create a supply chain plan (as described below).
- Gate 2 reviewed the output of the 'work book' studies until an agreement was reached on the plan. There were usually several iterations of this gate.
- Gate 3 bought off the plan with the associated set of baseline assumptions and actions. This then formed the input to the business plan for the board and, once approved, was the executive basis to instruct and align all resource, capital and financial planning across the company.

Once the final business approval was given, a formal launch event was held. These events were held globally and provided a clear executive signal to commence work in a *synchronized* way. Just as importantly, it also demonstrated that the leadership of both parts of the organization were collaborating, so setting the tone for teamwork across the organizational boundaries that would be needed later.

3 *Integrated supply chain plan*

Our experience had shown that the best way to get the supply chain ready to receive a new product was to actively engage it in creating a credible plan for its introduction.

The first level of engagement started early in the product evolution and influenced the design concept itself. This was achieved by establishing a regular forum for the CBU/future products and supply chain development teams to confirm that the baseline product concept and its associated business plan requirements could be met by the supply chain capability and footprint. This included not only any novel manufacturing capability that needed to be developed, but also any new supply chain strategies to address issues such as cost, joint ventures, partners, government offset etc. Regular reviews were put in place to work through these issues to get to an early agreed position on these significant strategic items.

The next level of engagement, started later but running in parallel with the above, prepared the detailed plan using a structured 'work book' process. In simple terms, this was a document that captured the assumptions and agreements between the CBUs and the SCOUs. This process was led by the central NPI team over a 4- to 6-week period. It ensured there was a documented formal baseline and set of assumptions based on the following key agreements:

- a preliminary Bill of Material (BoM) defining the product, at an appropriate level;
- an achievable programme timescale plan;
- a confirmation that technical and supply chain capability was at a suitable level of readiness consistent with the baseline BoM;
- an assessment and agreement on the supply chain design and its unit cost;
- supply chain capital and budgetary requirements;
- supply chain headcount requirements by skill and timing;
- identification of any additional supply chain capacity required, ensuring that capital and resources were planned to deliver it;
- identification of key risks and confirmation that there were strategies, budgets and resources in place to mitigate them.

This output was then formally committed to by all parts of the business through the gated launch process (Gate 3) and thereafter subject to rigorous change control as the concept design developed.

There are always competitive pressures on a company to take risks to secure market, and discussions internally as to where to focus and prioritize resources and capital. An important lesson here was to formally agree with the affected SCOUs an acceptable level of risk to take and, further, to ensure that the treatment plan describing funding and resourcing had been included in the 'work book' agreements. This was important in winning the commitment and 'hearts and minds' of supply chain personnel, who are often left holding the baby when things go wrong.

4 *Build a single global team*

Experience had shown us that there can be an 'us and them' mentality between product and supply chain teams. This was partly addressed by the organizational structure and process implemented above, which naturally brought people together in a common cause. But this process alone was not enough.

There was a significant investment in a team-building event over a period of a full week involving both the key product and supply chain personnel to 'jump start' the creation of a truly integrated team. Like many similar events, it set out goals and vision but, perhaps more importantly, it focused heavily on establishing a behavioural model to create a high-performance culture within the team. The event provided fun but also addressed issues such as trust, accountability, motivation and self-awareness; further, it broke down barriers and allowed the team to see individuals not just as role owners in the organization but also as human beings sharing a common purpose. Note, however, that this was not a one-off event and the process required continual reinforcing mechanisms.

So what are the key messages to ensure supply chain readiness in a new product launch? Each organization will be at a particular point along the journey of adopting and implementing the four critical areas described above, and some may put more emphasis on one aspect than another. In this case, the success of the approach described above was such that it has now become the standard. So, in summary:

- The benefit of softer behavioural team-building activities should not be underestimated, as relationships and behaviours in the team will be critical to success in the execution phase of the programme. The shadow that leadership casts here is critical.
- Consciously create a core competence in product introduction both in organizational design and in process.
- Give it a respected leader with strong relationships across the company.
- Engage the supply chain early and jointly build robust plans.
- Control and synchronize launch into the supply chain elements.
- Create 'one team' between the product and supply chain teams and build 'emotional capital'.

Getting ready for M&As

In *The New M&A Playbook*, Christensen *et al* (2011) identified that $2 trillion is spent on acquisitions each year. Their study also highlighted that between 70 and 90 per cent of mergers and acquisitions fail to deliver the benefits that were expected, because most acquirers do not know how to think systematically about what they are buying and what it might do for them. The implication here is that a fixed plan or system can be defined which will cover all the key needs of bringing about the desired change. In our experience of complex change initiatives, especially around M&As, success does not come about from a structured plan alone. Plans tend to address the *hard* elements around process, structure and procedure, and rarely do we find the *soft* elements such as integrating organizational cultures, mindsets (impacting what we can sense), values (influencing our actions) and skills (competencies and behaviours).

CASE STUDY

A small UK electronic manufacturing organization, ABC, with fewer than 50 staff, was acquired by organization XYZ, with around 500 staff. One of the outcomes of this acquisition was to implement a unified information system (IS) for integrated material requirements planning (MRP).

ABC was in the early stages of growth and XYZ was well established in the international market. As a result of the acquisition, ABC was catapulted into the international market and XYZ's product portfolio was increased along with its customer base. This was an acquisition with a win–win outcome; however, after a few months it became clear that there were particular challenges to be managed. In particular, the robust IS that XYZ was using and wanted ABC to adopt did not scale down to an efficient size for it to add value to ABC, the smaller operation. Rather than reducing costs, the new system was increasing costs owing to the need for additional staff to support the new comprehensive yet complex system.

At first, XYZ felt that there was some hesitation from the smaller organization to adopt its IS, since the project was not progressing as it had anticipated. The IS performed perfectly in XYZ, so why not now? People were flown from one continent to the other to sort the problem. Slowly over time, as both organizations started to discuss the issue rather than to posture, realization dawned that although the IS was perfect for the one organizational context, it was not the perfect solution for the acquired organization.

This was a gift at the time: business implications were minimal yet the learning was significant for the new integrated organization. The result for ABC was a vastly improved, albeit different, IS to what it had used before the acquisition. The business value-add was increased operation efficiency. Both organizations managed to achieve their objectives, just not in the way they had initially anticipated. Interestingly, both organizations realized that they were able to learn from each other and as a result a strong bond and trusting relationship evolved. There was no 'them and us', only 'us'. Open and meaningful discussion exploring the issues resulted in a robust solution, provided the opportunity to better understand the capabilities each brought to the table, and provided a strong basis for future collaboration across continents.

So what was the key learning? Size and context do matter, especially in relation to the relative strengths of both acquirer and the acquired; in this particular case, the issue happened to be a software system for MRP. Also, understanding different perspectives and inviting collaborative decision making delivered a successful outcome. Learning that the approach that the larger acquiring organization had taken had value in terms of insight and the knowledge; however, in terms of specific implementation, ABC still needed something relevant to its actual size of operations. By integrating ideas and knowledge from both organizations, something stronger emerged.

Conclusion

Operational 'readiness' is an ambiguous concept and one typically given insufficient time and thought. One proven method is 'reverse-engineering': working back from the target operational state to the current point in time, identifying key decision points and dependencies along the way. The nature of these plans means that they must be continuously revised as dependent activities change and as better insights are gained into the scope of preparations for 'Day 1' and beyond. Change programmes that embed operational readiness from the outset typically identify risks earlier, mitigate design issues when they are less costly to resolve and build highly capable teams.

Focusing on process, technology and structure is critical, but not the whole picture. We also need to ensure that the human element is suitably covered and dealt with, with equal attention and focus.

Create a 'one team' approach regardless of geography or function and actively engage each part in creating a credible operational readiness plan, understanding that operational readiness delay or failure can represent value destruction for the business.

Start planning for operational readiness as soon as possible. Do so early on in the programme and involve those who will be directly affected or who will be required to take action, ensuring that personnel understand from an early stage what will be required of them and what action they will need to take. Finally, allow for iterative work. Training materials won't be right first time, equipment won't pass acceptance tests, suppliers won't necessarily keep their promises, so contingency planning and the ability to flex your resources will help to avoid the potential reputational damage that poor operational readiness planning can cause.

Key questions

How does your organization ensure it is operationally ready for change in terms of:

- process
- governance
- people?

References

Balogun, J and Hope Hailey, V (2004) *Exploring Strategic Change*, Pearson Education, Harlow

Christensen, CM *et al* (2011) The new M&A playbook. *Harvard Business Review*, **89** (3), pp 48–57

Deloitte (2012) [Accessed 9 August 2016] Effective operational readiness of large mining capital projects: avoiding value leakage in the transition from project execution into operations [Online] http://deloitteblog.co.za/files/icp/Effective_Operational_Readiness.pdf

Deloitte (2013) [Accessed 9 August 2016] Mastering the people side of operational readiness: Operation Go-Live! [Online] http://www2.deloitte.com/uk/en/pages/infrastructure-and-capital-projects/articles/operation-go-live.html

Managing change in Asia and the West   12

Different windows, different views

KEVIN PARRY

Introduction

This chapter will explore how our education system, national culture and business environment shape our perceptions of how change should be designed, managed and embedded in organizations. Four linked short case studies and a final case study will highlight some of my own first-hand experiences and those of close colleagues to illustrate these differences. In particular, I will show why we have different ideas about change in China and the West, noting that Chinese culture has some similarities with other Asian cultures such as Singapore and Korea (Huntington, 1993). By 'the West' I mean the UK and United States primarily and their cultural allies.

Our culture and education affect our perspective, expectations and values which in turn determine our behaviour. These are crucial in managing change and at their most dangerous when not considered or are taken for granted to be the same. The influence of China in Asia, not only through its diaspora and massive economic growth, but also by migration and the creation of new communities in other countries, has made it the most important new factor in business and social culture over the past two decades (Ackerman, Hu and Wei, 2009).

The chapter will therefore look at how change is both experienced and managed, since even those who are managing it go through the experience of change even if at an intellectual level they know what they intend and why. This is especially true when change is imposed by external events or by people with more power than the change leaders.

We know from our own experience that influencing someone else's behaviour depends on either meeting their expectations or changing them to expect something different. What we consider 'normal' includes these expectations, and at both senior executive level and more junior employees these expectations are the key difference between managing change in Asia and the West today.

Change management concepts in conflict

Where organizations direct change from the same cultural and educational background, agreement may be easier and ideas more readily aligned between those directing change and those affected. However, where there is a mix of Asian and Western cultures, misaligned expectations are almost inevitable. This can affect morale, staff turnover, productivity and ultimately the future survival of the business. The stakes could not be higher.

Western middle and senior managers can be seen as outspoken, challenging authority, disruptive and demanding excessive consultation by Chinese executives or board members to whom they report. Conversely, Chinese managers can be seen by Western leaders as autocratic and secretive; in some cases, even as subversive in not voicing concerns and not contributing. Western leaders expecting 'engagement' may get only 'yes' and apparent agreement.

These same Western senior managers may helplessly see what appears to be demotivation by Asian staff as people grapple with structural and process changes, but do not question directions and answer affirmatively to instructions out of respect and deference. These are examples of unmet expectations on both sides, often manifested in the loss of trust between those in charge and their staff.

Let's consider how these different perspectives originate, first looking at Asian business change management from the Western perspective. In both cultures, change is usually driven 'top down' from the CEO and board, but the underlying assumptions are very different in terms of the design, details and method of managing change. In China, one cultural norm is that 'big brother knows best', whereby the state, leadership or seniors know what is best for 'little brother' or 'sister' (Anthony, 2007). This comes from many sources, most notably Confucianism and political theory in which 'Tian'

(Heaven) is the source of all legitimate authority on earth; choosing the most worthy person which gives them the mandate of heaven (Yuval Noah Harari, 2015). From this comes the expectation of respect for, and obedience to, seniors and elders. Contrast this with the rise of the individual as 'knowledge worker' in the West. In the United States or the UK, the same attitude and behaviour may be seen as authoritarian, secretive and autocratic, whereas the Chinese executive is simply acting normally in deciding what is best for those who report to him or her.

Chinese senior managers will also seek information from trusted sources rather than consulting their subordinates, and are less likely than their Western counterparts to involve a wider circle of managers in the change design or approach. These trusted sources will be based on personal relationships or first-hand recommendations by trusted advisers. As such, they are unlikely to include aspects of change design, which is very much a Western concept.

Stakeholder management is an important aspect of managing change in both China and the West. In Asia, it is often carried out on a more intuitive basis based on relevant information sharing 'at the right time' and typically later in the implementation stage of the change than is considered 'good practice' in the West. This approach may be seen by Western stakeholders as a little patronizing, and highlights the difference between engagement and notification, of being in or out of the inner circle of the change leader.

Chinese senior managers rarely admit what they don't know, since this would lead to a loss of face. The concept of 'face' or Miàn zi (面子) in China reflects the reputation and prestige of an individual in the different aspects of a person's life. In Chinese society, status can be increased or lost in multiple ways and is often seen relative to the status of other people rather than on personal achievements. Compare this with the West, where such an admission by executives is more likely to be seen as showing integrity and openness; ambiguity and knowledge gaps are typically tolerated more than would be expected in China.

In Asia, motivation tends to be by competition and fear of the consequence of failure, which includes the loss of face. Enforcement of compliance is expected from the obedience and hierarchy assumed from the belief that big brother knows best. Teams comprising a mix of Western and Chinese people will therefore experience this differently and so adjust to changes by seeking harmony first and foremost, or resistance and confusion, depending on cultural background.

Let's now look at the Western world through Asian eyes. In the West, we increasingly understand change to be a process, not an event. To Asian eyes, this may be seen as slowing the change, or as weak leadership, while endless consultation takes place without making the urgency clear enough. In Asia, once change is decided, it is soon executed. The ideal leadership style is more patriarchal and based on the mass assembly of employees in meetings or company-sponsored formal meals, or 'gatherings' to hear what is to happen. By the time this happens, many of the details have already been decided. A Western leader presenting the direction of change without including the way it will be implemented would be seen as unclear and premature. This may even cause a loss of face in the eyes of their Chinese subordinates.

Chinese celebration of success in the achievement of a milestone is still in many organizations more of a religious ceremony. This will involve a ceremonial cutting of a roast suckling pig, with prayers to the gods and on an auspicious date, by the senior executives and honoured guests. Everyone present will get a freshly cut piece of the pork to share in the celebration. This also reflects the more superstitious beliefs of Chinese people, which can comfortably co-exist with a top business school education (Leung, 2015).

The Western view that managing change is a specialist function, with external consultants advising management or with internal specialists, would be seen in China as giving up far too much power and control. In Asia, it is always the collective interests of the group or organization and the maintenance of harmony which matters. There is less interest in the individual change experience, except where this results in non-conformity or resistance to the new requirements for work performance.

Chinese business culture in managing change

The aftermath of the Cultural Revolution in China, and in Hong Kong after British rule, has created a melting pot of ideas, management styles and some re-interpreted Western concepts (Ralston, Gustafson and Cheung, 1993). This is not to suggest that such change is not effective, but the effectiveness of this approach greatly depends on the type of change involved. The main Chinese change concepts used in recent times are:

- tactics that are diagnostic in nature;
- tactics that provide information;
- tactics for communication;
- compulsion or enforcement tactics.

Tactics that are diagnostic in nature

Tactics that are diagnostic in nature, such as gathering information concerning organizational dynamics, aim to understand how the organization works and the target benefits or fears that people may have towards the change. This is based on military thinking and strongly reflects the command and control style of management.

CASE STUDY 1 The new cargo terminal at Hong Kong International Airport

The Chinese CEO wanted to know the views of the local management team in Hong Kong on outsourcing over one thousand unskilled labourers for the cargo-handling business of a major airline. He was considering what would work best; for example, using one external organization or two. He met with his senior management team and his programme manager to sound them out on this and how it would affect their teams. In particular, he wanted to know at what level their own junior managers should be placed to oversee the contactors, and whether these junior managers would be capable of managing third-party staff.

A key consideration was the ability of these contract staff and their middle managers. A suggestion of a management workshop to 'walk through' the 24×7 operation was rejected in favour of separate one-to-one conversations to gather information. A recurring theme was the requirement to avoid differences in views being aired in open discussion, which would lead to a loss of face for a manager whose views were openly overruled. It became clear that this was not about forming ideas collectively. It was about testing already formulated ideas for flaws and employee resistance before implementing them.

Key questions

- Are there advantages to holding one-to-one briefings first by the CEO and the company over an open discussion with the group?
- What are the disadvantages and what do they depend on?
- What risks are increased by this approach?
- If you were briefing the managing director ahead of these meetings, what would you advise or want to have prepared in advance?

Tactics that provide information

These are tactics deployed by the leaders in Chinese businesses to establish information ahead of taking action and provide the basis of the timing and speed of change to be implemented. The main purpose of these are motivation (stress the positives) and delegation (what you need to do now).

CASE STUDY 2   The new cargo terminal at Hong Kong International Airport

The transition from testing to live operations at the new business was designed to take place over three stages, separated by four to six months. This would ensure that the sophisticated materials handling system (MHS) to move and direct the flow of cargo, and the hundreds of offices and huge floor layouts, would be tested progressively in pairs of floors from the ground floor up.

Contractors and managers would be hired on a just-in-time basis to control the substantial payroll and contract costs of employing more than 2,000 people before any revenues were received, but it was clear that this would impact the front-line staff considerably. These people would have to repeat the same actions as precisely as possible over a period of weeks to test equipment, and then revert to normal operations after a successful transition stage.

This meant that not only would the rules change from testing to operations by the content of the work; it was highly likely that procedures would be refined after trial and even in the first weeks of live operation. Rain and high winds were a risk in the huge open space. Later testing would be in warmer weather and it was estimated that temperatures of 40 °C were likely in the huge concrete structure open to the runway at the back and the airport perimeter road at the front. Meanwhile, manual labour was needed to move the cargo against tight deadlines to meet operational performance targets in the heat and dust.

The decision was taken to establish a Works Council to provide regular briefings and consultation, but suggestions to include representatives of the unskilled front-line staff and that the CEO should chair it were rejected as too risky. The view was that adverse publicity from information leaks and from the implied ability to press for change was not the message that management wanted to give. Instead, the Works Council had only middle management representation and was chaired by the Personnel Department.

It was another form of information capture for the consideration of senior management and, although useful in this regard, it was not a consultative body before changes were introduced. Briefings to front-line workers were carried out by line managers on a daily basis and they reported any grievances back to the Works Council. As Chair of the Works Council, the Head of Personnel was expected to brief the managing director (MD) and take any instructions from him on how to handle any issues or concerns raised.

Subsequently, it was more difficult to separate the repetitive and probably boring tasks as a model for real operations in which considerable variation would be experienced, from the technical problems as software defects and hardware failures were ironed out. This postponed the testing of processes and procedures in a meaningful way until later.

Key questions

- What should this kind of consultation normally be part of in planning terms?
- What should we know before such engagement begins?
- What was the primary consideration of the MD in this case?

In the above two case studies of a major change project based in Hong Kong, the positions of Personnel Manager and Communications Manager were two of the earliest positions hired. These were seen as critical in managing industrial relations when implementing change.

To explain a little of the background, relations at this time between contract staff and management at the shipping cargo terminal in Kowloon had reached breaking point. This was seen to be damaging the reputations of the companies concerned and of their suppliers. It was front-page news for several days in the Hong Kong press, the headlines making the management look indecisive and ineffective.

The company was naturally anxious to avoid this kind of reputational damage. However, they needed to ask hundreds of contract staff to take part in testing, which was not, strictly speaking, in their contract or normal course of duties. It was a delicate balance between learning from the experience of manual workers before volumes increased later in the transition to full operations, and appearing to be open to negotiation or changes by the workers and their supervisors.

Although communication was widely agreed to be necessary for success, for many of the Chinese senior managers, especially older managers, communication was essentially about marketing. Although quite beneficial in some respects by reminding managers of how far the business had come and what future plans were, these communications were not designed to invite feedback on ideas which at that stage were still untested.

There were many good reasons for this view: the risk of information leakage when plans were commercially sensitive and the risk of encouraging dissent, so creating extra work when the main objective was to move at pace. Nonetheless, the implied lack of trust was evident, along with the assumption that the operational staff's motivation was not the success of the enterprise on which their jobs depended.

Tactics for communication

More recent developments in Chinese change management include new tactics for communication which are beginning to include some two-way discussion between individuals and groups. These include the growing importance of even semi-skilled workers in the organization, their freedom of movement to other employers if not treated well, and the value of experience in productivity and safety at work.

However, there are two important caveats to this apparently more liberal approach. First, culturally it is difficult if not impossible to question any fundamental assumption by senior management except by a superior, such as a board member. Second, such discussion is likely to be within functions such as IT services or finance, rather than between functions. For this reason, change management in a Chinese-run organization is more about the implementation of new structures than a process of shaping, scoping and designing change (see Figure 12.1).

Enforcement tactics

Enforcement tactics are often used to impose change. These can include the use of task forces or briefing workshops. Unlike the Western idea of workshops in which problems are jointly explored and solved, the Chinese concept of briefing workshops is closer to a carefully choreographed briefing, with any questions being tightly controlled.

CASE STUDY 3 The move to live operations at the cargo terminal

The new MD was appointed a short time before the second of a series of workshops with the major customers, management and other stakeholders was due to take place. These workshops were designed both to provide peer-review progress and to test out plans with those departments and users who would be affected. Part of the workshop involved 'breakout sessions' in which cross-functional groups of 8–10 people spent 20 minutes discussing some of the most difficult problems identified. Each table then presented their findings to the plenary session.

Good ideas were generated and, just as importantly, some cross-functional discussion preceded it. They were not necessarily the right answers, but added some options that the programme team had not considered. They also had the additional benefit of showing the managers how complex and ambiguous some of the issues were.

People were encouraged to raise risks and concerns in open forum so that these could be discussed and, if possible, a consensus could be reached. There were no 'show-stoppers', but the programme team were dealing with 'known unknowns' and 'unknown unknowns', so the Western consultant wanted to get everyone's minds working on whatever their experience could contribute.

Afterwards, the MD made it clear that he thought the workshop of limited value and that the breakout sessions didn't contribute to the programme. This was a good example of expectations not being met, which could affect the relationship if not addressed quickly.

In talking to the MD and other senior managers, it soon became clear that the next workshop had to be quite different. The workshop must first involve slide presentations, which would be scripted carefully and edited in advance for consistency.

As a result, the consultant worked with each senior manager on their slides to help them to communicate their plans, progress and issues consistently. No major issues were to be raised; instead, these should be handled 'off-line'. The workshop would be a briefing to the stakeholders and other department heads rather than a problem-solving forum. Importantly, it should not contain any surprises and instead be primarily motivational and confidence-building.

Key questions

- The use of workshops in this example did not allow for engaging stakeholders, so the opportunity to discuss issues and uncertainties was lost. However, there were advantages to this approach too. Consider how you could turn this into an opportunity; what other options could have been used in this situation?

- What is the underlying concern and expectation shown by the MD's point of view?

- How could you deal with this concern and establish trust so that other ways of solving problems and dealing with uncertainties could be used?

Figure 12.1   The traditional Chinese change model

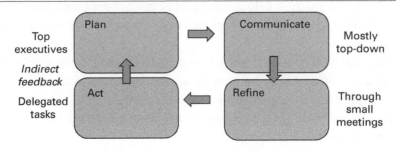

Pilot tests are also used to prove the value of the changes, to build motivation and to develop staff involvement in their implementation. While this may seem very familiar to Western readers, this is typically carried out to confirm that senior managers know best. Results that fall below expectations are looked at first as compliance and then as technical problems rather than revisiting the fundamental design of the process, although the severity of problems in operation may later make this inevitable.

These mechanisms primarily avoid loss of face and are based on the belief that big brother knows best. However, such discussions were not absent; they were simply held in private with the MD.

Figure 12.1 brings together case studies 1, 2 and 3 and shows the impact of the military command and control origins of Chinese management thinking (Martinsons and Hempel, 1998). Here, demarcation between senior officers and junior officers as well as the chain of command is more pronounced than in the West.

CASE STUDY 4   The transition to live operations at the cargo terminal

The transition management in the airport terminal was designed to avoid the risks of a single operational cutover from zero to full capacity. This had been a disastrous approach for the first terminal at the new airport when it opened in 1998, resulting in hundreds of people being employed to physically sort the cargo after computer system problems, and training gaps leading to an unsustainable build-up of unprocessed cargo and missed flights.

Not only had this been the experience in Hong Kong, but similar problems were experienced in London Heathrow Terminal 5 at opening and in Denver, Colorado.

It was therefore decided that three stages would be used to test operational readiness. Each stage required an operational trial (OT). These were carefully designed to simulate the speed and accuracy of teams using the highly automated materials handling system (MHS), training effectiveness, internal coordination and the functions of the Integrated Control Centre (ICC).

The ICC was the nerve-centre operations room using the advanced IT systems to control the flow of information not only within the terminal, but also with its customers and supplier organizations such as the ground handling supplier.

To manage these operational trials, an OT Management Group and an OT Supervisory Group were established. The ICC would monitor the trials, and the OT Working Group would meet each day following the trials, bringing suppliers, managers and the advisory consultant together. Each week the OT Supervisory Group, MD, Head of Commercial Operations and the programme manager would then consider the lessons learnt and adjust the trial targets for the following period.

These trials would simulate the operation and stress-test the systems, but were focused on whether front-line staff and systems could perform as expected. In Stage 2, this proved to be critical, and various factors combined to create a backlog of unprocessed cargo.

An investigation took place into how the trial was handled by the workforce and concluded that, in part, the advanced IT system used by the ICC had been frequently overridden by managers who did not trust it to manage the vertical and horizontal workflows against a tight schedule of delivery and despatch.

Despite being told that the IT system could manage the workflow, even duty managers wanted to take decisions based on what had worked previously in quite a different environment and terminal design. Each one tried to optimize his part but lost sight of the connectedness of the process and the sheer complexity of thousands of pieces of cargo in vertical and horizontal movement against different time priorities.

This reversion to past experience, despite training and documented new procedures, was almost disastrous, a consequence averted only by senior management taking over the direction of operations.

Key questions

- To what extent was the change process designed, and what gaps existed in the planning?
- How were the change lessons applied to refine the testing, and what did this depend on?
- What was this management style aiming to achieve, and to what extent did it achieve this objective?

Western business culture in managing change

Western education has gone through a rapid evolution from the 1950s teaching of project management by the American Association of Cost Engineers formed in 1956, and the start of teaching about the concept of scientific management by Frederick Taylor from 1911 (Taylor, 2014). These treated organizations as machines to be optimized and made more efficient: ways of thinking that were widely adopted in Asia following the Second World War, notably in Japan, through Total Quality Management and later Six Sigma.

However, since the 1980s, managing change has become an area of special study in the West as the social sciences began to apply new models to the way that organizations really function, replacing earlier machine metaphors. This research and theory development has further accelerated both the development of ideas in this field and new models of change as a dynamic and complex chain of events.

A recent example of this thinking is the work by Colin Carnall and Rune Todnem (2014) on managing change in organizations. It has also been complemented by the increasing development and professionalism of organizational change practitioners.

The Western view puts the emphasis on change as an individual experience as well as in groups and teams made up of individuals who affect each other (Figure 12.2). The idea of this being a psychological adjustment as well as a knowledge or performance difference is widely accepted, and from this has emerged the concept of the designed change.

Figure 12.2   A comparative Western change model summarized

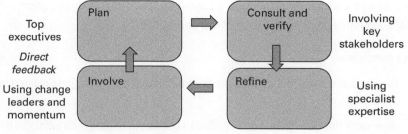

CASE STUDY 5 The international telecoms business transformation

A global telecoms company was embarking on a fundamental business transformation. The senior executive in charge of the change management was the Chief Information Officer (CIO), based in the UK. He determined that the existing IT development portfolio of more than 1,400 projects was unsustainable, so he worked with consultants and his senior leadership team to define 29 major programmes of work. Everything outside these programmes would be terminated, and he obtained the backing of the MD and the leadership team to follow this policy.

He assembled the senior and middle managers of the IT delivery organization and told them that the way the business worked had to change, that there was no alternative and that anyone who did not feel they wanted to be part of it could leave now without shame. Those senior programme leaders who chose to stay were put through a rigorous evaluation, including psychological testing and evaluation.

From this, a new team of 29 programme directors was appointed, who would then lead the change within a rigorous discipline of agile development. Although the direction of the change was highly directive and top down, once these new leaders were selected they were consulted on how the new portfolio would be run. They were given additional training and coaching to support them, and large teams to run.

The empowerment came as something of a shock, since the responsibility that had been distributed among a wider group was now in the hands of a few people. They were also put in competition with each other for the scarce resources, since many of the resource pool were redirected towards fee-earning customer delivery, with around 60 per cent left for the internal transformation, based on new and higher standards of expected performance.

Key questions

- How did this example reflect the process in Figure 12.2?
- What are the strengths and potential weaknesses of this approach?
- Would you expect this approach to be faster or slower than a purely top-down change management approach?
- What next steps would be needed to make the change sustainable in this example?

Conclusion

Perhaps the first important point to make is that the business environment around the world is undergoing an unprecedented period of change as a result of globalization, information technology, international air travel and the global market for higher education. As a result, it seems that differences are increasingly submerged, as people work in multicultural teams and supply chains.

However, the different models used in China and the West affect every aspect of how planning, leading and implementing change is applied in China and the West, even at a time when managing change appears to be converging and increasingly based on Western ideas.

The new challenge for change designers and change leaders is to increase the speed and reduce the difficulty of making change happen, in such a way that it can be understood and accepted by people of different cultures spanning thousands of miles, time-zones and perspectives.

The key will be to translate the change effectively into a narrative that is understood in terms of the part each person and group must play, united by a vision that makes the emotional connection real in every culture involved. It won't be easy, but we can start by understanding the importance of culture in how we design and deliver change.

Key questions

- How would you test the potential cultural barriers to change before designing a change programme in China or the West?

- What factors are essential in leading change where people of mixed cultures are involved?

- What should you, as a change leader, consider about your own cultural influences before embarking on a business change?

References

Ackerman, D, Hu, J and Wei, L (2009) Confucius, cars and big government: impact of government involvement in business on consumer perceptions under Confucianism. *Journal of Business Ethics*, 88 (Suppl 3), p 473

Anthony, M (2007) [Accessed 2 May 2016] The New China: big brother brave new world or harmonious society? [Online] www.sl.hariomtech.com/mindfutures

Carnall, C and Todnem, R (2014) *Managing Change in Organizations*, 6th edn, Pearson Higher Education, Harlow

Harari, YN (2015) *Sapiens: A brief history of humankind*, Harper, New York

Huntington, SP (1993) The clash of civilisations. *Foreign Affairs Journal*, **73** (3), p 28

Leung, K (2015) Beliefs in Chinese societies, in *Oxford Handbook of Chinese Psychology*, ed MH Bond, Oxford University Press, Oxford

Martinsons, MG and Hempel, PS, (1998) Chinese business process re-engineering. *International Journal of Information Management*, **18** (6), pp 393–407

Ralston, DA, Gustafson DJ and Cheung, FM (1993) Differences in managerial values: a study of U.S., Hong Kong and PRC managers. *Journal of International Business Studies*, **24** (2), pp 249–75

Taylor, F (1914) *The Principles of Scientific Management: The early sociology of management and organizations*, Harper & Brothers, New York

Suggested further reading

Lewis, RD (2005) *When Cultures Collide: Leading across cultures*, Nicholas Brealey International, London

Hon-Fun Poon, I (2010) *Human Resources Management Changes in China: A case study of Banking Industry*, Lambert Academic Publishing, Saarbrücken, Germany

Denison, D *et al* (2012) *Leading Culture Change in Global Organizations: Aligning culture and strategy*, Jossey-Bass, San Francisco

Boncori, I (2013) *Expatriates in China: Experiences, opportunities and challenges*, Palgrave MacMillan, Basingstoke

Wolff, C (2008) *Project Management in China: Soft skills as success factors*, Diplomatica Verlag GmbH, Hamburg, Germany

Developing change capacity and capability in organizations

ROBERT COLE AND SARAH COLEMAN

Introduction

Change initiatives are increasingly being used to help increase and embed an organization's competitive position and respond to emerging trends in the market. Organizations typically struggle to design the 'right change' and to deliver it correctly. One of the crucial questions organizations ought to be asking themselves is whether they have the ability to undertake change: do they have the skills, budget, capital equipment, time and other necessary resources to do this over and above what they are doing as business-as-usual? This question helps boards, leadership teams and managers assess where they may have capacity or capability gaps, and where the areas of difficulty may lie in making organizational change happen. Further, do they have the ability to change the business while running the business at the same time with little or no detriment to performance? These are all questions and issues for the strategic level of the organization, and are part of what is known as 'organizational change management'; that is, establishing the right environment, culture and process for successful change. Reports suggest that approximately 70 per cent of change is not successful (Nohria and Beer, 2000), and although this figure continues to be challenged, we can infer that organizations have room for improvement.

Two basic concepts for shaping, scoping, designing, implementing and embedding organizational change are having a sufficient volume of resources to do change (change capacity), and ensuring that those resources have the right skills and are working efficiently (change capability). Organizations often tell us they face 'too much' change. This is typically a combination of the stream of change initiatives agreed at senior level and the result of insufficient capacity and/or capability. Organizations have finite resources and many of the important decisions within organizations involve the allocation of resources against priority, whether these resources are personnel, expertise, budget, capital equipment or technology. Change is certainly no exception, and our experience is that change initiatives are hugely demanding on organizations in terms of cost, time and resources.

In this chapter we will look at the typical issues around change capacity and capability that organizations face when they want to shape, scope, design, deliver and embed successful change, and we will focus on personnel, rather than any other type of resource. We'll use our own experiences and case studies to describe how organizations typically resource change; we'll also offer suggestions as to how organizations can improve both capacity and capability for change.

Capacity for change

The capacity of an organization to undertake successful change is essentially the resources the organization can put towards change that is in excess of the resources needed to do business as usual. Human resources are quite elastic in the way they can be counted and contribute. This has advantages in that organizations often ask for, and get, more effort for specific actions such as change. The disadvantage is that it is very hard to quantify how much resource is available for change at any given time.

Resource capacity

Kotter (2012) proposed thinking of an organization as two systems: (1) an operational system, which runs the organization's business as usual, and (2) a strategy system, which is responsible for changing the operational system.

Different structures and processes are needed for each system, but people move between the systems as required. This separation makes it easier to identify change resources, or requirements for resources, and to organize them. The strategy system uses a network organization to make it flexible and to encourage interaction between people regardless of function, grade, or experience, which govern relationships in the operational system. This systems approach leads to consideration of the whole cycle of change and managing multiple cycles. The change system encourages holistic system thinking about how to do change effectively and efficiently, just as the operational system is optimized to run business as usual.

CASE STUDY

Senior management in a UK government Department were spending a significant amount on organizing change projects, trying to improve efficiency through cost savings and the introduction of new technology. External consultants were hired to run a programme management office, best practice methods were adopted and spend on software to track projects and programmes exceeded £1 million.

Each executive-level manager had their own pet change programme, often ranging over parts of the Department where they had no control. An inevitable catalogue of delays, failures and poor implementation brought the situation to a point where the business was struggling badly. As a result, an internal manager was identified who had the capability to take charge of change across the programmes.

This new change manager was most concerned about the impact of all the changes on the front-line staff, where he had spent much of his career. He organized a workshop for all the project and programme managers to identify the full range of resources they needed from the workforce to implement their changes: full-time staff seconded to projects, part-time support, effort for testing and user acceptance, and staff development. All ideas, requirements and issues were documented using Post-It notes posted onto wall charts around the room. Everyone then went round and tallied up all the required resources for the next 15 months. The canny change manager held this workshop in the corporate board room and ensured that the wall charts were left up. When the next executive board meeting was held, the senior managers asked about the wall charts, providing the change manager with the perfect opportunity to explain the demand on front-line staff for the range of changes the executives had put in motion, and demonstrating that capacity would not allow the Department to do the changes as planned and meet their operational targets at the same time.

The Department started to develop a portfolio approach to monitor and control the change initiatives across the business. The immediate resource problem was helped by an enforced long delay in one of the bigger change programmes, which was subsequently cancelled after much debate about wasted investment.

Many organizations try to deliver change from projects by asking line managers to deliver the required changes alongside running day-to-day operations, but there are inherent problems in this. The ability of busy operational teams to implement and absorb change is limited. As we are often told by line managers, the biggest challenges are their lack of time, which leads to lack of focus, and their uncertainty about their priorities ('should I concentrate on the business operationally, or on the change?'), where the answer is often an ambiguous keeping everything in balance. Under these circumstances, it is perhaps understandable that line managers choose their own priorities, the result often being a piecemeal implementation across the organization with some parts being successful and some parts not changing at all.

By using separate resources whose priority is doing the change (the strategy system), the line managers (the operational system) can prioritize business as usual. Obviously the two systems must work together, but their different priorities are clear.

Too much change (or not enough capacity) is an increasing phenomenon among organizations worldwide. Prosci (2014) reported that 77 per cent of respondents were near, at or past their saturation point for change compared with 73 per cent in 2011 (see Figure 13.1). Typical symptoms reported included:

- disengagement and apathy among staff for change;
- anxiety, stress, burnout and fatigue among staff;

Figure 13.1   Change capacity in organizations

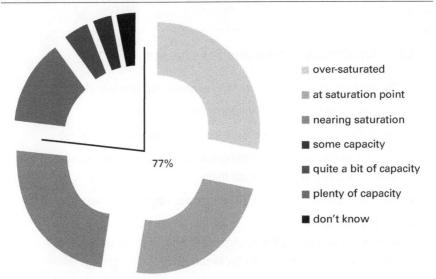

over-saturated

at saturation point

nearing saturation

some capacity

quite a bit of capacity

plenty of capacity

don't know

77%

SOURCE Graph derived from data found in Prosci (2014)

- automatic resistance to any type of change;
- lack of focus on operations;
- attrition and higher staff turnover along with low morale throughout the organization.

Introducing additional capacity by buying in resource, either by recruiting for full-time roles or recruiting contract/interim personnel to take these roles, has the benefit that these resources will be focused on the change without being distracted by operational issues; however, this solution also results in a hit to the bottom line, at least in the short term. Some organizations, which have been restructuring over the past several years, have chosen to reskill and redeploy staff who otherwise faced redundancy, some into change roles.

Process and monitoring capacity

Increasingly, organizations are insisting on well-thought-out and realistic business cases for change. Financial and other resources are finite and there is inevitably internal competition for these, so that organizations have to decide how they allocate them, impacting which change initiatives go forward and when. Not only do business cases address the crucial questions for change (see Box 13.1), helping organizations understand the implications of what they are asking for, but they also provide the basis for prioritizing change initiatives so helping capacity planning.

From our experience, many organizations undertake large numbers of change initiatives in one guise or another. Too often these initiatives trip

---

Box 13.1: Crucial questions for change

- The strategic question: What's the rationale and relevance?
- The stakeholder question: What are the expectations?
- The activities and processes question: What will we need to do?
- The capabilities and capacity question: Do we have the necessary resources, skills and bandwidth to do this?
- The impacts question: What do we want to happen as a result?
- The learning question: How can we learn from this and how will we share it throughout the enterprise to help improve what we do? (Adapted from Coleman and MacNicol, 2015)

each other up by duplicating work and benefits, or even working at odds with each other. This is especially noticeable when the organization is spread over different locations, whether within a single region or across geographies. How can organizations provide the capacity necessary to do essential change? Part of the answer lies in the phrase 'essential change'. Most organizations suffering from change fatigue appear to be doing large numbers of change initiatives, some of which may not be essential.

By 'successful' change we mean two things:

- Organizational change success: where the organization achieves its anticipated value and goals by way of the change.

- Change management success: where the change is well managed. This would include *efficiency*, ie completing the required scope within time and budget. At the strategic level, questions should be around capability and impact.

Portfolio management

The Project Management Institute (PMI, 2015) reports that 'the two most commonly acknowledged weaknesses in the management of strategic projects are project termination (30 percent) and resourcing (24 percent)'. On average, survey respondents reported that one-fifth of current projects should be terminated and that nearly one-half aren't resourced properly, with 29 per cent receiving too few resources and 19 per cent too many.

One mechanism to manage change capacity and the range of change initiatives in an organization is the use of portfolio management. At the very least, the portfolio needs to cover all strategic change initiatives; including operational continuous improvement will ensure a balance between the two and avoid conflicts in resource allocation and benefits realization. The purpose of managing a portfolio of change is in providing a comprehensive view across the organization, so making the best use of the available capacity; it is also to ensure that the performance of the change initiatives and the benefits associated with them are monitored.

Change portfolio management has a few basic concepts:

- It ensures that all change is aligned to the strategy of the organization.

- It allocates appropriate and timely resources to change initiatives and flags resource gaps.

- It allows the organization to measure and manage its change capacity and capability.

Success with a change portfolio starts with a clearly defined strategy and strategic objectives, which are themselves prioritized. Business cases for change initiatives are developed, reflecting the organization's own hurdle rate, risk profile and priority, before going through any ratification process to be accepted. It is also at this point that trade-offs between change initiatives happen, particularly in respect of their resources and timing. We've sat in leadership team meetings where prospective change initiatives have been introduced, their business cases agreed and still they are not given the go-ahead; after all, any organization has a finite amount of capacity and capability to deliver change, and that includes the option of buying in resource. But it's not just the financial impact that organizations are focused on: they are looking at all aspects of value perceived by customers, employees, suppliers and others. This wider use of a 'balanced scorecard' approach (Kaplan and Norton, 1993) has encouraged more varied thinking about impact on customers, competitive advantage, the organization's own employees, process, supply chain and other areas.

CASE STUDY

The UK arm of a European holding company had decided to change the focus of its sales strategy from finding new customers to generating more sales from existing customers, since they had identified that the market was saturated. Owing to a recent spate of mergers, the board had two sales directors. One sales director was very enthusiastic and provided a lot of drive to his next-level managers to implement the change; these in turn worked on their areas but with differing degrees of enthusiasm (often depending on which side of recent mergers they were from). The result was that most of this part of the organization did implement the changes, but the speed of change varied enormously. Eventually most of the benefits were seen.

The second sales director was not enthusiastic and did not support his next-level managers with time or encouragement. The changes in this area of sales just did not reach the front line and few benefits were achieved – although everyone was trained up.

The other board directors saw this change as a 'sales thing' and nothing to do with them. A problem quickly arose when the sales team succeeded in getting bigger orders from their existing customers. This meant that these customers would owe the business more money (delivery of goods in 24 hours, payment in 30 days). The credit control department in Finance was not aware of the change in sales strategy, so they refused extra credit to the customers, which severely frustrated the sales staff. The change had been conceived and kept within a silo (sales). Similar problems happened with logistics. A proper systems design of such a strategic change would have identified the linkage with credit control and developed mechanisms to support the extra sales. After a review by the incoming chief executive, the organization set up a programme management office to form the core of a systems approach to change across the organization.

Change roles

Organizational change requires a variety of roles and capabilities, from governance to assessing business readiness, from designing total operating models to delivering them. The role of change manager has become more prominent in the past several years, with a variety of responsibilities assigned to them. Some organizations use the change manager role as a project or programme manager, others use them as a behavioural change agent.

Change architect, change manager, change sponsor, change champion, change readiness specialist, change disrupter, change maker, change adviser: we increasingly see a variety of titles and roles in organizations, usually each with a different interpretation of responsibilities. There is no industry standard for these roles, just as there is no single recognized or professional body providing quality control or consistency around change management standards, qualifications and resources. In the absence of clearly defined standards, it can be difficult for professionals and organizations to identify the knowledge, skills and competencies required to successfully design, deliver and embed effective change. However, it is not in anyone's interest to allow individuals who are unprepared or who lack the necessary skills to take roles in designing, coordinating or directing change.

Regardless of what titles organizations choose to give their change roles, they highlight that organizations recognize a rebalancing between the doing or delivering of change and creating the environment, opportunities and space for change; also the rebalancing of hard technical skills with those softer, relationship-based skills of good relationship building, communication, influencing and leadership for change.

Of course, there are less visible but just as relevant roles which support organizational change. Communications experts, human resource and organizational design professionals, technology specialists, business analysts, customer experience personnel and risk managers are all part of the blend.

CASE STUDY

A global engineering organization needed help in clarifying the sponsorship role for major expenditure and transformation projects within the business, and in developing and supporting existing and potential senior-level sponsors within the business to meet these responsibilities.

The organization had already given considerable thought, investment and effort to the professionalism of their project, programme and change communities. It delivers projects, programmes and change which are diverse, complex, multi-geographic, multicultural, high profile and high risk across major capital expenditure, new product introduction and business transformation initiatives.

As a natural progression and maturity the organization wanted to clarify what sponsorship meant for them, to define and implement a robust and appropriate sponsorship process at senior level as part of change and project governance, and to support this by the training and development of existing and potential senior-level sponsors. They recognized that the sponsor role can have a tremendous impact on success. However, typically the sponsor role is very unclear in many organizations: sometimes the sponsor is very hands off due to lack of interest, other priorities or time constraints; sometimes they are too involved and try to act as a sort of 'super manager', which generates its own conflict and problems. Moreover, trying to find a single person to be the 'unblocker' (who owns the business case, can be the business conscience and make things happen for the change) is a tall order.

Our solution was to hold facilitated workshops with senior stakeholders in order to clarify the issues and views, and then to design, develop and deliver workshops to vice-presidents from the UK, Europe and South America to develop and support existing and potential senior-level sponsors within the business. These vice-presidents were flown into the UK for development workshops where particular capabilities, behaviours and responsibilities for sponsors were identified. Subsequently, a specific sponsor role definition and process was adopted as part of the standard governance process for projects, programmes and change.

The time and effort taken by staff to implement a change can vary widely across an organization and can be surprising. The example below demonstrates a situation where additional change resources were needed to help a particular group of staff through a seemingly simple IT change.

CASE STUDY

A corporate IT department planned to implement a common desktop on all personal computers across the organization. It could no longer support the different versions of operating system and applications that had accumulated over years of mergers and acquisitions. To most people the change involved a slightly different layout on their computer and hence required a little familiarization time. To some older administrative staff who had acquired skills in earlier versions of the software through learning little scripts, this was a major threat to their efficiency and effectiveness. Some felt so threatened that they considered suing the company for constructive dismissal.

The department recognized that the initiative was about to fail spectacularly. Rapidly, change champions were identified and sent on additional software training supplemented by soft change skills. These champions provided expert support to their colleagues and were able to break through the resistance, providing reassurance. This extra effort was not foreseen by the IT department, who had not originally involved stakeholders in their planning.

Change capability

The other side of the equation is capability, ensuring that change capacity has the relevant ability to do what they need to do successfully.

Levels of change capability

The way management skills are used in organizations can vary enormously, leading to different levels of capability for change. A capability model is a key tool in assessing and developing the capability of an organization to do change: it provides a basis for understanding what the organization is doing well and what needs improvement. Moreover, it provides a route map for the improvement of capability across the organization.

Figure 13.2   Change capability model

Use of change management is sometimes proactive, but isolated and idiosyncratic. Change is occasionaly successful.
Managing change occurs in isolated pockets, ignored at organisation level.

There may be an ad-hoc business case for investment.

Use of change management is always proactive and performance is measured. Change is nearly always successful.
Realistic business case is used to justify investment, control delivery and test for success.

Managed

Reflective

Use of change management is tailored and fully integrated as learning is embedded.
Successful change is the expectation.
Change management is part of the knowledge management and improvement culture of the organisation.

Heroic   **Structured**

Use of change management is mostly proactive and uses organisation wide processes.
Change is often successful in terms of outcomes.
Change management is part of the management language, implementation quality varies.
Most change has a business case, used to justify investment, often unrealistic. Not used to test success.

Chaotic

Use of change management is reactive to implementation failure.
Change is rarely successful. Managing change is not part of the language or culture.
There is no business case.

SOURCE Reproduced with kind permission of the Centre for Change Management

A capability model typically has two dimensions: a set of capability levels and specific areas of competence. There are usually five capability levels, from level 1 (virtually no capability) to level 5 (best capability). The Change Capability Model (see Figure 13.2) developed by the Centre for Change Management (www.c4cm.co.uk) uses four areas of change competence, and each capability level attempts to capture the main change behaviour seen at that level.

The four areas of competence are:

● Leadership and governance: the continuing and consistent support at senior level, senior management taking on new behaviours as exemplars, setting role accountability, are the most cited critical success factors in change, and their lack is a common factor in change failure. In our experience, leadership and governance of change are difficult areas to improve, because it revolves around senior managers and their perception of their roles.

● Processes and roles: the use of formal project, programme, portfolio and change methods within the organization. This can range from the formalization of job titles, job families, roles, responsibilities and accountability to the adoption of industry-standard methodologies or the development of in-house methodologies.

- Knowledge and skills: what each role is expected to know (or have experience in) and what skills they need in order to deliver their responsibilities.
- Managing change: the organization's own holistic view of how change will be managed. Typically, this includes input from clients, employees, suppliers; the range of change methods, tools and techniques adopted by the organization; quality and innovation in change initiatives; how the end-to-end change process will be driven.

Assessing change capability

A change capability model is a tool to start a conversation: it prompts discussion about what 'good' change capability might look like. It helps an organization understand where they are with their change capability, identify where they would like to be and plan how to get there. So the model needs to be turned into an assessment tool. The basis of an assessment is always the observable behaviour of people within the organization. Each cell of the matrix specifies the set of competencies expected. An organization will only be said to be working at a particular level if all the areas are measured at or above that level, and it is quite usual for an organization to be higher in one particular area than in others. This model supports the organization in assessing and planning for capability by focusing on what it needs to improve, and at the same time ensuring it maintains its capability in areas where it is already strong.

Figure 13.3 shows how the levels and competences form a matrix, each cell describing the behaviour expected.

Figure 13.3 Change capability matrix

	Areas of change competence			
	Leadership & Governance	Processes And Roles	Knowledge and Skills	Managing Change
5. Reflective				
4. Managed				
3. Structured				
2. Heroic				
1. Chaos				

levels

SOURCE Reproduced with kind permission of the Centre for Change Management

CASE STUDY

A global telecoms business benchmarked its current change delivery competencies to understand its capability and plan for further development. It used four levels (entry, core, expert and leader) and a range of capabilities (stakeholder engagement, team leadership, scope and quality management, accelerating delivery, planning and tracking, risk and issue management). Each level and capability was defined to prevent confusion, and each individual within the organization who had been identified as playing a role related to delivering change was required to complete the capability questionnaire. Each individual initially completed the capability profile from their own viewpoint, in preparation for discussions with their resource manager and feedback from stakeholders who had been involved with their change initiatives. This provided the organization with a snapshot of where their strengths lay, and allowed them to plan what would need to happen next in terms of capability development to upskill their personnel.

Both change capacity and capability are fundamentally about people. The following case study about one award-winning initiative will illustrate this very effectively.

CASE STUDY

Cheshire West and Chester Council (CWCC) had established a change team as a corporate function, which represents the strategy system from Kotter's model. This function was resourced with full-time business analysts and project managers who were responsible for designing and implementing system changes across all council departments. Changes could be proposed by senior managers, department-level managers or the change team itself. As a separate corporate function, the change team soon obtained a reputation of 'doing change to' the staff, rather than with the staff.

To address this disconnect, the council proposed establishing change champions to interface between front-line staff, the management hierarchy and the change team to help promote and facilitate change. These champions would be part-time but with a guaranteed time allowance for their role. We worked with CWCC to establish the initial cohort of 40 change champions.

The council had realized that its change resources were missing key skills to mediate between the strategy system and the operational system, and ensured that additional resources were in place to cover this gap. The 'additional resources' comprised some 40 staff, all volunteers from across the council and management layers.

Simply adding people is never enough: the additional resources needed particular skills to do their work efficiently and effectively. The initiative to create the cohort focused on providing the change champions with the confidence to operate across the management hierarchy of both the operations system and the strategic system to facilitate change. We used 'confidence to be a change champion' as the main measure for progress and success.

The development programme for change champions included:

- Monthly workshops for the whole cohort of 40 staff to develop a community of practice, and to share problems, solutions and successes. These workshops also explored and defined the roles and responsibilities for the new concept of change champions. (Linking to the Processes and Roles capability area)

- Monthly action learning sets to focus on supportive problem solving and encouraging active interventions. (Linking to all the capability areas, but especially Managing Change)

- A training day to provide knowledge and skills early in the development programme. (Linking to the Knowledge and Skills capability area)

- A vocational qualification to demonstrate the application of knowledge and skills in the workplace. Success in the qualification was also used as a measure of the competence of the change champions. (Linking to the Knowledge and Skills capability area)

- Clear support from the council chief executive who addressed the launch workshop and backed up the change champions when they needed to break through barriers. (Linking to the Leadership and Governance capability area)

The development programme was influenced in particular by the concept of 70 : 20 : 10 (Lombardo and Eichinger, 1996; 70 : 20 : 10 Forum, 2015), where these proportions relate to how much learning as adults we derive from three contexts:

- 70 per cent through informal, on the job, experience based, stretch projects, and working on tasks and problems;

- 20 per cent through being coached, mentored and receiving direct feedback;

- 10 per cent through formal learning interventions, reading and structured courses.

Training played an important part in developing knowledge and skills, but small compared to the time taken in developing the roles, responsibilities and managing change capabilities of the cohort. By the end of the programme the change champions were supporting and learning from each other. The result was a functioning increase in the change capacity of the council, with a competence and confidence to improve the way the council managed change. The council went on to use the same programme to develop a further cohort of change champions.

Developing capability

There are many approaches to improving knowledge and skills. More and more, individuals are being given the responsibility of self-learning and developing their own careers, with support from the organization. The typical call is for formal training, but increasingly organizations are using a blend of approaches to suit a mix of learning styles (Kolb *et al*, 2001; Honey and Mumford, 1982), also acknowledging that organizations are less inclined to allow staff time away from work to complete three-day, five-day or longer training courses. Bite-sized learning (short development opportunities such as webinars or breakfast/lunch/evening events) are becoming more common. A carefully planned development programme delivered over a number of months – using a blend of face-to-face sessions, self-study, communities of practice, opportunities for practice, knowledge-sharing forums, and coaching and mentoring – is a robust way to increase both knowledge and skills, and to embed these. All this is a long way from a typical short, sharp, formal training course, which is easily forgotten once back in the onslaught of the day job.

Figure 13.4 demonstrates the broad spectrum of learning and development opportunities available for developing personal capability, from the formal learning to the informal. All fall within the 70:20:10 spectrum, each having their particular strength and relevance.

Capacity and capability can be developed in-house, bought into the organization as interim or contract personnel or recruited into the organization on a full-time employment basis. Research by Changefirst (2009) reported that 84 per cent of responding organizations believed that internal teams were the best way to implement change.

Figure 13.4 Spectrum of learning and development opportunities for developing personal capability

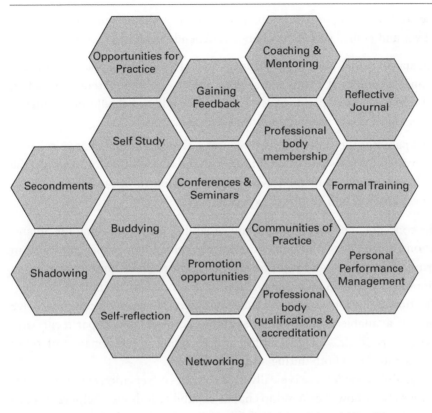

SOURCE Coleman and MacNicol (2015). Reproduced with kind permission of the authors

Where the organization has hired external personnel to help support their particular change initiative, the commitment of these individuals to sharing their knowledge and experience of previous change initiatives in other organizations and other industry sectors, and so helping develop in-house capability, would mark them out as being particularly valuable. No organization likes to think that the experience and knowledge gained by contract or interim personnel from the organization's own change initiative would simply walk out the door once the contract has expired. Organizations that ensure hired-in contract and interim change professionals share their own experiences and knowledge of change gained with other sectors and organizations enhance their competitive advantage in two ways: they develop their own capability for deeper learning and they develop good practice within their change community.

Conclusion

The ability of an organization to consistently shape and scope, design, deliver and embed successful change is dependent on two factors:

- Capacity: the ability to identify and deploy appropriate resources. Busy operational teams are seldom able to do this without impacting business-as-usual performance, so recruiting additional full-time or interim personnel is one way organizations overcome this.

- Capability: the skill of those resources. Organizational change requires a variety of roles and capabilities, from the very visible (for example, the change manager) to the less visible (communications, technology, business analysts and customer experience).

The concepts of change capacity and capability are far-reaching for organizations, since change initiatives are hugely demanding on organizations in terms of cost, time and resources. Organizations have finite resources, so adopting a portfolio management approach is one way to support the identification and prioritization of change initiatives; to ensure a comprehensive view of available capacity and capability across teams, departments and divisions regardless of geography; and to monitor performance of those change initiatives both during and after delivery.

Capability models are typically used to start conversations within organizations about how they develop change capability in-house, helping them to become self-sufficient. The most visible of change roles is the change manager. Increasingly, individuals are expected to take responsibility for developing their own abilities and careers, with support from the organization.

Key questions

Here are some questions to help focus you and your organization to develop change capability and capacity:

- How are change initiatives shaped, scoped and designed within the organization?

- How are change initiatives approved and prioritized? Are business cases developed purely in terms of financial return, or does a wider and more balanced perspective apply?

- How does your organization work with capacity for change? Has it adopted a portfolio management or other approach?

- Thinking about the change competency matrix, at which level would you position your organization? Which areas of competence does your organization favour?

- As an individual involved with organizational change, what are your own development needs and how will you achieve them?

- As an HR or OD professional working within the organization:

  - What change capacity and capability do you need for the future?

  - How can you best support your people to develop their change capabilities?

References

70:20:10 Forum (2015) *70:20:10 Framework Explained*, 2nd edn, FastPencil, Inc, Campbell, CA

Changefirst (2009) [Accessed 7 November 2016] Making change your business [Online] http://www.changefirst.com/uploads/documents/Making_change_your_business.pdf

Coleman, S and MacNicol, D (2015) *Project Leadership*, Gower, Farnham

Honey, P and Mumford, A (1982) *Manual of Learning Styles*, P Honey, London

Kaplan, RS and Norton, D (1993) Putting the balanced scorecard to work. *Harvard Business Review*, **71** (5), pp 134–47

Kolb, DA, Boyatzis, RE and Mainemelis, C (2001) Experiential learning theory: previous research in new direction, in *Perspectives on Learning, Thinking and Cognitive Styles*, ed Robert J Sternberg and L Zhang, pp 193–210, Lawrence Erlbaum, Mahwah, NJ

Kotter, J (2012) Accelerate! *Harvard Business Review*, **90** (11), pp 45–58

Lombardo, MM and Eichinger, RW (1996) *Career Architect Planner*, Lominger, Minneapolis, MN

Nohria, N and Beer, M (2000) Cracking the code of change. *Harvard Business Review*, **78** (3), pp 133–41

PMI (2015) *Implementing the Project Portfolio: A vital C-suite focus*, Thought Leadership Series, Project Management Institute, Philadelphia

Prosci (2014) *Best Practices in Change Management – 2014 Edition*, Prosci Inc, Fort Collins, CO

Risk and organizational change

14

RUTH MURRAY-WEBSTER

Introduction

In this chapter I will argue that risk and change are closely connected: a reciprocal relationship that it is important to manage as a whole rather than as two distinct parts.

At the heart of this is the fact that change – a disruption of the status quo – triggers uncertainty about the future in the hearts and minds of the people in the situation. When I talk about risk in the context of change, I am thinking about those uncertainties perceived by stakeholders that would matter to the change effort if they occurred. Some risks are negative threats – they would make things worse than planned if they happened. Some risks are positive opportunities and things would be better if they could be seized. Attempts to manage change are likely to be compromised if we do not understand the myriad of threats and opportunities perceived by stakeholders. This is the part of the risk – change relationship that requires us to work with perceptions of risk in order to shape, design, deliver and embed change so that intended benefits are achieved.

The reciprocal aspect of the risk – change relationship arises because, in most organizational groupings, the ability to collectively identify, analyse and manage risk is a practical challenge. Changes in practice are required. When a change is something that an individual has decided to embrace, implicit in the decision is a trade-off of risk and reward. The decision may be risky but the person has probably thought about it, made some mental contingencies and is prepared for the consequences that go with the choice.

At an organizational level, there are many people who are affected by change who are not the people who decided that the change was necessary in the first place. These people may not have made the same choice themselves, nor do they really understand the potential consequences, so it's difficult to be mentally prepared for what might happen next. In the absence of a collective approach to understanding and managing risk, the people who are integral to delivering and embedding organizational change may not have a voice about the risks they perceive. This reduces the chance of the change being successful. Similarly, the investors in change – shareholders, donors, or other sources of funding – have no way of knowing whether the estimates of how much the change will cost are optimistic, pessimistic or realistic. In many organizations, therefore, the way that risk is considered and managed is itself a thing that requires change.

The remainder of the chapter explores common challenges of understanding and managing risk during organizational change. Examples and practical tips that can be applied in your organization are offered. This chapter is written for the change management professional. Where a more technical knowledge of risk management might be of use, references are made to other sources of information.

Change is risky

By definition, change requires us to disrupt what is usual, and in doing so start to deal with situations that are unusual, and therefore uncertain. This is the case whether the change is being introduced using a formal project-based method, or not. In some organizations, a project-based methodology for managing change is well established and there are well-defined practices in place to formally consider risk through the project lifecycle. In other cases, the organization is not 'project-like' and transformation efforts need to establish skills for risk-based planning and reporting as part of the change. In both cases, it is vital to consider multiple views in deciding how to take account of risk as the work proceeds. This chapter is 'method-agnostic'; that is, it does not promote any particular change or project method or language. Regardless of the steps in your organization's change/project-based process, it is important to think about the relationship between change and risk when *making investment decisions* – shaping/scoping/designing change, when *protecting previous investment decisions* – delivering new processes, systems and ways of working, and when embedding and sustaining new practices and behaviours to realize the intended benefits.

The focus of this chapter is on risk and change, rather than risk in projects *per se*. Many projects are focused on delivering outputs that the organization can then use to deliver benefit/value, but they do not concern themselves with broader change managed through an overarching programme, or strategic portfolio. I will attempt to avoid getting into a terminology debate between projects, programmes and portfolios but instead focus on those planned change endeavours that start with a need to make a step-change in organizational capability and end when the people in the organization are using the new capability to create value.

This next section focuses on the challenges that arise when *making investment decisions* if risk is ignored or downplayed. Causes of this problem are outlined and practical tips offered for the change professional. The same format is followed in the third section where the common problem of over-reliance on risk registers is explored in relation to *protecting previous investments decisions* during delivery of new capabilities and benefit. Together, the most common problems when applying risk management during organizational change are explored and summarized at the end of the chapter.

Making investment decisions

I have encountered many situations when early work to approve investment in a change has been completed. Expectations have been set in the minds of senior leaders about what change will be delivered, when and for what cost, yet no one has explicitly considered risk at all.

This situation is bad, but worse still is when the business case for the change has been presented as if risk has been considered, for example to present a notional 'worst', 'expected' and 'best' case net present value (NPV) or internal rate of return (IRR) but where the thinking and analysis behind the estimates are partial and therefore misleading.

CASE STUDY

In a mid-market manufacturing company, a complex set of more than 100 information systems had been developed over time. The lack of past investment to provide an integrated solution had become a business issue. Senior members of the management team decided that a significant investment in an enterprise resource planning (ERP) solution was warranted to replace 100+ disconnected legacy systems with one integrated business platform. The leaders tasked with the early lifecycle work to scope the change and select software and a system integrator led a competent process with sound underpinning choices. The business case was presented to decision makers at its first decision-gate, providing a 'worst-case', 'expected' and 'best-case' range of options based on a range of logical assumptions but no explicit risk analysis.

Six months later, after the next phase of high-level design had been completed, the worst-case cost had increased by 40 per cent and the IRR decreased by 4 per cent. Although the investment was still sound with the revised estimates, such a large shift in a short time shook the confidence levels of those investing in the change and cast doubt on the competence of the team to deliver the ambitious programme of business change.

This sort of deviation from early estimates happens often in all sorts of organization. Why is this?

Causes and effects

There are two, very real, psychological phenomena at play when people are taking the first steps to shape, scope and design change initiatives and present information to support decision making. These can be described as 'delusional optimism' (Flyvbjerg *et al*, 2013; Lovallo and Kahneman, 2003) and 'groupthink' (Janis, 1971).

Delusional optimism

If you are leading a change, either as a senior executive, or as a manager or consultant employed as a change expert – what is your main objective in early lifecycle? It is human nature to want to 'sell' the change – to convince investors and other decision makers that they should back the proposal and align behind the vision and intended benefits. Not only is this human nature, but there are many positive benefits of such a mindset. Everyone knows that change brings uncertainty, so the last thing that the organization needs is doubt in the minds of the people who need to lead the change. It's really important to have a strong vision of what is possible and to align people with that vision. It is vital to have 'belief' that challenging targets can be achieved. We know that doubt and hesitation have a direct impact on motivation and success.

But how many change initiatives have you led or observed where the enthusiasm to proceed and the positive belief that things can be achieved have 'skewed' judgements? Researchers into delusional optimism, or optimism bias, have used the term 'strategic misrepresentation' to describe how change leaders often behave to present the change in a mainly positive light. At one level this might be interpreted as some form of deliberate deception or manipulation of 'truth', but the reality is that when it comes to predicting future outcomes from change, there is no truth – only estimates – and we naturally deceive ourselves in our desire to push forward. Some organizations, knowing this, make an adjustment to all estimates to 'correct' for optimism bias. This is a crude macro solution, but perhaps better than doing nothing.

Groupthink

The perfectly natural and normal tendency to adopt a 'can do' attitude and associated optimism can be compounded by a group effect known as *groupthink*.

How many times have you observed, or been part of, a group that is faced with a decision to make, and the group comes to a decision without exploring differing perspectives? Sometimes this is inevitable, because the leader of the group speaks first and others follow without challenge. Sometimes this is because there is a time limit for the discussion and individuals feel under pressure to 'go with the flow' and not take the time to ask the questions they have. This can be exacerbated in early lifecycle change when the vision and ideas are shared between a relatively small number of organizational members for reasons of confidentiality, or when a wider group of (usually) more junior team members can see that estimates may be optimistic but do not feel empowered to say so.

Groupthink, a highly researched psychological effect, happens when the subconscious desire for social cohesion trumps the desire to explore differing perceptions and options and come to the optimal answer in the situation.

The combination of the completely normal tendencies for people and groups to fall foul of optimism bias and groupthink often results in wildly optimistic estimates of what can be achieved, by when and for how much being passed off as realistic. Expectations are set, funds are invested on the basis of estimates and the change is off to a start that seems full of promise, but is really a delusion. What can be done about this?

Practical tips

In my experience, the solutions to the challenges raised need to address the human causes of the problem. It would be easy to impose a formal, 'textbook' risk management process on early lifecycle change, and in an organization where the culture for risk-based decision making is mature, this will be an expected and useful thing to do. In such situations, decision makers would expect to see estimates of 'best', 'expected' and 'worst' outcomes (expressed as NPV or IRR or comparing cash investments with a range of financial and non-financial benefit measures) backed up by probabilistic analysis of scenarios to model the combined effect of uncertainty and risk on objectives. You can read further on these ideas with Pullan and Murray-Webster (2011) and Hillson and Simon (2012).

My practical experience is that few organizations have mature enough risk cultures to carry out leading-edge risk management during early lifecycle change, so in these situations what practical steps can be taken? There are two things that I always try to practise, which we will visit next: talking about uncertainty and risk in everyday language, and expressing estimates in ranges, not single points.

Talking about uncertainty and risk in everyday language

Risk management at one level is a highly technical subject, but at another it is the most basic and intuitive of human capabilities. Most people consider things that might happen quite naturally. They talk about what they are concerned about, worried about, wonder about. Equally, they talk about what opportunities or 'lucky breaks' might occur. As a change leader, I make it my business to engage as many people as possible in conversation about their perceptions of uncertainty and risk, but using everyday, not technical, language. This provides a much wider perspective on the situation and provides invaluable data on the organization, the culture, the market conditions and other variables that are certain to influence the outcomes of change.

When working with clients as a consultant, it is relatively easy to have such conversations, adopting the role of a neutral facilitator. In such circumstances it can be easier to challenge and help the client avoid 'sleepwalking' into skewed decisions.

CASE STUDY

In the early lifecycle stages of a very large government programme, I was able to convince the programme director of the benefits to him and his team of having a good understanding of the chance of achieving challenging targets. The programme would realize 'game-changing' benefits for the UK if successful. The programme was led by visionary, energetic leaders and the vision for change was widely shared. To challenge that vision was career limiting in the organization at the time.

My team and I talked to hundreds of people involved in the programme to understand the challenge and the risks involved, and we were able to build risk models to demonstrate to the programme board of senior civil servants and elected Ministers the true confidence they should have in their plans. Even when faced with this information, however, the senior team found it hard to believe that the worst could happen. Risks were seen as negative blockers to their vision. They wanted to plough on regardless, ignoring the information that things could be far worse than they had planned, with significant impact on policy and taxpayers' money.

Changing this perspective took an approach to flip perspectives of risk. Rather than thinking about uncertain events that could make progress worse than planned, I used a technique for contingency planning that focused the group on the future state through a spoof tabloid newspaper account of the situation they did not want three years on. By providing an opportunity for the group to suspend core beliefs for a day and to think the unthinkable, we were able to pull together a different plan that dealt with the risks without the word risk ever being used. More information on the technique used can be found in Klein (2007).

This sort of perspective-challenging exercise is often easier to perform as a consultant rather than employee. When employed by the organization investing in the change, it is important to recognize the degree to which you are part of the problem, where you are as susceptible to the hidden traps as any other member of the team. Sometimes it is good to engage an external and neutral facilitator to expose the organizational blind spots so that you can participate as a team member.

The second practical tip relates to how to express estimates in a meaningful way.

Expressing estimates in ranges, not single points

This is a general point that has the greatest relevance when making investment decisions, but applies throughout a change lifecycle. When implementing risky change, the cruel reality is that the statistical chance of achieving a particular outcome, be that a budget, a timescale or a benefit, is close to zero. The reality is that there is a range of possible outcomes, and a good estimate is one that falls within the expected range.

We won't talk here about how to determine the expected range, but even without specific technical knowledge of risk management we can learn to talk in ranges and to qualify our estimates so that they are more realistic.

What does this mean? When senior leaders ask me about expected benefits from change, I talk about the measures we will use and the range of outcomes we could expect from the investment. For example: 'We expect to have an effect on employee engagement that would be seen in reduced sickness absence from the current level of x per cent to between y and z per cent.' Or when asked about budget and timescales, I talk about the potential range of outcomes and ask them what level of confidence they want in estimates.

CASE STUDY

In a recent conversation with non-executive directors of a logistics company, I asked what confidence levels in estimates were needed for a forthcoming major investment decision. A good conversation ensued where the group admitted that they had not talked about it, and they learnt quickly that they had differing views across the board. As a result of the conversation, it was decided that for an early decision-gate they wanted to know the worst-case position; that is, that the change would cost no more than £x million and would return cash benefit of no less than £y million. This provided the motivation for the senior team to do a thorough analysis of threats and opportunities in order to be able to provide these data. The focus on the worst case did not limit ambition to do much better than that, but it did mean that the decision makers were 'anchored' to the worst case where the odds for a better outcome were high, rather than an optimistic case where the chances were that they would be disappointed with the outcome and the team.

The very positive experience shared above does not always happen. I have worked with major, global organizations where change leaders are convinced that their senior managers would not tolerate a discussion about ranges and that single-point estimates must be provided, perhaps with a ± tolerance range. Sadly, most people, when faced with a presentation that tells them that a change will cost £10 million ±20 per cent, go away with the £10 million figure firmly anchored in their memory. Presenting the same data using the range £8–12 million usually triggers a beneficial conversation; for example, what would it take to achieve an £8 million out-turn? If this conversation isn't already part of the conversation about change, it is most definitely worth raising.

Considering risk when making investment decisions

If the tendency is to downplay or ignore risk when making investment decisions, my experience is to overcome this challenge by: (1) talking about uncertainty and risk in everyday language where possible, and (2) expressing estimates in a way that communicates that things aren't certain.

Conversation and challenge are key to progress. Analytical risk techniques can definitely help in the right situation, but my experience is that they are not always welcome or appropriate for the culture of the organization in question. In such circumstances, it is possible and highly effective to be able to facilitate conversations about risk without the audience particularly realizing it.

Protecting previous decisions

Once an organization has decided to invest in change, and hopefully understood the risks associated with that decision, the ongoing role of risk management is to protect that investment decision.

All risk management processes and methods advocate the use of a risk log or register as a repository of risk information. There is an unavoidable need to hold risk information in one place. The challenge arises when completing the risk register becomes the goal, rather than a means to a different end. Of the hundreds of risk registers that I've reviewed, audited and worked with across a wide range of organizations, there are few where I have felt that the risk information truly connected with the objectives at risk.

The primary purpose of a risk register is as a repository for a prioritized list of uncertainties that would matter for the change effort if they occurred. It is the main record of the risk management process, examples of which can be found in Office of Government Commerce (2010). When the change team is at the peak of activity, with many people involved in delivering multiple tasks, being able to keep track of the most important risks is very important. Whether your organization has a risk register in a simple tool, or a more complex database linking risk information with assumptions, issues and decisions (a 'RAID' log), what value is it adding to your efforts to deliver the changed capabilities and benefits?

CASE STUDY

In a recent consultancy assignment within an international energy company, I was reminded how easy it is to have a 'compliant' risk process that adds little value. The organization had recorded many risks in a risk register and created colourful reports which were provided to various governance forums, yet the risk information contained in the risk register was unrepresentative of the 'real' risks in the situation.

One of my colleagues refers to this as 'paper risk management' – a process that ticks all the boxes, withstands audit, makes people feel comfortable but adds no practical value. I saw here first-hand how team members were contributing to the risk register with thought and enthusiasm, and where the portfolio management office (PMO) was performing a variety of analyses to summarize the information. Unfortunately, these summaries ended up reporting pointless information, such as 'how many risks raised this month', or 'how many risks open for more than 3 months', as well as reporting the 'top risks'; none of these represented the 'real risks' in the situation. When change teams are committed to doing risk management well, why does this happen?

Causes and effects

The two most significant things that destroy the power of a risk management process to protect previous investment decisions are poor risk descriptions and a static or partial process.

Poor risk descriptions

There are many books, guides and other sources of information that explain how a risk management process is intended to work. It's a logical, step-wise process at one level, but it completely relies on descriptions of risks that communicate what is really important and enable the most accurate assessments of likelihood and size of impact possible. A good decision also makes it crystal clear where any additional work to reduce uncertainty should be focused, that is, whether the path to greater certainty is by treating the cause and/or mitigating the effect. Other authors have written the 'rules' about good risk descriptions and why it matters (Hillson and Simon, 2012). In short, it's vital to be able to succinctly separate causes (facts now) from the uncertainty (something that might happen) from the impact on the change objectives. Take a look at the risk registers in your organization – do they do that? Is it clear what is risky and why? If not, the steps in the risk process that follow identification are likely to be suboptimal.

A static or partial process

Describing risks well assumes that you have understood what stakeholders perceive as risky in the first place. How are stakeholder perceptions of risks captured and assessed? How do you make sure that relevant voices are heard over time? The risk 'workshop' is used in many organizations to bring together (in person or virtually) relevant stakeholders to share views and capture risks. With great facilitation to limit human bias (Pullan and Murray-Webster, 2011), such risk workshops can be really useful sessions that enable people to share perceptions and perspectives, build on ideas and capture meaningful information about the change and the associated risks, good and bad, to achieving the benefits. But after the first session, how is the risk information kept current? Often risk information is just a 'point in time' and not representative of the emerging threats and opportunities with the work. To avoid a static risk process, it is increasingly common for workflows to be established whereby individuals working on a change can input risk information as an individual when it occurs to them. This helps to keep the process dynamic, but then risks the information being partial, or parochial, that is, the risk register only contains the perspectives of the people who take the time to contribute.

So, even where your organization embraces risk management for its change initiative and wants to do a good job, the combination of poor risk descriptions and a static and/or partial process can destroy good intentions and create a bureaucracy that adds little practical value to the task of protecting previous investment decisions. What can be done about this?

Practical tips

The challenge in focus here is an over-reliance on risk registers to protect previous investment decisions, that is, believing that if you have a process where people are inputting their perceptions of risks into a register on a regular basis, all will be well. There is obvious value in doing this and in getting the information to be clear and current, but my experience is that greater value from risk management is created when the focus is taken away from the 'system' and instead is placed on the quality of conversation about organizational change objectives and uncertainties.

As a change leader, here are two things that I encourage you to practise: (1) talking to the team and other stakeholders about objectives and plans, and (2) preparation for governance meetings.

CASE STUDY

A global mining company engaged me to help them transform their risk management culture and practices from a 'tick-box' exercise to one that added business value. I worked with the organization for more than three years, addressing multiple aspects of this challenge. The most significant part was getting people to realize that if they talk about their objectives and plans, it's then a natural step to also talk about the things that could happen that would make those plans more or less effective. It's a completely natural human process and one that we often stifle when we come together in workshops to talk about *risks* rather than coming together to talk about *objectives that are at risk*. People who had previously contributed to risk workshops, and reported that they had 'lost the will to live' and 'got no value' from the process, where amazed when they came to sessions to talk about achieving objectives and plans and that an output (created and shared afterwards) was a really meaningful risk register. One project I supported in that organization stands out in particular. It was political, high profile and had very short time-frames to achieve a difficult restructure. The project leader had worked with me on other projects and asked me to facilitate a session with the team with the objective of identifying, analysing and planning responses to the key risks. The team arrived for the meeting expecting a boring albeit necessary session. They left having had a really valuable discussion, everyone sharing their views in different ways, but thinking we hadn't talked about risk. The day afterwards I shared the risk register that they had created, but hadn't realized it.

This example picks up to some degree on the practical tips above and illustrates the importance of finding a way of talking about risk in a way that opens up thinking rather than closing it down. Often it's better to do that without using the 'R' word (ie risk), because for many people this triggers either negativity or boredom.

The bigger point that is illustrated by this example is that often the focus on a risk register happens in such a way that the objectives at risk and the plans to achieve them are lost or missing from the thinking. This has a direct impact on the quality of risk descriptions, the quality of prioritization and the quality of responses. Switching the conversation to objectives first and current plans second can have a transforming effect on the outputs of a risk process.

The second practical tip relates to preparation for governance meetings. These may be called steering groups, programme boards, or some other title for the meetings that are designed to track progress and make ongoing decisions to protect the investment in change. The contents of a good risk register will help you prepare for successful governance meetings; however, reporting on the content of the risk register without relating this information to the 'bigger picture' is often done, but is usually pointless.

Use risk information to prepare a compelling story

In governance meetings we need to do some simple things:

- Focus decision-maker attention on plans and outline the current status.
- Outline challenges (issues now and future risks) and the significance of these on objectives and plans.
- Decide what, if anything, to do differently to keep the change on track.

The success of such meetings relies on people being able to sum up status and challenges, and then be able to make compelling recommendations about what to do so that decision makers can provide guidance and steer the change.

CASE STUDY

A recent steering group meeting for a major transformational change programme reminded me how difficult people often find it to tell their story in such a way as to get good value from governance. If you have a good understanding of what you're trying to achieve, how you're doing now, and the problems and uncertainties that need to be managed, all you then need is to craft a story that outlines all this in a way that highlights options and makes a recommendation.

In this particular situation, the team were putting forward four options as responses to a major risk that was about to cause a material delay to the programme if left unmanaged. In the slides provided for the meeting, both the root cause of the risk and the validity of the four potential responses were obscured by colourful charts of progress since the last meeting, current plans (with no visualization of the impact of the problem shown on them), excerpts and 'stats' from the RAID log, and pros and cons of options that seemed to have been put together by different people with no reference to each other. All the data presented were valid but they did not tell a logical and coherent story and therefore did not help the decision makers to make an informed judgement about what to do next. The meeting was messy, the change team felt beaten up, and the senior leaders felt confused and left the meeting with reduced confidence in the change team.

When preparing for a steering group or similar decision-making meeting, I was taught that the most important thing was to tell a logical story and to make sure that the visuals produced in support of the story (the slide deck, handouts etc) were simple, leaving no room for ambiguity. The part of the story that draws on risk information is rarely helped by cutting and pasting information from the risk register into the deck, nor providing statistics on the risk *process* rather than reporting on risk *content*. The content of a useful risk register provides lots of information, but it needs to be used in a way that supports the story being told, rather than providing information to distract the audience. This chapter does not have space to share information on how best to shape a compelling story and recommendation, but practical and invincible advice can be found in Minto (2008).

Over-reliance on risk registers to protect investment decisions

My own observation is that change teams often believe that if they have a risk register that is well populated, this ticks the box for risk management.

It is a fact that if risk registers are populated with well-described risks that really speak to the objectives at risk, and are dynamic and in touch with emergent situations, they will be an asset to the change effort. Risk registers, however, are only a repository for risk information, and it is a major pitfall to see the task at hand as 'filling out the risk register and reporting on the content of it' rather than 'ensuring good conversations are held about risk and compelling recommendations made to deal with emerging situations'.

Conclusion: managing risk during organizational change

This chapter has drawn out a number of areas that are important if those people charged with delivering organizational change are to handle risk well. The core argument is that understanding risk and how to manage it is an essential part of organizational change, because change is inherently risky. Many change practitioners realize this, but struggle to know how best to get value from the risk management processes offered in textbooks and standard methodologies. Change to the way risk is managed is often needed.

Practical advice offered in this chapter has addressed the following areas:

- The need to appreciate some of the underlying reasons why it is natural to underplay risk when making investment decisions. We all have a tendency to an optimism bias when we are trying to progress novel ideas. Our natural behaviour in groups can lead us to 'go with the flow' rather than challenge and explore alternative perspectives. Both of these things need to be handled if investments in change are to have a good start.

- The need to talk about uncertainty and risk in everyday language to help to overcome any tendencies to avoid thinking about risks that could be detrimental to objectives. It is also very useful to express estimates in ranges rather than single points to open up minds to the fact that the outcomes from change can never be predicted with certainty.

- The need to avoid a singular focus on risk registers. Risk registers are necessary to hold information about risks that are perceived by stakeholders and the plans to manage them. Unfortunately, many risk registers are rendered useless by poor risk descriptions that are not clear and lead to inaccurate prioritization of risks and ineffective responses. Risk registers are also misleading when they are assumed to hold complete information when in truth they hold a 'point in time' and partial picture.

- The need to talk to the team and other stakeholders about objectives and plans to engage people and draw out the 'real' risks that are perceived. These risks can then be captured and shared using good descriptions that clearly separate causes (facts now) from the uncertain event (that may or may not occur) from the impact on objectives if it did. This method also makes sure that people are not limited in expressing their perceptions of risk by the limitations of the fields in the risk register.

- The need to use the content of the risk register to support options analysis, recommendations and future decision making. Rather than believing that the role of governance is to understand the health of the risk management process, the skilled change practitioner knows how to draw on risk information to help the organization take the optimal path through the change.

Managing organizational change is challenging, but can be made easier by effective engagement of people to really understand the risks they perceive to objectives. Expressing those risks, in words in risk registers and as ranges of expected outcomes, can be really useful. Risk management is often done badly and seen as a necessary evil to meet the requirements of governance. Hopefully this chapter has helped you to think how you could do things differently to make risk management a core part of decision making when investing in and delivering benefits from organizational change.

References

Flyvbjerg, B, Buzelius, N and Rothengatter, W (2013) *Megaprojects and Risk: An anatomy of ambition*, Cambridge University Press, Cambridge

Hillson, DA and Simon, PW (2012) *Practical Project Risk Management: The ATOM methodology*, 2nd edn, Management Concepts, Vienna, VA

Janis, IL (1971) Groupthink. *Psychology Today*, 5 (6), 43–46, 74–76

Klein, G (2007) Performing a project premortem. *Harvard Business Review*, pp 85 (9), pp 18–19

Lovallo, D and Kahneman, D (2003) Delusions of success: how optimism undermines executives' decisions. *Harvard Business Review*, 81 (7), pp 56–67

Minto, B (2008) *The Pyramid Principle: Logic in writing, thinking and problem solving*, 3rd edn, Financial Times/Prentice Hall, London

Office of Government Commerce (2010) *Management of Risk: Guidance for practitioners*, The Stationery Office, Norwich

Pullan, P and Murray-Webster, R (2011) *A Short Guide to Facilitating Risk Management: Engaging people to identify, own and manage risk*, Gower, Aldershot

Embedding and sustaining change

ANDY WILKINS AND KATE STUART-COX

Introduction

This chapter represents some of the key insights in our research and experience over the past 30 years to better understand what it takes to embed change in organizations.

The Final Report of the Change Management Consortium (Balogun and Hope Hailey, 2009) revealed a negative picture of change and change capability inside organizations, mainly because of:

1 an over-reliance on a machine metaphor for conceiving organizations, leading to an emphasis on structures, systems, methodology and lots of rhetoric;

2 a lack of learning about change at senior levels;

3 a lack of approaches, tools and concepts to translate the strategic rhetoric into tangible implications for the organization and the individuals in it.

We believe that an organization is a group people working together to help another group of people get its needs met, so our approach is to work from an individual perspective and then help this diffuse to the organizational level over time. The keys to embedding change we offer here address the challenges identified by this research, other recent research and our own experiences. In particular, we focus on the aspects that those involved in leading and managing change might develop in order to embed change and so keep individuals engaged and moving forward.

We will share our key insights to embedding and sustaining change by using case studies of three organizations we have worked with and continue to work with:

- embedding innovation in a large food company;
- embedding organizational flexibility in an international consultancy firm;
- embedding a culture change in an international marketing company.

We have learnt that many people hold the view 'I will believe it when I see it'. But if you hold this view you will miss many things. So building on our deep belief in the power of education to help our mind see with new eyes and so see things afresh, we encourage people to also experiment with the idea 'I will see it when I believe it', in order to observe and notice new aspects of situations that maybe hitherto were unseen. We believe that this is one of the secrets to embedding and sustaining change; after all, the eyes are useless if the mind is blind.

CASE STUDY 1 Embedding innovation in a large food company

This food manufacturing company operates mainly in the UK, with a turnover of £1.6 billion and approximately 15,000 employees. It has many divisions and many household brands.

The phone rang and I answered. 'Help!' said the caller. 'I have been asked to explain to my company how to embed innovation. I know I innovate but I am not sure I know how I do it or can explain it to my colleagues in the company. The chairman has asked me to explain how to do it to all the top bods in the company and then develop and embed innovation across the company. I am off to an innovation conference in LA tomorrow to try and find out.'

The caller was the New Product Development Director for one of the key divisions, and I suggested we meet up at the airport the next morning before the flight to walk him through a framework that would help him understand what he would hear on the west coast. I also mentioned some people he may wish to look out for while there. We met over a coffee for 45 minutes and I shared with him that the essence of innovation is ultimately all about creative approaches to problem solving.

My listener, Jeffrey, flinched. 'Problems are something to be avoided, so how can innovation be all about creative problem solving?' he said.

Key #1: Be credible

Embedding this innovation change would require Jeffrey to change his own mind and behaviours first. It's challenging because we immediately bump into tensions and potentially conflicts of views – the new ways in contrast to Jeffrey's old ways.

To generate movement towards the new requires a clear message but more importantly a credible messenger, since so much of change is about communications and the communicator. You have probably heard the saying 'You won't believe the message if you don't believe the messenger.' It originates from Aristotle and has been developed by O'Keefe (1990) and others. Change involves influencing others, and in our experience it is important to earn the trust and confidence of the people we are influencing and attempting to change. So while many involved with change talk a lot about all the latest models, the buzz words from books and the enormous number of tools they have to hand, few consider the most important tool in their toolbox – themselves, and the question 'Are you credible in change management?'

Research has found that credibility is not based on job titles, hierarchy or the size of your toolbox but with the human being. It may be an inconvenient truth, but if the people you are attempting to change don't believe in you as the messenger, they won't believe in the message. Or put another way, if people don't believe in the change manager, they won't believe in the change nor in what you say.

A credible change manager is a leader who understands that they are not an island and that their effectiveness depends on the willing commitment of their constituents. So what does it take to lead change? For 30 years, Jim Kouzes and Barry Posner (2011) have been asking the question from the perspective of the follower, the person being changed. The question is simply: 'What personal values, traits, and characteristics do you look for and admire in a leader, someone whose direction you would *willingly* follow?' It turns out that people look for many special qualities in those they are *willing* to follow as opposed to those people they have to follow because they have no choice, or follow out of curiosity.

Kouzes and Posner have found that the four attributes of *honesty, competency, inspiring* and *forward looking* are what we require from people we choose to follow. More recent research also shows that these same four factors are cross-cultural and enduring: they have consistently ranked as the top four factors across different countries. They seem to form an 'essential character test' that an individual must meet before others are willing to follow them. These four characteristics form the basis of leadership credibility: those whose direction we would *willingly* follow.

Jeffrey believed in us and therefore started to believe in what we were saying. He believed we were credible and now we needed to help build his credibility in order to ensure there was a chance of embedding and sustaining any organizational change.

The aspect of credibility is important, of course, to change management in general, but it is critical when thinking ahead to what it will take to embed and sustain change. Following someone and a change because we want to (*commitment*) feels very different from following someone and a change because we have to (*compliance*). Willingly following means that when things get a bit difficult, stormy and bumpy, and our anxiety starts rising, we are still committed and prepared to dig deeper to find the courage, resolve and energy to carry on because we believe. Whereas if we have to follow and things get difficult or frustrating, we use strategies to avoid putting in any extra effort – strategies such as deflecting, avoiding and distracting. At worst, people sometimes also seek to disrupt and even seek retribution at some time in the future.

Key #2: Use a flexible framework

CASE STUDY 1 (contd)

Jeffrey and I talked about how to ensure that innovation could be sustained. I shared the longest-serving (most sustained!) framework for innovation that is used by many organizations around the world: the 4Ps of innovation. Jeffrey liked the concept of the 4Ps but was still very unsure and unconvinced about the language when he left for his flight. We agreed to meet when he returned.

About two weeks later, Jeffrey and I met in Henley-on-Thames. Jeffrey returned a little more convinced that the 4Ps would be a useful approach in helping to embed innovation.

He also told me of an informal yet fortuitous meeting he had with one of the original founding-father gurus of creative problem solving, Sid Parnes, who was also at the conference and whom I had mentioned to Jeffrey at the airport two weeks earlier. Jeffrey explained: 'While there, I met Sid and talked with him about his work and this "creative problem solving" idea you mentioned to me at the airport. Sid and I sat down and had a coffee together. I said to Sid: "If you were to take Mrs Parnes (Bea) on holiday to Paris, would you see this as a problem to be solved?" Sid answered "Yes." I then said: "Ok, so choosing a hotel to stay at is a problem to be solved?" "Yes" said Sid. "And once in Paris, if you wanted to take Bea out for dinner, would you see this as a problem to be solved?" Sid again answered "Yes."'

With that conversation, Jeffrey understood the mindset of Sid and many others who understand the power of broadening their language to include other areas such as creative approaches to problem solving as a foundation for innovation and change.

Innovation, like many other types of change, is what some have called 'wicked'. Rittel and Webber (1973) coined the term 'wicked' as distinct from 'tame' to describe situations where various aspects are woven together interdependently. The difference between tame and wicked becomes really useful to those of us involved with designing, implementing and embedding change, in that it helps to guide our approach.

Give people a description of a problem in their area and they will most likely come up with a solution, quickly. In the 21st century, in many organizations, that's what people believe is expected of them. But some problems – especially wicked ones – probably can't be solved quickly. That's why they remain problems. The approach to addressing tame problems differs from strategies appropriate for wicked problems (Table 15.1). It's worth remembering that in reality most situations involve a mixture of tame and wicked problems.

Table 15.1 Strategies for approaching tame and wicked problems

Characteristic	How to Approach Tame Problems	How to Approach Wicked Problems
Source of power	Management based – bestowed on you by boss	Leadership based – bestowed on you by followers
People	Creates groups, committees, task forces	Collaboration across a wide spectrum of people
What gets set	Sets guidelines, milestones, and deadlines or due dates	Sets the climate – the 'press', the container – and the approach
Delegation	Can be delegated	Cannot be delegated
Approach	Addressed through process and action	Addressed through fair process, values, and dialogic conversation

The key is to address something that is wicked using a flexible and systemic framework such as the 4Ps, which focuses on all the appropriate areas.

The 4Ps framework for creativity, innovation, problem solving and change was first established in the 1960s (Rhodes, 1961), so the system has pedigree. There is, of course, no perfect recipe for innovation and change, but the 4Ps is a recognized and widely used framework for sustainable change that highlights the four key aspects that need to be focused on:

- Two 'hard' aspects:
  - *product*: the needs and resultant products, outputs and outcomes that are required and which include new products and services but also include new behaviours or integrating a new process or organizational structure;
  - *process*: the methods and tools that involve the deliberate structures, operations, steps and thinking to enable and implement any desired changes.
- Two 'soft' aspects:
  - *people*: the heart of the system, which includes the characteristics and behaviours of people to be ready, willing and able to change;
  - *press*: the physical and more importantly the invisible psychological environment which 'presses' on us.

The key to making any change sustainable is to ensure that all 4Ps are addressed. The favoured mindset for change tends to focus on the two hard aspects at the expense of the two soft aspects; however, any change that does not balance all four areas is likely to achieve limited results, so not be embedded and sustainable (Isaksen and Tidd, 2006; Isaksen *et al*, 2011).

Key #3: Embrace loose tight

By *loose tight* we mean the organization giving people freedom, autonomy, independence and opportunity to develop, grow and experiment when appropriate; at other times to be specific, directing, controlling, fixed and rigid as needed. Why is this important? Innovation and change, like many fields, are diverse, with many points of view. The 4Ps framework provides enough clarity to frame and direct the critical aspects of what needs to be done but also leaves plenty of room for freedom of choice. For example, another area where this idea of *loose tight* arises is with the language of change. Our experience across geographies and across industries is that:

- Different industries and groups of people use a slightly different language to talk about change.

- When people do collaborate across multiple functions, industries and cultures they often use the same words but mean different things. This inevitably produces confusion and at worst misunderstandings, tensions and conflict.

We have found that, on the whole, *creativity, innovation, problem solving* and *change* are ostensibly, and for all practical purposes, the same. Or put another way, change can be seen as just problem solving!

Now we appreciate that this may provoke some people – like Jeffrey – to flinch at this strange idea, and we accept that there may be some differences. Yet from a practical change perspective, holding them all as ostensibly the same thing from different contexts is not only a useful perspective, but it also means we can broaden and rebalance our language and approach to innovation, problem solving, creativity and change (Figure 15.1):

- The so-called creative industries such as media, marketing, fashion and the arts tend to use the term *creativity*.

- The so-called heavier and more output-based industries tend to use the term *innovation*.

- The term *problem solving* tends to be used by engineers, the health service and many other professionals.

- The term *change* is often used by those in human resources, learning and development, and by consultants.

Figure 15.1   Creativity, innovation, problem solving, and change are ostensibly the same: tension resolvers

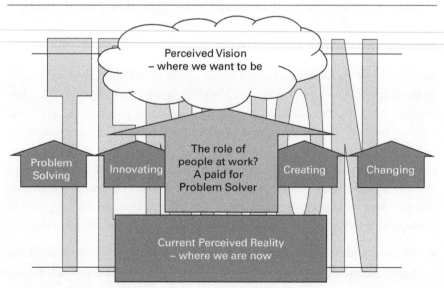

This rich tapestry helps us extend the language, mindset and knowledge resources available to everyone involved with change.

Jeffrey had to reframe his own mindset and he started to appreciate that in order to influence the changing world around us and acquire what we need, we have to think. Thinking is the way by which we solve problems, and it is the same process that produces creativity, change and innovation. All involve moving (or trying to move) from a current state to a desired state. Therefore a helpful definition we use for creativity, innovation, problem solving and change is: 'newness that is useful (at least to the creator)'. Embracing loose tight enables us to access all the insights about change from across multiple disciplines; it enables us not to be so precious about our view of the world, and prepares us for the inevitable sense of muddling along that comes when embedding change involving people.

CASE STUDY 1 (contd)

Jeffrey adopted the 4Ps and adapted them into the 4 Pillars of Innovation for the company. He used this framework at the chairman's talks, which also went well, and shortly afterwards Jeffrey was promoted from the Head of Innovation for one division to the Director of Innovation for the whole group.

There were two key reasons Jeffrey was chosen to lead the programme to embed innovation: one was that he had created a fabulous climate for innovation and change in the division he was in, and still today this is one of the best we have ever encountered. At the time, he had successfully launched products worth over £1 billion. The other reason was that at the chairman's events, he projected credibility (Key #1) and clarity (Key #2) by using the 4Ps as a way to frame what the company needed to do to embed innovation.

Jeffrey set about embedding the 4 Pillars of Innovation across the whole company over the next 7 years. Some of the ways he did this were to:

- diffuse the 4 Pillars of Innovation across the organization with highly interactive one hour workshops called 'Beginnovators';
- build impact by running highly effective workshops, known as 'Same Day New Product Development' workshops, with multiple stakeholders all together at the same time, such as consumers, retailers, suppliers and industry experts, as well as the company itself;
- demystify innovation and create a shared interest in and language for creativity and innovation by writing articles and talking at internal and external events about the 4 Pillars of Innovation as often as possible;

- develop and embed an innovation strategy and metrics in business units that focused on measuring innovation;
- strengthen individuals' innovation capabilities based on a programme called 'Focused Innovative Thinking', which encapsulated the 4 Pillars and taught people:
  - the key thinking skills of generating and focusing evaluating options;
  - how to lead others to do the same.

He commented many years later that: 'Without doubt, the 4Ps model for understanding, developing and applying innovation is a really helpful framework for embedding the necessary changes we were trying to make.'

CASE STUDY 2 Embedding organizational flexibility in an international consultancy

This 6,000-person global engineering consultancy firm was used to addressing engineering challenges, but over time these engineering challenges were being interwoven with more and more aspects that vexed them and their normal approaches. They needed new strategies in several areas, including the following:

- Clients were asking not only for great engineering but also now wanted innovation.
- The work-winning process was not working effectively and, if not addressed, would see the organization's decline.
- The global strategy development process was not working successfully and was producing conflict.
- There was poor horizontal collaboration and communication across the organization.
- Senior management teams seemed to be increasingly ineffective and operating in too much of a 'cosy us' syndrome.

In contrast to the typical problems faced at the company and the typical approach taken to make and embed changes, these challenges were characterized by their ambiguity in problem formulation and challenges in gaining acceptance to the approach to address them, often referred to as 'wicked problems'. To address these, the company initially began adding some new language: the language of creativity, innovation, problem solving and change; the language of collaboration; and the language of wicked.

As one of the board directors said to us: 'Challenging me and the company to sometimes hear and see what, to be honest, we sometimes didn't want to deal with was one of the key changes from the work. And over time, we became better able to figure out many of the challenges ourselves as we developed our ability to address wickedness.'

Key #4: Develop people while developing the business to enable self-embedding

Despite all the rhetoric about the need for organizational flexibility (currently more trendily known as agility), there is still corporate inertia. Typically two quite different approaches to change are used:

- One has its intention focused on shorter-term development of the organization's economic results. It is typically driven from the top, is planned and programmatic, and almost always changes formal structures and systems, and uses incentives.

- The other has its intention on development of the organization's social capital to be able to develop more economic value in the longer term. It is typically enabled from the top, is often emergent and less planned, and often changes engagement, leadership behaviours and, over time, potentially the organizational climate and culture.

These approaches are based on very different mindsets, assumptions and views about the purpose of and means for change. In the engineering company case study above, the organization approached the change by integrating these two approaches: developing their personnel while at the same time developing the business – this built into their personnel the capability to constantly change and, at the same time, become more resilient to the waves of change the organization faced, understanding that change is not a one-off nor even a series of events, but a constant. What we have noticed is that as the capability to change develops, the language around actively and deliberately *embedding* change reduces: as people learn how to consistently self-embed change, it becomes part of the natural operation of their professional lives.

Key #5: Accept that everyone has their own path to high performance

One of the signs of an organization or a person who is stuck in a bit of a rut is that they tend to see things from their view only, or they are so bogged down with administrative standardization that they lose the ability to see other viewpoints. One of the most useful tools for change we use is VIEW™, which assesses an individual's preferred style of problem solving. VIEW™ provides deep insights into preferences that are aimed at helping people consider who they are working with and they are working on; it also helps individuals and teams understand how creative collaboration works across projects, functions, and cultures.

VIEW™ has three hugely important and useful dimensions of people and their preferences for change:

1 *Orientation to change*: this scale describes preferences in two general styles for responding to and managing structure, novelty, and authority, when dealing with change:

   – developer style – thinking and working to improve within the accepted paradigms;

   – explorer style – thinking and working beyond the accepted paradigms.

2 *Manner of processing*: this scale describes preference for how and when people use their own inner energy and resources, the energy and resources of others, and the environment; and for different ways of handling information when managing change:

   – external style – with other people throughout the process;

   – internal style – thinking and working alone before sharing ideas with others.

3 *Ways of deciding*: this scale describes the preferences for balancing and emphasizing task concerns and personal or interpersonal needs when making decisions and moving towards taking action:

   – person style – maintaining harmony and interpersonal relationships;

   – task style – emphasizing logical, rational, and appropriate decisions.

Recognizing and using these preferences initially enables us to see that everyone has their own path to high performance and that we don't all think about change in the same way. This then leads to a more effective understanding of what it takes to embed change and also to prevent the unwitting creation of invisible resistance caused by not valuing other people's thinking preferences and at worst trampling on them.

CASE STUDY 2 (contd)

Several people in the engineering consultancy company with existing credibility helped to spark and pioneer the changes to get things started. They started by: (1) using VIEW™ to develop a better understanding of how people change and to help dissolve potential barriers to agreement; and (2) building the organization's change capability through a programme called 'Facilitative Leadership and Creative Problem Solving'.

Over nine years, the company worked on the many key areas using the new language of VIEW™ to help address new challenges such as innovation, bid process, strategy, collaboration and senior team effectiveness.

VIEW™ was shared at a number of global company-wide conferences involving 500 of the most senior people and the change activists who had been selected in the company to start to share and embed the new language.

A Perspectiv programme, Facilitative Leadership and Creative Problem Solving (FL&CPS), was first applied directly to the work-winning process and over the years the win rate went from 1 in 3 to 1 in 2. It was also estimated to have saved £15 million in bid costs in the first few years.

Shortly afterwards, as VIEW™ and FL&CPS were embedding, they were also then applied to the strategy process. This led to the company being ready, willing and able to begin moving to the next level of 'developing people while developing the business', especially in the senior management teams and how they were interacting with each other. As the new language and thinking was embedding and diffusing across the organization, the CEO and a number of the divisional directors had started to want to raise the bar on the quality of their teams. They started to use one of the most powerful tools we know of: skilful conversations with dialogue (see Key #7 for more).

Key #6: Build in commitment, not compliance, using fair process

Although companies use different names to characterize engagement, the common thread between all definitions is *discretionary effort*. This is the effort that employees choose to give above the required effort. With high engagement we see a different attitudinal attachment to work and the organization: an intention to act in the organization's best interest, and a willingness to invest discretionary effort to achieve goals. This discretionary effort has been estimated at 40 per cent of the effort people can or do put in at work.

How do we build the type of engagement that produces this discretionary effort? There are two types of commitment we experience when making decisions: emotional commitment and rational commitment:

- *Rational commitment* primarily relates to the change outcome itself. People ask themselves:

    - Does the change make sense?
    - Is the outcome fair in the context?
    - Does it seem logical and rational?

- *Emotional commitment* primarily relates to the process by which the change was achieved. People ask themselves:

    - Was the process by which the change was achieved fair?
    - Who by and how was the outcome achieved?
    - How was the process determined?

But the important factor here is that research suggests emotional commitment is worth about four times more than rational commitment:

- People care four times more about the fairness of the process through which a change is produced than they do about the outcome itself.

- People in general appear always to be making procedural judgements, and these judgements tend to be important to them.

- People's justice perceptions of what constitutes a fair process are determined by similar principles across cultures.

Fairness does not mean equality. Equal means the same; fairness is not necessarily about treating people the same, but it does mean treating people with what they need to be effective. The aim is always to try to be fair, but this means that things will not always feel equal: what one person needs and what someone else needs may be very different. So what's the key to fair process? The three Es of fair process (Kim and Mauborgne, 2005) are:

1 *Engagement*: involving people in the decisions that affect them by asking for their input and allowing them to challenge the merits of one another's ideas and assumptions.

2 *Explanation*: everyone involved and affected should understand why final decisions are made as they are. This does not mean that they necessarily agree with the decision (outcome), but they do understand the logic and reasoning on which the decision is based.

3 *Expectation*: building clarity so that once a decision is made to change, leadership clearly states the new rules of the game.

Like all aspects of change, this is easily said and less easily done. It's worth remembering that fairness is not only a global human value but also a professional skill that needs to be observed, developed and practised. With fair process, the chances of embedding a change rise significantly. Without fair process, the chances of embedding change are inhibited and the best to expect will be compliance; if you break fair process repeatedly or extremely, prepare for retribution.

CASE STUDY 3 Embedding a culture change in an international marketing company

This company operates in seven markets across Europe, the United States and Asia. It comprises around 75 people. New, unexpected competition and volatile market forces in its industry forced this organization to rethink its vision, strategy and values. Figuring out how to really up the ante on working together across the world – clichéd though it may sound – was to acknowledge the need to work as 'One Global Team', to share collective wisdom rather than operate in independent silos. Embedding a collaborative culture was vital for survival.

To embed this sort of change requires people to adapt their mindsets and behaviours from independent to collaborative. The first challenge was to clearly articulate and gain acceptance from the CEO and leadership team that putting down these roots for collaboration would not be achieved in a one-off event! They needed to be in it for the long term, and sustained interventions would be necessary for the culture to embed.

A new way of thinking

The starting point was to engender a new way of thinking – flexibility, mental suppleness, emotional agility – which would help people manage this change and equip them to move more easily from one change to another. A number of methodologies and assessments were used to enable learning and continuous self-reflection for them to become better 'observers of themselves': to understand the effect of their mindsets and mental models on their ability to change; to understand their personal values and the impact on their behaviour; their problem-solving style; their attitude and approach to conflict; their preferred defence strategies and approach to learning and self-reflection.

A new way of speaking

In order to embed a collaborative culture where sharing, openness, relationship building through trust, and respect for differences became a norm, we needed to enable people to communicate within their teams and across markets to build lasting relationships beyond the confines of their silos. The company learnt and used a skilful conversations approach to communication, which fostered trust and openness. Building 'skilful conversations' capabilities combining self-reflection, listening and feedback created a new way of speaking, which employees could use to support each other through any change.

Key #7: Learn how to have skilful conversations

Skilful conversations are a bit like *extra-strength conversations* which, if used with care, can help people to have difficult, crucial conversations in order to talk through important issues. Dialogue is an approach to skilful conversations involving listening to and talking through important topics such as team relations and strategy – without defensiveness – to reach a new level of understanding of a situation or problem hitherto concealed, misunderstood or misinterpreted.

The international marketing company above, like many others, was wasting considerable resources by working to solve the wrong problems and by not being aware of the real, often deep-rooted problems. Leaders and managers pressurized by today's need for economic short-term value frequently apply 'band-aid' solutions which address the symptoms but not the cause. They often forget or ignore a significant problem inherent in any group of people working together: that is, the people themselves.

From an early age we are taught to prepare ourselves to speak and defend our point of view, but we are rarely taught to listen. The process of dialogue enables a group of people to move beyond just 'talking' to new means of listening and responding to each other that provides in-depth insights for individuals on the impact they themselves have on the issue. It increases their awareness of the real opinions, attitudes and behaviours of the other people involved. Dialogue diagnoses the cause: it 'gets to the heart of the matter', 'digs below the surface', because only when the 'root cause' has been diagnosed can targeted and effective solutions be found and implemented. Used with skill, dialogue can also support organizational change.

CASE STUDY 3 Embedding a culture change in an international marketing company (contd)

This common language provided a means to get people collectively talking about the realities of any change in forums for inclusive conversations about their behaviours: to voice the tough realities of change; to have a voice; for that voice to be truly heard. It enabled teams to uncover the hidden 'elephants in the room' that were hindering performance and only when the real challenges had been identified expending energy and resources to collectively solve them. Change in its infancy is new, different and unproven and in the early days, challenge and debate are vital.

This approach also respected and valued the 'canaries' for the points and challenges they made. Canaries were placed in mines from around 1913 to detect carbon monoxide primarily. The birds, being more sensitive, would become sick before the miners, who would then have a chance to escape or put on protective respirators. So, the canaries in the company who looked at change and foresaw potential flaws and pitfalls were valued for their inputs, sharing their views without fear of reprisal or fear of being dismissed as resisters, naysayers or whingers.

A new way of doing

Introducing a new way of thinking and a new way of talking with each other had already kick-started behaviour change. But embedding these new habits required further initiatives. There is frequently a yawning gap between knowing what to do and actually doing it. Narrowing this gap, mastering a new skill and changing a habit need practice. Practice requires support, the freedom to try and learn from practice, and the opportunity to experiment in small ways.

We introduced processes to appraise progress on behaviour change regularly and consistently. Behavioural charters with guidelines and expectations were generated and evaluated in meetings. Meetings were monitored not only on the quality of the task outcomes but also on the quality of behaviours. Desired behaviours were integrated into recruitment, induction and performance management systems. Peer-to-peer support groups were established in teams to engender encouragement in behaviour change and mutual accountability.

A new way of leading

Unsurprisingly, the leaders who role-modelled well – who inspired the change, set examples of their own behaviour change, observed behaviour changes in others so they could reward and celebrate those making efforts, and encourage those who were struggling – were most successful in embedding the change.

Leaders ring-fenced budget for developmental training and coaching. They upheld the training as a priority. They shifted their own mindsets from developing people being a 'nice to have' to a 'must have' for high performance. They shifted from blame to mutual accountability. They shifted to a preventative 'car service' mindset – the cost of regular attention and care which keeps the car running smoothly and efficiently is significantly cheaper than fixing the major repairs caused by deliberate ignorance and neglect.

Collaboration became hardwired, part of their DNA and the 'way we do things around here'. People live the habits. New recruits notice the culture and are frequently astonished by it. People who have moved to other organizations miss it.

To embed and sustain change, those involved in change need to understand the importance of both listening and engaging in skilful conversations. As people start to understand any change, they also become more engaged with the change itself. Additionally, the increasing democracy of the workplace means that people have greater expectations to ask questions which cannot just be labelled 'resistance' or 'difficult'. Having, enabling and welcoming adult skilful conversations with legitimate questions is a sign of a change-mature individual and organization.

Conclusion: the seven keys to embedding and sustaining change

Some change is authoritative and some changes are discretionary. We have little choice but to abide by laws made in a country, or to follow policies and organizational changes made by management. But for many other changes we have a choice: this choice might be whether to adopt a new performance improvement process, to update our skills, to fully support and get behind a change of direction.

Strings of change variables in impressive formulae may provide an illusion of progress and make us feel in control, but as Wheatley (2012) wrote: 'Any moment now, the earth will crack open and I will stare into its dark centre. Into that smoking caldera, I will throw most of what I have treasured, most of the techniques and tools that have made me feel competent.'

We suggest not a formula but some keys to think about embedding change in the 21st century. Change management can be a catalyst to help organizations react, flex and adapt by reviewing their own mindset and capabilities about what it takes to make effective change happen. This opportunity will place significant demands on change practitioners to also embed some changes in themselves.

Our seven keys to embedding and sustaining change are:

- Key #1: Be credible.
- Key #2: Use a flexible framework.
- Key #3: Embrace loose tight.
- Key #4: Develop people while developing the business.
- Key #5: Accept that everyone has their own path to high performance.
- Key #6: Build in commitment not compliance.
- Key #7: Learn how to have skilful conversations.

Key questions

- Do you agree with Kouzes and Posner's four leadership attributes of *honesty*, *competent*, *inspiring* and *forward looking*:
  - for functional leaders?
  - for change leaders?
- How well do you score against these four characteristics?
- How do you rate your own organization against the seven keys for embedding and sustaining change?
- What skilful conversations has your organization had to have in relation to change? How successful were these conversations?

References

Balogun, J and Hope Hailey, V (2009) *Final report of the Change Management Consortium*, CASS Business School, City University London, London

Isaksen, SG, Dorval, KD and Treffinger, DJ (2011) *Creative Approaches to Problem Solving*, 3rd edn, Sage, Thousand Oaks, CA

Isaksen, SG and Tidd, J (2006) *Meeting the Innovation Challenge: Leadership for transformation and growth*, John Wiley & Sons, Chichester

Kim, WC and Mauborgne, R (2005) *Blue Ocean Strategy: How to create uncontested market space and make the competition irrelevant*, Harvard Business School Press, Boston, MA

Kouzes, BZ and Posner, JM (2011) *Credibility: How leaders gain and lose it, why people demand it*, Jossey-Bass, San Francisco

O'Keefe, DJ (1990) *Persuasion: Theory and research*, Sage, Newbury Park, CA

Rittel, H and Webber, M (1973) Dilemmas in a general theory of planning. *Policy Sciences*, 4 (2), pp 155–69

Rhodes, M (1961) An analysis of creativity. *Phi Delta Kappa*, **42**, pp 305–10

Wheatley, M (2012) *Leadership and the New Science: Discovering order in a chaotic world*, Berrett-Koehler, San Francisco

Change innovation

16

JOHN PELTON

Introduction

Innovation and change can be considered to be symbiotic. Yet all too often the nature of the relationship between them is confused or in conflict. The UK's construction industry routinely responds to some extraordinary engineering challenges and yet it is often characterized as being resistant to change. Crossrail, currently the largest construction project in Europe, has taken a pioneering initiative and introduced an innovation programme, Innovate18. This chapter explores the impact this innovation programme has had in terms of the changes that have resulted within the Crossrail organization and whether the initiative has provided a catalyst for change in the wider industry. The conclusions may provide lessons for the management of change in organizations and within an industry.

The Crossrail innovation programme

Crossrail is a £14.8 billion project that will deliver a new east–west railway across London (Figure 16.1). It comprises 42 km of bored tunnel, 8 new underground stations, 100 km of upgraded over-ground rail line and 30 upgraded surface stations.

Once operational, the Elizabeth Line will deliver 24 trains per hour, so increasing London's rail capacity by 10 per cent. Each 200[th]m long train will comprise nine air-conditioned, Wi-Fi enabled coaches and will carry 1,500 passengers.

Figure 16.1   The Crossrail route

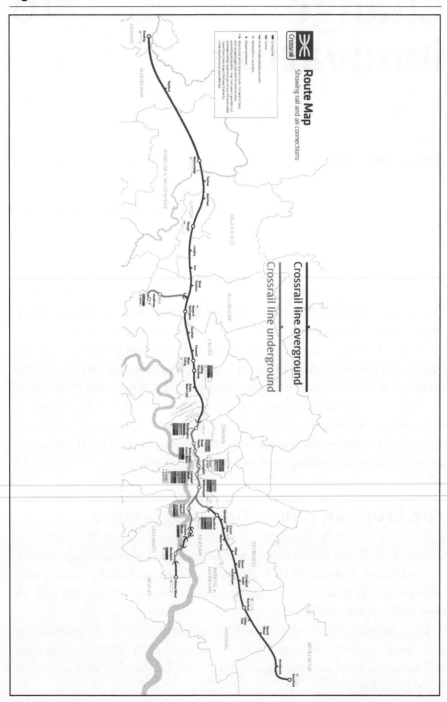

SOURCE Crossrail Ltd

Crossrail recognized an opportunity to lead UK construction industry innovation by sharing ideas from all those involved in the project. Innovate18 grew from a partnership with Imperial College, which developed an innovation strategy for Crossrail (Crossrail, 2013). Davies *et al* (2014) set out the genesis of the programme, describing its application in the 'leveraging' innovation window. Innovate18 is based around the three 'Cs' of Collaboration, Culture and Capability. Fundamentally it is about collaboration, enabled by the unique funding mechanism adopted by the programme. Each chief executive/managing director was personally invited by Crossrail Ltd's chief executive to join Innovate18 by investing £25,000 and agreeing to participate in the open sharing ecosystem that it involves. In return, Crossrail agreed to match fund the investment. This encouraged the contractors' active engagement in the programme. Although an essential prerequisite, it was not, however, sufficient.

Therefore, an innovation team of four people was set up by Crossrail, under the direction of the Strategic Projects Director, to bring the innovation programme to life across Crossrail's work sites. The team established a network of over 140 innovation 'champions', people who were prepared to take on this additional role and lead the innovation activity. These champions then identified and supported the 1.000+ innovators that provided the innovation 'engine room'. This geographically dispersed group represented around 10 per cent of the entire workforce. Drawn from across Crossrail's organizations, it was brought together by a common desire to try out new ideas as part of an open sharing environment. The mantra was 'pinching with pride', that is, any idea could be 'pinched' by anyone provided they improved it and shared the results.

All this activity was enabled by a web site, the 'Innovate18 portal', which allowed ideas to be uploaded, shared and discussed via a blog, underpinned by a basic relational database. The software rapidly became the only universal sharing mechanism on Crossrail. To complete the picture, a 'light touch' governance process (Figure 16.2) was established to process the ideas that required funding from the innovation fund. The resulting 'mini-projects' were delivered by innovation champions/innovators or the innovation team.

Since Innovate18 was launched in April 2013, it has triggered over 1,000 innovations. An independent benefit assessment completed in 2015 (Vernet, 2016) assessed the likely return on the investment to be around 3th:[th]1 by the half way stage. The increasing maturity of the programme during its second half should allow the final ratio to be more than twice that figure. The report noted that there were also significant unquantified benefits around

Figure 16.2   The Crossrail Innovation Programme governance process

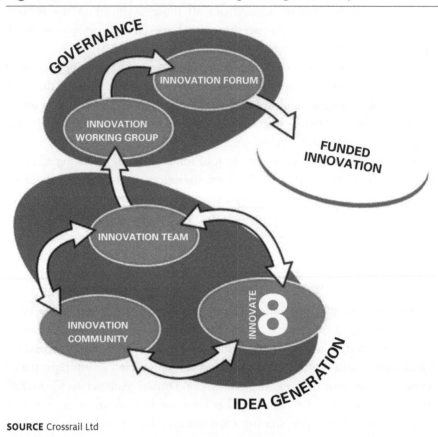

SOURCE Crossrail Ltd

collaboration, motivation and performance. The success of Innovate18 has resulted in demands for an industry approach building on Crossrail's legacy. Therefore, Crossrail began migrating the concept into an industry platform which allows sharing across the major infrastructure programmes.

Leadership

In 2014, Crossrail was awarded the NEF Innovisions award (www.thenef. org.uk) for innovation by a public sector programme. Crossrail also won the 2014 British Construction Industry Award for programme management for its collaboration and innovation. But why did it take so long for innovation to be appreciated and why did it not emerge until four years after the start of the Crossrail project?

'In delivering London's new east to west railway, we hope to raise the bar in the construction industry, now and for future projects. To achieve that, we need to think differently about how we share ideas and implement them.' (Andrew Wolstenholme OBE, Chief Executive Crossrail)

The Latham (1994) and Egan (1998) reports considered how to overcome the construction industry's poor reputation for delivering on time and budget by developing new ideas and learning, and also by adopting successful practices from other industries. Both reports emphasized the need for innovation. Later, Wolstenholme (2009) restated the earlier reports' findings, again emphasizing the need for innovation, while the Armitt Review (2013) attributed the success of the London 2012 infrastructure delivery to, *inter alia*, the transfer of innovation from the Channel Tunnel Rail Link (HS1) and Heathrow Terminal 5. Some of this systemic learning benefited Crossrail during its procurement process. The NEC3 contracts also encouraged innovation and collaboration through incentivization and risk sharing.

However, the decisive factor for Crossrail was Andrew Wolstenholme's key role in initiating the innovation programme by engaging Imperial College and setting up a Crossrail team to deliver it. He provided the strategic direction and executive support needed. He invested at risk throughout the formative stages of Innovate18 and also championed the programme, its successes and potential benefits. However, while the chief executive's role was key, he was not the only leader that ensured its survival in its early stages and at a time when detractors could have snuffed out the flame before it had 'caught' and demonstrated its potential. The Tier 1 contractors were key partners in the process, and the support of chief executives across the supply chain sent a powerful message to people on Crossrail and across the industry. The innovation leads from several of the Tier 1s also played key roles in active engagement in the programme.

Academia too played a role: without the personal commitment of Professor David Gann and his team from Imperial College, together with the consistent support of the Cambridge Centre for Smart Infrastructure and Construction (CSIC, an Innovation Knowledge Centre funded by EPSRC and Innovate UK), the programme would have struggled.

Finally, the young team from Crossrail and its programme partner Transcend (a JV comprising CH2M, Nichols and AECOM providing programme management services) showed leadership and strength of character. They took this novel and often contentious concept into the canteens, work sites and offices across the programme in their efforts to practise their passionate belief that innovation is essential to the industry.

The time was right to introduce Innovate18 in 2013, but it still took a strong client lead to unlock its potential. Once the strategic direction was provided, contractors, academia and Crossrail Ltd personnel took up the challenge. However, it was not always easy, and required a sustained effort to ensure that progress was maintained. The challenge for the future is to maintain the industry-level leadership to sustain the process beyond the immediate future.

People and behaviours

The construction industry's reputation is for adversarial behaviours, disputes and a philosophy of 'go in cheap and make it on the claims'. The 1990s saw a dramatic shift in thinking with the evolution of approaches such as partnering, set against the backdrop of Latham and Egan's recommendations. The emergence of the NEC3 contract enabled incentivization, rather than punishment. It also established the criticality of behaviours and set a collaborative context for successful innovation. Innovate18 focused on collaboration, which defines the culture and the capabilities required to support the programme (Figure 16.3).

Figure 16.3   The '3Cs' that enabled Innovate18

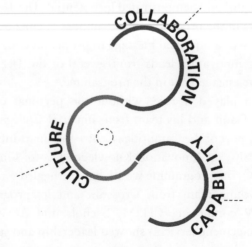

SOURCE Crossrail Lt

Crossrail's leadership commitment ensured senior engagement and enabled innovation by people, secure in the knowledge that they were supported by committed leaders. The 50 per cent gain share incentive in the NEC3 target cost contracts was also a key factor. However, the novel nature of a programme such as Innovate18 can also lead to risk and change aversion, and so there was a need for a 'nudge' to start the process. Andrew Wolstenholme's challenge to the Tier 1s to co-invest provided the necessary encouragement and at the same time created the funding to provide the innovators with the confidence that investment funds were available. This approach encouraged all the major Tier 1 companies to join Innovate18, creating an innovation fund and committing them to the programme's future. This modest investment enabled personnel from each company to become involved in Innovate18 with confidence.

The next challenge was to mobilize the potential of everyone working on Crossrail. The innovation team was allocated four positions: programme manager, knowledge manager and two innovation 'coordinators'. Their specific roles reflected the programme's needs. All team members were also assigned the task of visiting the Crossrail projects. Their mission was to find 'innovation champions'; that is, people prepared to be Innovate18's agents and then help them develop networks of innovators on each site.

Techniques varied between sites depending on the work, the contractor's culture and the people involved. However, they were all essentially face-to-face personal engagements, often over coffee or 'bacon buttie breakfasts', but included forums through to full workshops. Initially they remained site focused, but gradually expanded to sharing and exchanging ideas between different sites. The coordinators rapidly built their networks and quickly identified areas of acceptance and resistance. Engagements had to be tuned to the people and context: there was no templated standard solution. Sometimes it did not work, usually due to a lack of leadership interest or a challenging site context. However, for most, it was a highly successful approach, with 140+ innovation champions and 1,000+ innovators, nearly 10 per cent of Crossrail's workforce engaging with Innovate18.

Why did people become so involved? Some felt it their duty; some saw an opportunity to experiment, to do things differently and better. Many became passionately and energetically involved; some became 'serial innovators' delivering many new ideas. Others were caught up by the enthusiasm and engaged with energy. The small innovation team and the champions were disproportionately effective in fanning the sparks of innovation into flames.

After three and a half years, there were over 1,000 ideas on the innovation database. Of these, 300+ have been shared between sites or contracts and over 130 have received funding, representing around £500,000 at the time of writing with a further £250,000 available during the programme's final year.

Some interesting correlations began to appear. The most successful innovation sites were also the highest performers overall (Figure 16.4). While not a cause-and-effect relationship, there was an evident symbiosis between the behaviours for innovation success and those that deliver project performance. The implication is that a focus on the conditions for innovation can also improve performance. Examples include process innovation, erection of a reinforced earth wall enabling a significant production rate increase, halving construction time and enabling completion on time and without penalty. In another case, the discussions around safety innovation played across some difficult interfaces, highlighted some interesting innovation activity (hydrogen-powered lighting towers) and triggered discussions which led to an innovation coordinator engaging with the workforce around further innovation.

Above all else, it became apparent that people are at the heart of innovation. If excited by the opportunity and supported and encouraged, then they

Figure 16.4   Performance assurance data for Crossrail's projects showing generic (cost/schedule) project performance against innovation activity)

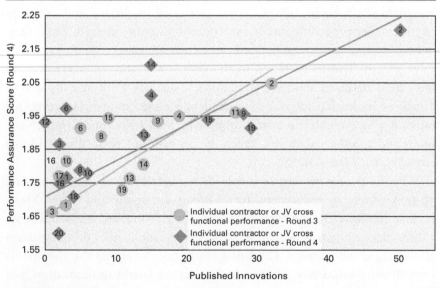

SOURCE Crossrail Ltd

will commit. They will often work together with an unexpected passion and will also share, support and build on each other's ideas. Unleashing this wave of positive, constructive behaviour allowed changes to endure and the organizational culture to evolve.

Resistance

Barriers can, and do, exist and must be realistically assessed. One that had been greatly anticipated was the protection of intellectual property (IP). The concern was that people would be protective, either of their own 'invention' or of releasing ideas across organizational boundaries. Therefore, the innovation programme stated from the start that where a specific form of IP, for example a patent or copyright, existed, then Crossrail acknowledged that it had a legal and ethical responsibility to respect it.

However, Crossrail also challenged the contractors and its own staff to share ideas developed through Innovate18. The mantra 'pinched with pride' (having been 'pinched with pride' from the safety community) was adopted as a *crie de coeur* for sharing ideas and improving them, rather than stifling them under IP protection. In essence, Innovate18 challenged Crossrail's supply chain to accept that the collective benefit of sharing ideas was greater than that due to protecting ideas for individual organizations' gain. With effective leadership and constant effort by the team on the ground, the principle was largely upheld: forums that engaged people from across organizations demonstrated the benefits. The contractors' ability to realize value away from the programme, based on the learnings and innovation from Innovate18, helped to reinforce their engagement.

There were detractors, both people and organizations. Some rejected ideas 'not invented here'. Some just did not tune in: some people were uncomfortable with the programme style; those who found the, often loose, approach challenging; those who were reluctant to share. Innovate18 specifically sought to manage one specific group: those engaged as project managers or key decision makers at programme level. These were people whose responsibilities spanned across projects, who had the heaviest workloads and who most needed to prioritize and delegate their activities. They also proved the most likely to see innovation as non-core activity and become inadvertent blockers.

Therefore, the innovation programme included a separate 'light touch' governance process. This enabled agile and responsive decisions for innovations that required and merited investment. Some middle management saw the merits and became supporters, even innovation champions in some cases. Many did not, but tolerated the innovation activity, a reluctance that is probably an inevitable consequence of the combination of an intense workload and an industry culture that is slow to change. Crossrail, through Innovate18, has started that change: success may ultimately be judged by deeper penetration of the management behaviours on future projects.

Commercial boundaries also created problems. Some organizations decided to adopt other solutions; for example, Six Sigma process improvement. In one particular case, the organization was very averse to 'programme money' being invested in match funding the innovation programme and yet its people were some of the most active and productive innovators. At times the commercial tensions were simply too strong for innovation to flourish. Innovate18 relied on willing commitment based on a shared understanding of the mutual benefits. It was never a coercive or contractual activity, and so whenever the resistance became too strong the response was to refocus effort to where the greatest value could be delivered.

Success in overcoming these barriers should be set against the industry context. In construction, as elsewhere, the structure of the industry itself and the resulting commercial construct have become barriers. Risk aversion across the industry, including clients, design consultants and contractors, remains high and can limit the exploitation of innovation opportunities. The lack of research and development investment may also be a contributory factor, with the industry as a whole investing as little as 0.05 per cent of revenue compared with, for example, manufacturing, which can exceed 5 per cent (Casey and Hackett, 2014).

Benefits

The case for change starts at an industry level. The UK's construction industry is a mature and technologically advanced industry supported by a world-class academic base. It is engaged in numerous major programmes which provide an opportunity for change. and in Construction 2025 it was presented with a timely 'call to arms' (Construction 2025, 2013). The industry attracts the brightest and best people (though arguably not enough of them), and has a demonstrable capacity to provide innovative solutions.

However, the industry is also fractured, comprising a multitude of companies operating across the infrastructure lifecycle and value chain. The commercial climate, despite Latham, Egan and Wolstenholme, still features low margins, and there is a constant forming of new joint ventures, making start-ups the most common organizational form at the commencement of a project; an inherently wasteful approach. Despite the manifest efforts of the various representative bodies, the industry still lacks a coherent approach to innovation, research and development. The information revolution, which previously transformed sectors such as aerospace and automotive, has now reached the infrastructure sector, and bodies such as the Construction Leadership Council (created in 2013 to identify and deliver actions, between industry and government, supporting UK construction in building greater efficiency, skills and growth) are creating an awareness of the need to work together to change and compete against international competition. However, companies must make a profit and clients must stay within their budgets. Therefore, demonstrating value to the supply chain as well as to clients is essential if innovation is to become an industry change dynamic.

Crossrail asked its supply chain to take a leap of faith by investing in Innovate18. The risk was minimized by the relatively low level of investment required, and most companies were able to sign up immediately. For some, what followed was about recovering their investment; for others, it was about the potential return; for some, it was about committing to change in the industry; while for others, it was simply about being in the club. Crossrail took the view that all of these were fine as long as the companies joined and that the programme showed the benefits, which is where the challenge really began.

The academic advice was that tracking benefits would distract from the main effort, which was to encourage innovation. This reflected pragmatism at the start, allowing a focus on generating numbers of innovations irrespective of each one's value, emphasizing the value of mass, rather than focusing on a small number of potentially successful ideas. This approach also tolerated failure and encouraged experimentation. Failure was considered an essential part of innovation. To assess every idea's benefit early in the development cycle risked switching off maturing innovations or ideas that could inspire others. Later, specific innovations did have to demonstrate a business benefit, but only once they had shown potential and required further investment. Therefore, Innovate18 declared financial benefits only at a programme level. In 2013, the metric for performance was simply the number of ideas and was tracked monthly (Figure 16.5). The results showed that there was sustained innovation effort throughout the programme. It also provided some interesting insights. For example, the programme launch coincided with the arrival of the 2013 graduate intake: a group that brought fresh thinking, energy and enthusiasm to Innovate18. They were a significant factor at the start of the programme.

Figure 16.5   The cumulative number of innovations for Innovate18

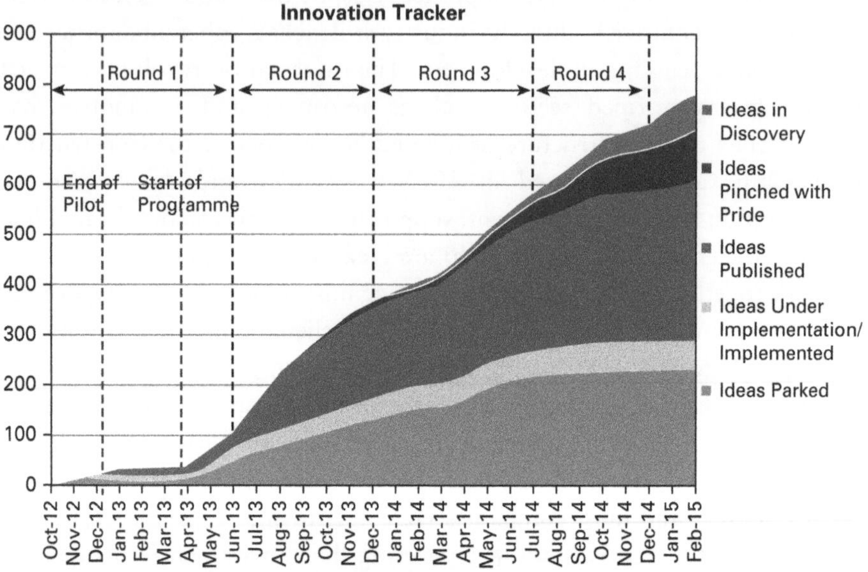

Innovation Tracker

Legend:
- Ideas in Discovery
- Ideas Pinched with Pride
- Ideas Published
- Ideas Under Implementation/Implemented
- Ideas Parked

Labels: Round 1, Round 2, Round 3, Round 4, End of Pilot, Start of Programme

SOURCE Crossrail Ltd

Once Innovate18 was established, the focus shifted to the benefits. The programme had been triggered by a desire to benefit from sharing ideas. Therefore, it seemed sensible to develop a metric that reflected the rate of sharing. This became the Crossrail programme-level key performance indicator (KPI) for innovation and was calculated as follows:

$$KPI(\%) = (\text{Published Ideas} + \text{Implemented Ideas}) / (\text{Total Ideas} - (\text{Invalid Ideas} + \text{Duplicate Ideas}))$$

The underlying message was that this was idea sharing that would not necessarily have taken place without Innovate18. Therefore, Innovate18 can be considered to have brought benefit to Crossrail through the efficiencies achieved by sharing. The KPI variation across the programme suggests that sharing was achieved (Figure 16.6). It also suggests that Innovate18 was beginning to erode some established barriers across the programme: a welcome change!

As was seen earlier, the correlation between innovation and performance has also been tracked during the progress of the programme (Figure 16.4). The data show a consistently positive correlation that has remained broadly unchanged over the programme. Interpreting these data is not easy as, even with the scale of Crossrail, it is still a small statistical population. However,

Figure 16.6   The Crossrail innovation KPI (%) variation by period. Note the KPI is reset at the start of each year as the KPI is a Crossrail Programme KPI for in-year performance only

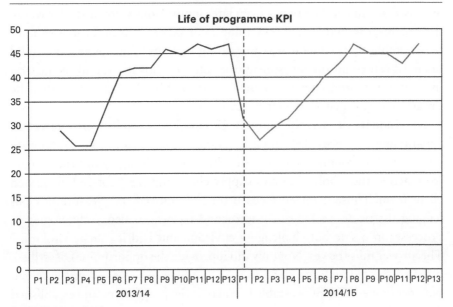

SOURCE Crossrail Ltd

there are some projects where performance has improved and innovation has followed the trend. This bears out the considered view that there is a link between effective leadership and innovation.

The programme has encouraged people to innovate and also to share across boundaries. The statistics also showed a positive correlation between performance and innovation. The programme has been praised for its courageous initiative and its pioneering role in the industry. But even at this stage there was still no proof that it was delivering against the bottom line – and, notwithstanding the initial stance, money has a persuasive power of its own.

Therefore, in early 2015, Crossrail commissioned Imperial College to carry out an independent assessment of the Innovate18 benefits. This study highlighted that 'there are a number of intangible benefits, such as Health and Safety benefits, behavioural benefits associated with an innovative culture, increased collaboration and team building, which should not be underestimated and are probably as important as financial benefits' (Vernet, 2016, p 3). It also provided the first estimate of the programme value in financial terms and suggested that the benefit-to-cost ratio was in the order of 6 or 7 to 1, extrapolating to the end of the innovation programme. This remains a conservative estimate, and the potential saving of around

£20 million is expected to be higher. A valuable lesson was learnt: the need to baseline innovations to enable the value to be more easily quantified.

From early 2015, several baseline techniques were used and more reliable assessments of the savings from later innovations were made. However, despite this, the study could only value some 20 per cent of the innovations. It is notable that, while it was reassuring to know that there was a solid financial return on the investment, the rate of innovations and the general interest in the programme remained unaffected by the knowledge that the programme was generating efficiency savings.

So visionary leadership allowed Crossrail to establish an innovation programme that provided opportunity for over 1,000 people to innovate and share. It encouraged collaborative behaviours, bringing together people from across the whole Crossrail supply chain and the Crossrail integrated client team. Those involved focused on and enjoyed the pleasure of challenging the norm, seeking new ideas and trying out new technologies or processes in a safe but challenging environment. Did it change Crossrail? The answer must be yes. Not only did it provide the opportunities described, but also created an 'ecosystem' in which innovation was not just accepted but encouraged. This was established across the programme and established Crossrail's reputation as a pioneering programme that encouraged innovation in everything.

For Innovate18, there were indirect actions that provided additional reinforcement of success. First, the Thames Tideway Tunnel project adopted the concept with some refinements: the ultimate 'pinched with pride' moment! As Innovate18 approaches the end of Crossrail, its portal is now shared with Thames Tideway as equal partners in seeking to share and improve through innovation. The second was the decision by the smart infrastructure and innovation sub-group of the Construction Leadership Council to propose, in October 2015, that the Crossrail Innovate18 programme be developed into an industry platform as an 'early win' in seeking to transform the industry and the council into becoming world-leading exemplars.

Developing an industry platform requires a different approach from that taken when only Crossrail was involved. The Construction Leadership Council workshops proved a valuable starting position by engaging the support of key industry leaders. An initial consultation with other major programmes suggested a number of principles that should apply:

- The ownership of innovation activity by a programme is a strong motivational force in the process, which should not be lost in developing an industry model.

- The need for strong leadership at both programme and industry level remained axiomatic.

- Sharing of innovation remains a primary activity – the 'pinched with pride' mantra should be sustained.

- Clients should lead the process and, in particular, provide the industry lead. However, any forum should also involve the supply chain.

- Funding would initially be the preserve of the contributing programmes, but the platform raises the possibility of pan-industry cooperation through responding to a common need.

- The central management of the platform, essentially managing the innovation-sharing database and secretariat roles, should be delivered by a non-aligned organization.

The first steps in this process are now happening, with the launch of the Infrastructure Industry Innovation Platform (I3P) – **www.i3p.org.uk** – on 18 October 2016 with 23 founder members including six major project clients. In the current context of rapid technology advancements and ever-greater pressure for cost and time efficiencies, the trend towards a more united industry approach, drawing on similar experiences from the aerospace and automotive industries, creates the ideal conditions for an industry innovation platform and in due course a greater emphasis on innovation and research and development. A spark of innovation struck during the midst of the Crossrail programme appears to have caught, and the flame has the potential to build into one of the most radical and challenging change programmes the infrastructure/construction industries have seen for a long time.

Conclusion

Crossrail, as the largest construction programme in Europe, has set a number of precedents, including developing the first systematic approach to innovation seen on a modern construction project. The programme, Innovate18, has been running for over three years, has involved over 1,000 people, generated over 1,000 ideas and innovations and been widely acknowledged as a highly successful initiative.

People are at the heart of Innovate18 and, therefore, effective leadership is axiomatic to its success. On Crossrail, this was provided by the chief executive, the leadership of the Tier 1 contractors, through the innovation programme team and the innovation champions drawn from across the

Crossrail organizations. Developing Innovate18 into an open innovation environment required a high degree of collaboration. This was enabled by the commitment and co-investment of the senior leadership and complemented by the intensive efforts of the innovation programme team to energize the innovation network into freely sharing its ideas and innovations.

There was resistance. Some resisted sharing; others were uncomfortable with the style of the programme; commercial boundaries intervened on occasions; and the sheer pressure of work on a busy project such as Crossrail inhibited commitment and consideration to innovation. Given the history of the construction industry, none of these were considered to be surprising. However, the benefits that began to accrue from Innovate18 helped to overcome the detractors. A strongly positive benefit-to-cost ratio likely to be more than 7:1 was demonstrated. The sustained rate of innovation, together with a high rate of sharing, showed its popularity with the people working on Crossrail, and engagement also proved to be symbiotic with high all-round performance.

Visionary leadership, a sound strategy and effective implementation ultimately combined to create the required collaborative environment on Crossrail. Together, they enabled this pioneering initiative to change the way that people responded to the construction environment. By migrating the concept into a platform shared between projects, it has also begun to expand the change process into the wider industry.

Key questions

In considering their own organizational change, readers may wish to reflect on the following questions:

- Is there genuine leadership commitment to change? If not, how should you go about creating the conditions for change? If there is the right leadership, how should it be supported and nurtured?

- Are the governance conditions right? Is the level of governance sufficient to provide the necessary scrutiny and assurance but not such that it constrains the organizational innovation processes?

- Will the proposed change align with the organizational context and culture? For example, if the organization is a temporary one, such as a programme or project, does the approach to innovation and change reflect this?

- Is the vision for, and purpose of, the change clear and does it provide a compelling reason for introducing it?

- What organization change is needed to design, implement, manage and then internalize the changes?
- Are the benefits understood and shared within the organization?
- What is the most appropriate way of measuring performance?

References

Armitt CBE, J (2013) [Accessed 10 February 2016] *The Armitt Review – An Independent Review of Long Term Infrastructure Planning Commissioned for Labour's Policy Review* [Online] http://www.yourbritain.org.uk/uploads/editor/files/The_Armitt_Review_Final_Report.pdf

Casey, M and Hackett, R (2014) [Accessed 10 February 2016] The 10 biggest R&D spenders worldwide. *Fortune*, 17 November [Online] http://fortune.com/2014/11/17/top-10-research-development/?iid=sr-link1

Construction 2025 (2013) [Accessed 10 April 2016] *Industrial Strategy: Government and industry in partnership* [Online] https://www.gov.uk/government/uploads/system/uploads/attachment_data/file/210099/bis-13-955-construction-2025-industrial-strategy.pdf

Crossrail (2013) [Accessed 10 April 2016] *Crossrail Innovation Strategy* [Online] http://learninglegacy.crossrail.co.uk/documents/innovation-strategy/

Davies, A *et al* (2014) Making innovation happen in a megaproject: London's Crossrail suburban railway system. *Project Management Journal*, 45 (6), pp 25–37

Egan, J (1998) [Accessed 10 February 2016] *Rethinking Construction – The Report of the Construction Task Force* [Online] http://constructingexcellence.org.uk/wp-content/uploads/2014/10/rethinking_construction_report.pdf

Latham, M (1994) [Accessed 10 April 2016] *Constructing the Team – Final Report of the Government/Industry Review of Procurement and Contractual Arrangements in the UK Construction Industry* [Online] http://constructingexcellence.org.uk/wp-content/uploads/2014/10/Constructing-the-team-The-Latham-Report.pdf

Vernet, A (2016) [Accessed 24 May 2016] *Crossrail Innovation Programme Innovation Benefits Evaluation Report* [Online] http://learninglegacy.crossrail.co.uk/documents/crossrail-innovation-programme-evaluation-report/

Wolstenholme, A (2009) [Accessed 10 April 2016] *Never Waste a Good Crisis – A Review of Progress Since Rethinking Construction and Thoughts for Our Future* [Online] http://constructingexcellence.org.uk/wp-content/uploads/2014/12/Wolstenholme_Report_Oct_2009.pdf

PART 2
The future of organizational change – opinion pieces from future thinkers

Opinion piece 1   17

The future and change

IRA BLAKE

Introduction

The way organizations do business is under intensifying scrutiny and increased pressure from government, consumers and campaigners to be more accountable. In the wake of multiple scandals, from unethical banking practices, misrepresentation of profits and tax evasion to a rising expectation of ecological sustainability and conscience, an unprecedented and sustained period of great change, innovation and commercial challenge exists.

Today, new workplace paradigms and drivers require organizations to make a fundamental shift from simply managing the numbers, closing gaps and managing performance, to building workplaces that people want to work in and feel they can contribute to and are appreciated. New-generation 'millennials' will own their portfolio-style careers and will make judgements on who will get to benefit from their talent and where they want to work. Through their increased connectivism and digital connectivity, millennials will select companies that foster innovation and value the uniqueness of individuals.

The implications of this changing landscape on businesses and strategic thinking are driving a shift that is being mirrored in studies across leadership and management. Hlupic (2014) explores the concept of 'Management 2.0' and emphasizes the significance of people and purpose as the determining factors in successful organizations. She explains this as *People + Purpose = Profit (private sector)* or *Pride in Service (public sector)*.

What all of this tells us is that we need to challenge or 'disrupt' our current way of thinking about change and that we will require different and innovative approaches to organization change. Disruption in this context equates to building successful change efforts by making them open,

Figure 17.1   Evolution to Change Management 2.0. © Ira Blake

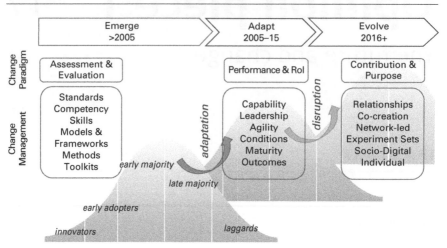

participatory and experimental; approaching change as a platform, and not a programme; mobilizing for emergent change, people-powered change and the co-creation of change through dispersed organizational networks.

Disruption can be viewed as a catalyst for changing the way change leaders and practitioners think about change. I believe it is one of many contributing factors creating a 'perfect storm', driving a fundamental change in both the direction and velocity of the way we deal with organizational change. This can be characterized as an inflection point (see Figure 17.1) representing the shift to Change Management 2.0.

Change management, like any function, service or discipline, is not static. Just a few years ago, change managers embraced, and adapted to reflect, a new methodology to become more agile (see Figure 17.1). However, this adaptation was still characterized by the same manifestation of change management, for example models, methods, toolkits, standards and so on. Most of what we currently do as change managers or practitioners is predicated on our current understanding, experience and assumptions about change.

Future change landscape

Social and technological shifts, such as social and enterprise networking, virtual organizations and the blurring of the line between work and life, are all changing the way people live and work. Research into neuroplasticity and workplace/environment psychology provides insight into how we learn, create and collaborate. This requires change practitioners to rethink their basic assumptions of communication, structure, location, roles and culture upon which today's organizations are designed.

By disrupting what we think we know about how people work best in organizations, we create the opportunity to design in individual and organization factors for success. These factors can be grouped under three key themes: competency, capability and contributing factors (see Figure 17.2). Each of the three themes applies and is controlled at different hierarchical levels within an organization. The development of competency is driven by individuals; capability – strategic and operational – is governed by the organization; contributing factors are external to organizational controls and include environmental, societal, cultural and technological enablers.

Figure 17.2 Individual and organization success factor model

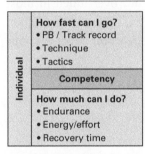

If we take the analogy of an athlete, they've done all their preparations, training, time-trials and have proved they have what it takes to get the job done. They've reached the necessary level of competency/qualification and now the athlete is standing at the starting line and has to initiate and deploy their race strategy – figuring out what *individually* they need to do, how and when.

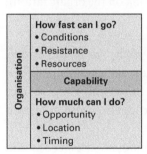

When formulating or selecting their race strategy, the individual has to evaluate the context or environmental factors that will influence how effective they can be – their operating landscape. What is in their favour and against them? Do they have the right equipment? What constraints exist that could influence how effective or successful they are? Is the right infrastructure in place to give them the best chance of success?

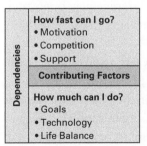

Individual athletes need to mentally rehearse their race strategies and be able to clearly picture themselves being successful. They need to be clear about their end goal, their reasons for doing this, who the threats are and how much help they can expect (human and technological) and what they are willing to compromise or trade-off to get there. By understanding the enablers and constraints to individual success, we also gain insight into the most significant determinants of change and organization success.

© Ira Blake

What this approach also shows is a direct correlation or relationship between individual and organization change. In our current constructs of change management, the ability of organizations to change is governed by their appetite and capacity for change, which is, in turn, constrained by their change capability, that is, the number of people with the specialist knowledge and skills. In the new Change Management 2.0 landscape, the complexity and unrelenting pace of change means that it can no longer be managed by a few 'experts'. Network-led change has the potential to exponentially expand capability within an organization, and the major constraint will be people's collective ability to absorb change, given existing bandwidth and workload.

Network-led change focuses on how we utilize and engage the collective asset we call employees. Neuroscience research, most notably by Itiel Dror and Amanda Kirby, highlights that our brains are not designed for 21st-century corporate life and that our cognitive mechanisms and natural ability to learn (neuroplasticity) are being stifled and overridden in most of today's organizations. The September 2015 CIPD 'Science of Human Behaviour at Work' conference reflected that our problem-solving brains operate most effectively when we are:

- given a clear picture;
- allowed time and space to understand;
- able to construct our own vision;
- engaged with and focused on vision (and not waiting on the organization);
- able to recognize our progress.

To stimulate and capitalize on people's natural ability to learn, leaders will be required to create opportunities for experimentation, positive reinforcement and recognition, and frequent practice. In turn, this will require employees to have space and reflection time to learn, engage and take individual responsibility for change.

New workplace models and ways to engage employees are needed and will require the development of specialist skills to leverage new opportunities, design new approaches and evaluate the effectiveness and sustainability of change.

In an environment of increasing ambiguity, greater regulation and risk mitigation, how will businesses create the space to transform? How will change management need to adapt to deliver within these new expectations of control, and what impact will this have on an organization's ability to absorb change – its resilience, capacity and response to organizational and environmental stress?

An organization's culture simultaneously shapes, and is shaped by, the context and environment. For transformation or disruption to be possible requires an internal culture that is receptive to, and promotes, a growth mindset. This growth mindset is characterized by mutual trust, aligned individual and corporate values, and diverse ways of working. Hope Hailey's (2012, 2014) research tells us that in times of uncertainty, trust becomes more important; and in the workplace, one distinct advantage of trust is its link to innovation. With innovation comes risk, and no one is going to take a risk unless they trust, and are trusted by, their immediate and senior managers. Workplaces with high levels of trust find it much easier to embrace organizational change – they can adapt faster and achieve better levels of employee engagement at all levels.

Organizational culture must also support the idea of:

● recognizing and rewarding contribution;

● ensuring that people have a clear line of sight between their endeavours and organization success;

● ensuring that people are valued for innovation and new applications of ideas.

I believe this all points to a future where organizations that build the individual into strategy and organization development will be rewarded by their people's energies, knowledge and creativity. This 'human dimension' is about:

● recognizing and valuing every person's unique contribution;

● putting relationships at the heart of the organization and enabling mutual responsibility;

● creating an environment for people to be their most creative and productive selves;

● being vulnerable, admitting mistakes and removing unnecessary pain.

Competency to contribution: the changing role of the change manager

The Change Management Institute (www.change-management-institute. com) defines a change manager as having 'mastery of the change principles, processes, behaviours and skills necessary to effectively identify, initiate and influence change and manage and support others through it'. This definition is robust because it remains relevant; it doesn't advocate managing change *per se*, and emphasizes the advisory, shaping aspects of the role that is manifested in Change Management 2.0.

'Change disruptors' such as Michelle Zanini (Management Innovation eXchange (MIX)) and Perry Timms (iPractice) may evangelize about the power of enterprise media platforms and the associated 'hackathons' that engage and co-create change through dispersed organizational networks and reject so-called change managers/experts as obsolete. My opinion is that this extreme view of the value of change management may work for a minority of entrepreneurial, forward-thinking and change-savvy organizations. However, the vast majority of organizations are still on a path to change maturity, that is, emerging or adapting (see Figure 17.1). This view is supported by the fact that as the velocity and density of change have increased – over the past few years especially – so have the emphasis on, and recognition of, professionalism and qualifications in change management.

In the Change Management 2.0 future qualifications, methods and toolkits will no longer represent competitive advantage (see Figure 17.3); they will simply be the hygiene factors which entitle change practitioners to get into the game.

Figure 17.3 Extract from Figure 17.1

Contribution & Purpose	The role of the change practitioner will necessarily migrate from manager to coach/advisor and their purpose will shift from delivering outcomes to navigating emergent changes in an
Relationships Co-creation Network-led Experiment Sets Socio-Digital Individual	adaptive change environment. Inevitably this will require a re-evaluation of competencies, and will place greater value on experience and expertise rather than rely on process, methodology and toolkits. This shift in emphasis will mean practitioner effectiveness will be determined on what they *don't* what they know.

Closing thoughts

There is a school of thought that we need to change the language we use to describe change management and change managers. New terms are emerging, including change disrupter, change architect, change maker, change adviser and so on. Regardless of what we call ourselves, the essential difference the terminology is attempting to highlight is the move from doing or delivering change to creating the environment, opportunities and space for change.

In the future, I believe that change practitioners may agree as a middle ground (or even as a transition) that to release the thinking, shaping and activities to make change happen, they will have to learn how to strike the balance between:

- relinquishing control without losing control;
- influencing towards an effective solution without stifling innovation;
- stimulating and nurturing creativity without diluting the purpose and strategy of the business.

New workplace models and ways to engage employees are needed, and we have to reinvent our change models, update competencies and develop new strategies for disseminating organization change. The capabilities, standards and toolkits, in which we invested so much, pave the way and equip us for Change Management 2.0; however, the deciding criteria for successful change practitioners will be their experiences, creativity and ability to influence the acceleration of the 'human dimension' in organizations.

References

Blake, I (2016) [Accessed 27 June 2016] Evolution and themes in change management: Change Management 2.0, 17 May [Online] https://www.change-management-institute.com/news-and-articles

Chartered Institute of Personnel and Development (2015) *Studies into Human Behaviour at Work*, London [Online] http://www.cipd.co.uk/research/behavioural-science

Hlupic, V (2014) *The Management Shift: How to harness the power of people and transform your organization for sustainable success*, Palgrave Macmillan, Basingstoke

Hope Hailey, V (2012) [Accessed 22 June 2016] Where has all the trust gone? *CIPD*, March [Online] www.cipd.co.uk/hr-resources/research/where-trust-gone.aspx

Hope Hailey, V (2014) [Accessed 22 June 2016] Cultivating trustworthy leaders, *CIPD*, April [Online] www.cipd.co.uk/hr-resources/research/cultivating-trustworthy-leaders.aspx

Opinion piece 2 18

Leading the agile organization

HEATHER BEWERS

Introduction

To date, change management has been seen as a project or a programme – something discrete and defined. In an increasingly VUCA world (volatile, uncertain, complex and ambiguous), change needs to become not a project but a core competence of the organization. In order to be able to respond (or even pre-empt) fast shifts in technology, customer demands, new competition or simply fresh revenue opportunities, the ability to change, almost in the moment, for staff to be empowered to make local decisions, for systems and processes to be agile and enabling rather than rigid and prescriptive, will be far more important than the ability to implement a single change programme. This overall corporate 'agility' will require a very different leadership style.

Drivers of change

So what's driving this need for agility? Different authorities quote a range of drivers but three (all of which are interdependent) occur regularly:

a The *pace of change* is visible to everyone. Moerdyk (2009) identifies that it took radio 38 years to reach 50 million users, TV 13 years, the internet 4 years and Facebook 2 years; today, for $1,000 and in 1 second, computing power equivalent to roughly a mouse brain is accessible; looking forward, by 2050–60 it is predicted that computing power equivalent to all the brains on the planet will be available for the same money/time. We don't consciously recognize the pace of change we are living through, nor are affected systems and structures adjusting within the same time-frames.

b *Technology*, and particularly mobile and digital technology, is creating the opportunity not just for new products and services (iPad, Oculus Rift virtual reality goggles, Tesla cars and drones are just some examples) but also facilitating an entire portfolio of new business models, especially those built to leverage platforms linking users/customers with suppliers/producers – think Airbnb, Uber or Etsy. Many of these are disruptive to incumbent organizations with their legacy systems and traditional approach.

c The *interconnectivity* of an increasingly digital network based on the internet means that companies are forced to respond to, or preferably pre-empt, external influences rather than simply controlling their internal environment. This connectivity can be beneficial – for example, crowdsourcing is increasingly used by a variety of institutions to provide fresh ideas, solutions and creativity (Kaggle, Foldit, Innocentive are just a few examples). Crowdfunding too has provided investors for everything from Oculus Rift through the Eden Project to the second Suez Canal. Equally, this interconnectivity can be a risk and threat as Quantas discovered when a false story spread over Twitter about one of its A380s crashing in Singapore (Stilgherrian, 2010) even before the plane had achieved its safe and normal landing there.

Corporate requirement for agility

The net result of all this is that companies need to be able to seize new opportunities and handle risks on a much more frequent and responsive basis. This impacts almost all aspects of organizational dynamics, but in particular:

- The discrepancy between the need for rapid decision making based on more data availability than ever before and hierarchies, reporting lines and approval procedures which currently assume a more relaxed time-frame. Automation, and the use of algorithms to drive decisions, is being promoted as one solution and regarded as a radical concept. In 2014, the Hong Kong-based hedge fund Deep Knowledge Ventures appointed an algorithm to its board of directors (BBC Technology news, 2014). The use of IBM Watson in medical diagnostics (and the creation of Watson Health as a major investment focus for IBM) represents enormous potential to change healthcare and provide incumbents with real-time data. Almost all organizations have access to more data than they use. The question, therefore, is how to turn those data into useful intelligence for change.

- Increasingly, organizations are recognizing that they no longer have all the answers within their boundaries, however large they are. As a result, many organizations are forming alliances (think ARM Holdings plc, which is a tiny company in comparison with many of its big technology partners but whose IP is central to the network), building corporate ventures (Diageo, Aviva are just two of many) to tap into start-up creativity, speed and entrepreneurial talent or converting themselves into more cooperative- type structures (Forbes publishing is now a platform open to 1,200 contributors rather than a centralized controlled hierarchy). All these options put a premium on an organization understanding their competitive advantage, the 'nugget' at the core of their business and what they do better than anyone else, and how that sits not only in their own value chain but in those of their potential collaborators.

- To achieve shifts in both of these areas, structures and hierarchies that create barriers, delays or a gulf between those facing the external world on a daily basis and those making decisions are having to be dismantled. Few organizations are going as far as implementing the principles of holacracy (Robertson, 2015), which creates peer working groups rather than hierarchical pyramids in a very formalized way, but increasingly companies are seeking to decentralize routine decisions to local management (for example, Whole Foods) and/or create multidisciplinary teams to make rapid decisions (P&G innovation was one of the first to bring together multi-functional teams). Collaborative tools such as social enterprise media (for example, Tibbr and Chatter) offer new ways to engage these virtual and remote teams.

Changing role of leaders

The good news is that it is not all an incremental burden on the leaders: instead, it is about doing less of some things and more of others.

Decentralizing and self-management mean fewer leadership decisions should be required at the centre and/or the top. Achieving this requires a big shift in mindset, which empowers local managers and staff to make clear decisions, and the criteria available for those decisions. So, for example, in relation to customer complaints, it would be extending the capacity of the customer service team. Many companies have already changed this – but not all employees see the accountability as theirs. And too often there is little clarity as to the overall direction of travel which those individual decisions are promoting. For example, is the end game to maximize revenue from an individual customer in the single transaction (ie decisions need to be focused around cross-selling, which potentially requires education and training), to create a long-term relationship (in which case selling may be the last thing needed) or is the customer to be a key evangelist for the service (support presumably may well be essential)? The change from one of these agendas to another remains the preserve and decision of the leader; how the detail of this translates at the coal face is often not fully developed, but it is essential to a decentralized decision-making process. In *Reinventing Organizations* (Laloux, 2014), such self-management goes hand in hand with greater consultation: the more important the decision, the wider (and higher) the consultation. However, the ultimate decision rests with the individual, not with those consulted.

Strategy is another key leadership activity which in the conventional sense may well be less relevant. In a rapidly changing world, to have a 5–10-year strategy may simply be a redundant exercise. Instead, strategic thinking needs to be done on a more fluid and frequent basis. Google revises its strategic priorities every 90 days, and there are now tools around, such as Shaping Tomorrow (www.shapingtomorrow.com), which are geared to a rapid review of external evidence and insight and which use technology and automation to help management focus on the real value-adding and subjective elements of the planning. More frequent review of strategy on this kind of basis may still involve less leadership time.

As many in change management know to their cost, change projects can be hugely demanding in terms of time and resources. Fewer discrete change projects and more agility built into the business can free up energy and resources at the leadership level and elsewhere. The combination of cloud computing, enterprise mobile apps and an increasing amount of low-cost, high-quality off-the-shelf capability (Dropbox, for example) means that the era of large-scale ERP-type implementation may be over – and those with current plans and projects may well find that these are overtaken by digital alternatives before their project expires.

So if leadership is doing less of the above, what is emerging instead? Role modelling and exemplifying the agility needed are critical. Driving the connectivity of the organization, and effectively removing the appropriate levels of corporate boundaries, is another. And finally, a leadership role is increasingly about people and relationships: to be a truly agile organization, the leader has to create an environment where everyone can be and is motivated to do the very best they can both inside and outside the organization.

Leaders need to create a culture where it is OK to experiment and fail (better than not to experiment at all) and where the development is about what good failure (a safe learning experience) looks like. This is by no means simple, and few companies are as open about it as Google: both Buzz and Google Glasses are examples of failing very publicly, but it is precisely by this method that the company progresses. Fostering curiosity and its companion humility to be constantly on the lookout for challenges, opportunities and ways to improve is another key aspect – but again not simple: how to create the time, space and resource for this, how to share knowledge in a way that means the sum is greater than the parts. And how to innovate effectively, to leverage those insights, is a further key component of agility.

Once daily decisions have been decentralized, those left to leaders are often the giant ones – when to change or even cannibalize the core business model, for example. Start-ups 'pivot' frequently (PayPal went through several iterations, starting life as PDA security software), but there are many examples of leaders being bold about change in established businesses too. For example, Nokia began life as a Finnish paper mill and moved on to manufacturing rubber goods before finally becoming the mobile phone giant. And those cases where the leaders should have pivoted and didn't are all too well known – think Kodak and Blockbuster.

The 'control' aspect of leadership is one that has very much been taken for granted in the past, and indeed most leaders recognizable outside their organizations are those very much associated with control: Steve Jobs is probably the most obvious example. And yet, for a company to be genuinely collaborative, to break down the company boundaries requires leaders to accept a lesser degree of control and potentially to work through mutual benefit and goodwill. Rarely are the collaborations mentioned above governed solely or even primarily by a legal joint venture agreement – it is instead about understanding the common ground and how to work together. Network Rail and the Samaritans have been working together for a few years around suicides on railways – a classic example of how both have a common aim, even though the strategic rationale for the institutions is very different. And increasingly, collaboration across the value chain is being seen as beneficial rather than competitive. McKinsey's report (2015) on the potential benefits of the circular economy in Europe discusses the multiple ways shifting from a linear supply chain to a circular economy can increase both revenues and profits – just one example of how collaboration will be key to driving growth and indeed agility in the future.

What does this all mean for people and the relationships between leaders and staff? Decentralized decision making and letting go of control implies huge trust on the part of leaders. It follows that 'people' cannot be the preserve of the HR function and processes; instead, leadership is responsible for setting the tone, culture and expectation across their workforce and externally too. Creating trust is critical, especially as, looking forward, there will be more and more speculation about automation and its impact on jobs.

Conclusion

The world is becoming ever more VUCA and as a result the operating environment is changing apace. The result is that internal change programmes, coordinated and controlled by reference only to internal criteria and priorities and done at a speed to suit the organization, are becoming a luxury that few companies can afford. Instead, the entire company needs to be able to respond, flex and potentially transform in response to, and in some cases ahead of, external factors. This requires not only a reappraisal of the systems, processes and policies but also a very different leadership style and culture. Rather than seeking to control all the resources required, networking and creating an ecosystem of collaborators may be one answer. Decision making needs to be faster and more disseminated. There is a much deeper need for trust to underpin empowerment and the decentralization of authority. And the organization needs to be fundamentally clear about what it stands for, and how much its operations can flex and seize opportunity without losing or damaging that central core. It is clear that the transformation from an established organization to one demonstrating agility is itself a major change, but only the first step needed.

References

BBC Technology (2014) [Accessed 15 April 2016] Algorithm appointed Board Director, BBC Technology News, 16 May [Online] http://www.bbc.co.uk/news/technology-27426942

HolacracyOne (2016) [Accessed 15 April 2016] Holacracy: how it works [Online] www.holacracy.org/how-it-works/

Laloux, F (2014) *Reinventing Organizations*, Nelson Parker, Brussels

McKinsey (2015) [Accessed 15 April 2016] Europe's circular-economy opportunity [Online] www.mckinsey.com/business-functions/sustainability-and-resource-productivity/our-insights/europes-circular-economy-opportunity

Moerdyk, C (2009) [Accessed 9 June 2016] It took radio 38 years to catch on; Facebook just two, *The Southern Cross* [Online] www.scross.co.za/2009/03/it-took-radio-38-years-to-catch-on-facebook-just-two/

Robertson, B (2015) *Holacracy*, Penguin Random House, Harmondsworth

Shaping Tomorrow [Accessed 15 April 2016] [Online] www.shapingtomorrow.com/

Stilgherrian (2010) [Accessed 15 April 2016] Timeline of misinformation: Twitter's plane crash down to human error, 5 November [Online] www.crikey.com.au/2010/11/05/timeline-of-misinformation-twitters-plane-crash-down-to-human-error/

Opinion piece 3 19

The shift from complicated to complex

HEATHER BEWERS

Introduction

Traditionally, change management has been a subset of project management, using many of the same tools and methodologies. Both rely heavily on a project (or indeed programme) plan with supporting relevant budgets, resource allocations, success and progress metrics and milestones, together with interdependencies and critical path analysis. As the operating environment of organizations becomes increasingly *complex* (where outcomes emerge on an unpredictable basis from multiple variables, both internal and external to the organization) rather than *complicated* (where multi-variable activities, however involved, are predictable – 'if this, then this' – and hence capable of planning, executing and controlling), this traditional approach may need to flex.

Traditional approach

Conventional change management is an approach that relies heavily on the underlying assumption that processes and structures to be changed are both rational and predictable – which, in the case of many businesses geared towards productivity and efficiency, has been a reasonable assumption to make. But there are circumstances where the approach is, even historically, notoriously less reliable. In early 2016, KPMG LLP (2016) indicated that 54 per cent of M&A executives agreed that cultural and HR integration was the most challenging area of merger integration. This is perhaps not surprising, since neither people, nor the collective culture they establish, are necessarily rational or predictable. To the extent that this has been addressed to date, there has been a tendency to identify the problem areas, and handle just those in a different way – for example, there are instances of crowdsourcing being used to help change to an innovative culture by engaging staff through seeking their ideas on how to change, save costs or drive revenue. But at larger scales, this type of solution is not necessarily feasible. The merging of two different cultures can be fraught with issues, many of which are not immediately obvious, since the parameters that give rise to them are often implicit rather than explicit in company analysis.

Just to take one example, merging a family-owned firm with a legacy of history and a long-term perspective on growth with a publicly owned entity with a schedule of quarterly or half yearly reporting and a commensurate focus on short term is likely to give rise to distinct problems. Some can be planned for – the reports, schedules and format of regular reporting can be introduced, but differences in the values behind decision making may only become apparent in the face of day-to-day resolutions needed. It may be possible to mark 'reporting schedule introduced' as green/implemented on the action plan – it will not always translate into smooth decision making on the same time frame (or ever in some cases). It may be that there is no easy agreement on the cost of working capital to use, or the length of payback to be met, but it could equally well be more fundamental and mindset oriented – a totally different perspective on the underlying rationale for investment, for example. Alternatively, the whole process could go really smoothly, simply because the respective investment managers happen to 'click' personally and work through their differences together. But the key point is that neither of these outcomes is predictable or guaranteed by a reductionist and deterministic process change focused on the structural and procedural elements alone.

A VUCA world

Why is this? And why does it matter to change management as we look forward? The answer is that the world is becoming more VUCA – volatile, uncertain, complex and ambiguous. The impact is that more of the change programmes as traditionally handled will have the hallmarks of people and culture issues – and, as a consequence, fewer will be susceptible to tidy action plans and success milestones. This is particularly true of the external operating environment, where connectivity is creating layers of interdependence and transfer of influence/control which are not necessarily capable of tidy planning looked at simply from the company's perspective. To explore what this means, think about the relationship with customers.

Look at Starbucks, United Airlines and a t-shirt company called Threadless. Back in 2012, Starbucks in the UK discovered that its public had a view on its company tax policy and on how much tax payment the company should be making in the UK. The blog post from Howard Schultz, Chairman, President and CEO of Starbucks, indicates just how seriously the company took that public opinion (Schultz, 2012) – he begins: 'Some of you may have been left with the wrong impression of Starbucks commitment to the UK.' It is clear that public perspective and conclusions have in this instance gone well beyond simply the tax policy to draw conclusions on the wider company. On a not dissimilar timeframe, there have been over 15.5 million views of 'United Breaks Guitars' (Carroll, 2009) on YouTube since the original launch around the issue – a response that far outweighs most planned advertising campaigns and which has benefited Dave Carroll far more than it has United Airlines. One small (from the company's perspective) instance of poorly handled baggage, and a reluctance to redress this through the usual complaints procedures, has escalated into a viral and very public statement of the company's now historic procedures. And to demonstrate that wider connectivity can be beneficial as well as opportunistic or creating risk, Threadless (2016) has built a business model around its customers providing designs for its t-shirts rather than commissioning expensive designers. All three examples indicate how interconnected these businesses are with their external audiences – and hence how sensitive to change those connections will be.

And it's not just customers and markets – Apple's App Store revenue is derived from products delivered by the Application Developers Network, none of whom are employees or suppliers to Apple Inc. Instead, they have a common interest with the company in publishing their apps – but they have alternative outlets through other phone companies that support the Android operating system, and Apple is not obliged to publish their apps.

The simple fact is that almost all organizations are now massively interconnected to their wider value chains and ecosystems (think how dependent most retailers are on their supply chains for just-in-time deliveries). And since external audiences will not necessarily (or even often) share exactly the same agenda, their response will often not be rational or predicable from the company's perspective. This interconnectivity and lack of predictability is a key characteristic of complex systems. Incidentally, complexity is not limited to the external environment, but suffice it to say that all sources of complexity are tending to require similar responses.

Impact on change management

The operating environment for change management is shifting fundamentally from *complicated*, where change has traditionally been handled in a reductionist (breaking it down into its component parts) and deterministic (a scheduled programme of specific process, structural and activity changes, which begins with the drivers (or causes) and delivers the desired outcomes (effects)) manner, to *complex*, where cause and effect are simply not determinable in advance and where local variations and context can create different and unpredictable outcomes.

This is not to suggest that all aspects of change management become complex, or that the entire project management capability is redundant. What it does mean is that a key part of the early change planning is to distinguish between those activities which are complicated and predictable (but still not necessarily easy to achieve!) and those which are more complex in nature.

In practice

For the latter, reducing the activity to set of component actions or processes, each of which is then programmed for change independently, is unlikely to be effective. Indeed, because cause-and-effect is not identifiable, the exact nature of the change needed, even at a holistic level, will need exploration. This need not be costly or time consuming – how often has a big systems implementation been done, only to find that a variety of teams around the organization are working their way around the system rather than using it in detail? The kind of insights from an analysis of why that's the chosen route is itself a form of exploration and probing, and will shed light on the type of changes that will be acceptable and effective for the local situation. For some cultures, the involvement of the relevant teams in the design is the right way to go; for others, a deeper understanding is needed of exactly where the real barriers are. Talking to the investment managers in the example above about exactly what they take into account, or how they go about making an investment decision, will help to identify early on where any differences lie, particularly if that is done jointly.

Together with a 'what if' discussion of options going forward, and an incremental approach to change (iterating/refining the process over time), this is more likely to create the desired outcome.

There are formal frameworks to help identify both the distinction between complicated and complex and the different ways to address these – Cynefin (Snowden and Boone, 2007) is one such. Here, the authors distinguish the complicated response – Sense, Analyse, Respond – from the one appropriate to complexity – Probe, Sense, Respond. As connectivity grows and complexity becomes more widely debated, expect to see more approaches, frameworks and decision tools becoming available.

Changing the mindset

But, as Boulton *et al* (2015) remark, handling complexity is more fundamentally about a change of mindset than necessarily doing things completely differently or needing a different toolkit. Curiously, as individuals, people are much more comfortable in their personal lives that not everything is predictable, and have a mindset that accommodates the potential for the unexpected much more readily. For example, holiday plans are made, but backed up with travel insurance and/or leaving a key with a neighbour – just in case. And planning is only done after exploration – for example, the TripAdvisor website is increasingly used as a way to explore (test) whether the destination looks like a great place to go before committing.

So, when it comes to change management in business, similar thinking is needed. There is a parallel here with *Thinking Fast and Slow* (Kahneman, 2011) and the distinction between the automatic System 1 brain pattern used all the time and the need to invoke the more analytical, more specific-to-the-situation System 2 thinking. The instinctive use of project management, the action plan and detailed scheduling needs to be tempered by adopting a more analytical and exploratory approach to ensure that those aspects which remain complicated are distinguished from the more complex at an early stage. Planning is still then appropriate, but more flexibility, more frequent checking can be built in to ensure that the plan is on track, especially around the complex elements. Pilot or test groups can be used in the early phases to check out the consequences of the change and to explore options before consolidating or scaling up for those areas. Above all, the plan will 'expect the unexpected' and build in contingency (budget, time or resource) to cope.

A quick note on language here: some of the issues around flexing change management methodology arise because words have become over-familiar and their meaning has shifted. 'Contingency' is a classic example: in a plan it is all too often greeted with 'if the plan's done properly contingency won't be needed', implying that it is some kind of balancing figure, when in reality a contingency means an unexpected (ie not capable of being planned for) event. In a complex world, with more unexpected events, genuine contingency will become more common, and potentially will require a larger part of the overall budget.

Conclusion

Change directors have long recognized that aspects of their programmes are not as susceptible to planning and prediction as others, people and culture being common instances. Looking forward, as the connectivity of organizations, their customers, employees and indeed all stakeholders increases, more and more aspects will fall into these problematic areas. That is the shift to complexity, accelerated by the rapid pace of change in the operating environment. The temptation is to separate out these specific aspects of the change programme; for example, crowdsourcing is being used to engage employees in some transformations today. But this incremental approach may not be sufficient. As complexity and rapid change become more and more the norm, the balance of the approach will need to flip in favour of exploration, validating and scaling up, with small elements of detailed planning embedded within the overall programme rather than the other way round as happens today – perhaps with an overall 'contingent' budget and smaller pools of money earmarked for small specific projects. Change management will assume a more iterative format as options are explored and decisions made to scale up change accordingly.

References

Boulton, J, Allen, PM and Bowman, C (2015) *Embracing Complexity: Strategic perspectives for an age of turbulence*, Oxford University Press, Oxford

Carroll, D (2009) [Accessed 14 April 2016] United Breaks Guitars (YouTube video) [Online] http://www.davecarrollmusic.com/music/ubg/

Kahneman, D (2011) *Thinking Fast and Slow*, Penguin Group, London

KPMG LLP (2016) [Accessed 14 April 2016] M&A Outlook Survey: infographic of key results [Online] http://info.kpmg.us/content/dam/info/ma-survey2016/images/kpmg-ma-outlook-2016-infographic

Schultz, H (2012) [Accessed 14 April 2016] Setting the record straight on Starbucks UK taxes and profitability [Blog], Starbucks.co.uk, 23 October [Online] http://www.starbucks.co.uk/blog/setting-the-record-straight-on-starbucks-uk-taxes-and-profitability/1241

Snowden, DJ and Boone, ME (2007) A leader's framework for decision making. *Harvard Business Review*, 85 (11), pp 68–76, 149. Available from https://hbr.org/2007/11/a-leaders-framework-for-decision-making/

Threadless (2016) [Accessed 14 April 2016] Threadless Design Challenges [Online] https://www.threadless.com/make/submit/

Opinion piece 4 20
The future and manufacturing

DAVID CADDLE

Introduction

Since the Industrial Revolution, Britain has been synonymous with innovation in engineering and manufacturing, and this innovation was an integral component to expanding the British Empire. There have been great pioneers in manufacturing and engineering: Richard Arkwright (textiles), George Stephenson (railways), James Watt (steam engines), Isambard Kingdom Brunel (rail infrastructure and steamships) and Frank Whittle (jet engine) are but a few.

From the early pioneering years in Victorian times we saw the introduction of mass production in the United States with Henry Ford, the founder of the Ford Motor Company and sponsor of the development of the assembly line technique. Although Ford did not invent the automobile or the assembly line, he developed and manufactured the first automobile that many middle-class Americans could afford. In doing so, Ford converted the automobile from an expensive curiosity into a practical conveyance that would profoundly impact the landscape of the 20th century.

In this chapter we will look at what manufacturing will look like in the future, addressing a number of areas, such as technology and innovation, market opportunities, skills and sustainability. To begin, we will look at why manufacturing is important to our economic wellbeing.

Importance of manufacturing to the economy

Previous UK governments have believed that the economy would survive and thrive with a heavy focus on the services sector, but the financial services sector crash in 2008 delivered an economic slowdown comparable to the 1930s depression. It is recognized that we need to rebalance the economy and that manufacturing plays a key role in long-term economic growth and economic resilience. It might surprise some that productivity growth of manufacturing outperformed that of services and the whole UK economy in the two decades to 2014 (EEF, 2016). Today, manufacturing benefits to the UK economy include:

- It contributes 11% to the economy: in 2012, it contributed £139 billion to the UK gross domestic product (GDP; PwC, 2013).

- It accounts for almost 75% of all R&D expenditure, compared with an average of 23% for other businesses (Awano *et al*, 2010).

- It employs some 2.6 million people directly, with many more in the associated supply chain.

- Fifty per cent of all UK exports are derived from manufacturing: £256 billion in 2012, compared with only 26% of non-manufacturers (Harris and Moffat, 2013).

- In 2011, remuneration in UK manufacturing was 10% higher in comparable occupations compared with the average across all industries, reflecting the high level of skills required in modern manufacturing roles (Foresight, 2013).

The UK manufacturing sector is diverse, with activities ranging from aerospace, automotive, pharmaceuticals and chemicals to food and drink. It is also characterized by a wide range of size of firms, with a disproportionate share of activity accounted for by a small number of large, often foreign-owned multinationals.

The future of manufacturing

The major trade body representing the sector in the UK, EEF (www.eef. org.uk), refers to the sector entering a new industrial age that will see big data (Columbus, 2014) and the internet of things play key roles in manufacturing. In 2013, the UK government published its Foresight report 'The Future of Manufacturing', which identified four key future characteristics of manufacturing:

1 technology and innovation;

2 exposed to new market opportunities;

3 increasingly dependent on highly skilled workforce;

4 more sustainable.

Technology and innovation

Manufacturing has traditionally been characterized as simply comprising the production process, that is, the conversion of raw materials into a finished product. Figure 20.1 shows the modern value chain, which includes the extended value chain rather than simply production, from research through to disposal and subsequent reuse, recycle and recovery. This also referred to as full lifecycle manufacturing.

Manufacturing technology in terms of plant and equipment stayed relatively constant throughout the 20th century until the advent of the integrated circuit, which completely turned the industry on its head. In the 1970s, computers started to enter the workplace. Initially, numerically controlled (NC) machinery started to appear on the shop floor to replace conventional manual machines, and quickly moved into all areas of manufacture: design, purchasing, test etc.

Computer-aided design (CAD) and computer-aided manufacture (CAM) are very much embedded in manufacturing, utilizing simulations to re-create the product in service, and now virtual reality is being deployed. The latest addition to this is 3D printing, which has been evolving since the 1990s; 3D printing, or additive manufacturing, is a process of making three-dimensional solid objects from a digital file. A 3D printed object is created using additive processes, laying down successive layers of material until the entire object is created. Each of these layers can be seen as a thinly sliced horizontal cross-section of the eventual object. Initially, 3D printing was seen as a way of producing prototypes quickly and more cost-effectively than traditional prototyping. It is now being seen as a method of producing production parts, and Rolls Royce is experimenting with producing jet engine components using this technology.

The entire digital capability, including sensory technology – electronic devices that monitor their surroundings and send signals to make something happen – is being brought to play in the extended manufacturing value chain. Robotics, long used in the production of cars, is now seeing its place in medium-sized businesses to replace laborious manual processes and other processes such as welding and assembly. On the logistics side of the value chain, automated guided vehicles can be seen buzzing around major distribution hubs and car manufacturing plants, collecting products to be collated and packed. The integration of sensors into networks of technology, such as products connected to the internet, will revolutionize manufacturing. New data streams from products will become available to support new services,

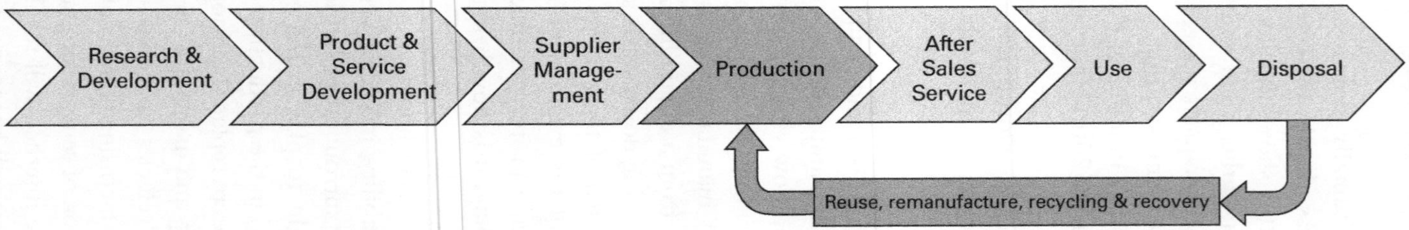

Figure 20.1 Simplified model of the modern model of manufacturing

enable self-checking inventories and products that self-diagnose faults before failure, and reduce energy usage.

The UK also has strong capability in developing new materials, including reactive nanoparticles, lightweight composites, self-healing materials, carbon nanotubes, biomaterials and 'intelligent' materials providing user feedback.

New market opportunities

In 2015, the UK's current account deficit was £96.2 billion, up from a deficit of £92.5 billion in 2014. The deficit in 2015 equated to 5.2 per cent of GDP at current market prices. This was the largest annual deficit as a percentage of GDP at current market prices since annual records began in 1948. The future of manufacturing will rely on exploiting more export opportunities outside its traditional European and US markets, so improving the UK's balance of payments and ability to continue as a leading developed nation. Germany's manufacturing sector accounts for more than double that of the UK, owing to its ability to export its reputation for high-end engineering and the reliability of its products – cars being a good example.

In recent years, the consensus has pushed UK exporters towards the emerging BRIC economies (Brazil, Russia, India and China). Recent analysis (EY, 2015) suggests instead that UK exporters, including manufacturers, need to shift their focus and have a more balanced portfolio, targeting high-growth and high-value markets (the ACE countries: America, China and Europe) and developing a stronger position in India.

Highly skilled workforce

Over the past decade, there has been concern over the impact of a possibly negative image of manufacturing among the public in the UK. There are similar concerns in the United States that manufacturing is seen as dull, dirty and dangerous. Negative attitudes to manufacturing can matter, particularly when these attitudes reflect an outdated perception which is being passed on to new generations of school leavers.

Most commentators cite skill shortage as being the main barrier to growth for manufacturing (Rowlands, 2008). New technology, manufacturing processes and process development require ever-increasing skill levels from both the current and the future manufacturing workforce; this in turn puts increasing demands on education and training institutions working collaboratively with business. Additionally, we have an ageing UK population and school leavers being encouraged to pursue a degree rather than embark on vocational careers. All these factors together have generated real concerns that skill shortages will constrain manufacturing growth. EEF's Skills Manifesto 2015 calls on the next government to prioritize sustained growth in the talent pipeline for manufacturing and for employers and higher education collaborating to play a greater role in driving forward the skills agenda. An example of manufacturing collaboration with higher education is Siemens and Lincoln University. We also need to continue to encourage children to embark on Science, Technology, Engineering and Maths (STEM) subjects at school.

The manufacturing sector of the future is likely to be characterized by:

- flatter management structures;
- a more highly skilled and IT-literate workforce capable of being reskilled in advanced technologies;
- working in multidisciplinary teams and having interdisciplinary expertise;
- soft skills for managing operations effectively;
- a better understanding of the customer.

Sustainability

Another key driver for the manufacturing sector is the natural environment. Interactions with the natural environment will be subject to a number of changes in the decades ahead:

- A growing and increasingly urban global population, predicted to be 3 billion by 2050, will raise demand for natural resources and influence the location of manufacturing (United Nations, 2013).
- Climate change is likely to increase the vulnerability of global supply chains and increase the pressure on manufacturers to reduce their greenhouse gas (GHG) emissions (Intergovernmental Panel on Climate Change, 2013). Climate change is firmly on the agenda for developed economies, a key component being to use less energy. Not only have manufacturers to ensure that products can be produced using less energy, but the materials have to be environmentally friendly and able to be reused or recycled. This is referred to as the *circular economy* and while initially seen as burdensome for non-enlightened manufacturers, it has spawned a new

sub-sector within the industry. We are also seeing symbiosis within the sector, where the by-product of a manufacturing process which would have previously been sent to landfill is being used by a completely different sector. One example is Denby, a manufacturer of household products in Derby. It had a problem with its ceramic waste, which was being sent to landfill at significant cost and environmental impact; after research, it now sends the ceramic waste to be recycled into aggregates to be used in the construction sector, with zero landfill as a consequence.

So the impact of sustainability for the future manufacturing sector to 2050 and beyond in a resource-constrained world can be summarized as:

- Products use smaller amounts of materials and energy.
- Material is not landfilled but is kept in a productive loop.
- Cleaner and quieter factories close to consumers and suppliers.

Conclusion

The sustainability agenda will be a big focus over the coming decades for manufacturing. The cradle-to-grave impact of a product will be assessed to ensure that it uses fewer scarce resources in design and production, and to ensure that it can be recycled or reused at the end of its useful life. The main scarce resource is oil, and the race is on to identify alternatives.

The new era of manufacturing will be marked by highly agile, networked enterprises that use information and analytics as skilfully as they employ talent and equipment to deliver products and services to diverse global markets. Identifying talent, developing skills and ensuring STEM skills will remain a priority. Highly talented skilled people are necessary to apply cutting-edge science and technology, systems thinking and smart services and processes effectively, across the entire modern value chain.

The future of the modern manufacturing value chain will continue to evolve, creating a multitude of challenges and opportunities for global manufacturing addressing technology, innovation, skills and where products are produced. The automotive sector, which leads on innovation in both product and processes, is already pushing the boundaries with trials of un-manned vehicles. Samsung (2016) predicts personal flying drones replacing cars and travelling holiday homes, as well as 3D printing of houses and furniture. All this sets a challenge for manufacturing to meet these future visions in a sustainable way.

References

Awano, G *et al* (2010) Measuring investment in intangible assets in the UK: results from a new survey. *Economic and Labour Market Review*, **4** (7), pp 66–71

Columbus, L (2014) [Accessed 29 June 2016] Ten ways big data is revolutionizing manufacturing [Online] www.forbes.com/sites/louiscolumbus/2014/11/28/ten-ways-big-data-is-revolutionizing-manufacturing/#7c5efc4e7826

EEF (2016) [Accessed 2 September 2016] Productivity: the state of the manufacturing nation [Online] www.eef.org.uk/resources-and-knowledge/research-and-intelligence/industry-reports/productivity-the-state-of-the-manufacturing-nation

EY (2015) [accessed 29 June 2016] Focus on the BRICs has hampered UK exports [Online] www.ey.com/UK/en/Newsroom/News-releases/15-11-09–Focus-on-the-BRICs-has-hampered-UK-exports-says-new-EY-report

Foresight (2013) *The Future of Manufacturing: A New Era of Opportunity and Challenge for the UK*, Project Report, The Government Office for Science, London

Harris, R and Moffat, J (2013) Investigation into trends in export participation among UK firms. UKTI Analytical Papers

Intergovernmental Panel on Climate Change (2013) *Climate Change 2013: The Physical Science Basis*, Cambridge University Press, Cambridge

PwC (2009) [Accessed 7 November 2016] The future of UK manufacturing: reports of its death are greatly exaggerated [Online] https://www.pwc.co.uk/assets/pdf/ukmanufacturing-300309.pdf

Rowlands, C (2008) [Accessed 22 June 2016] Report highlights trends in UK manufacturing 1997–2007 [Online] www.worksmanagement.co.uk/strategy-and-finance/news/report-highlights-trends-in-manufacturing/12848/

Samsung SmartThings (2016) [Accessed 22 June 2016] *SmartThings Future Living Report* [Online] www.samsung.com/uk/pdf/smartthings/future-living-report.pdf

United Nations (2013) [Accessed 29 June 2016] World population prospects, the 2012 revision [Online] www.un.org/en/development/desa/publications/world-population-prospects-the-2012-revision.html

Opinion piece 5 21

The future and local government

PETER GLYNNE

Introduction

The public sector has undergone radical change in recent years, primarily through a relentless focus on reducing public spending and ultimately the national budget deficit. Such radical change has impacted every public sector organization, ranging from significant job cuts to radical new ways of working to a greater reliance on external partners to deliver essential services. Much has been achieved along this journey and lessons learnt have significantly improved the change capability of the organizations involved. This scale and pace of change is unprecedented across government in the past fifty years.

Government is still facing significant challenges: the need to further cut spending, people are living longer, demographics are changing, national infrastructure requires major investment and the pressures on health and social care are ever increasing. Allied to this, economic competiveness is shifting to Asia, with China posing a continuing threat to the UK economy. There remains much more to achieve in the radical transformation of government, much of it dependent on the continued need to reduce the budget deficit, devolution and the opportunity to exploit the public sector's asset base to replace taxpayer funding with commercial income.

Ultimately, what does all of this mean for leaders of change across the public sector? There are six key factors driving the scale, pace and complexity of change across local government over coming years. They are described below.

1. Devolution of power

The biggest change agenda in local government for the next five to ten years is the devolution of power to cities and local areas. Devolving and decentralizing power and enabling local people to make decisions will create the conditions for sustainable growth, better public services and a stronger society. This is one of the most fundamental changes to government in the past fifty years and follows on from existing devolution to Scotland, Wales and Northern Ireland. The creation of the Greater Manchester Combined Authority in November 2014 and the concept of the 'Northern Powerhouse' have clearly heightened expectations across the UK. While this change agenda is still emerging, the challenge for public sector leaders is to respond with a fundamentally different approach to delivery of change under new models of local partnership and governance. Leaders of change across the public sector are planning their response through greater partnership, sharing of assets and looking at new ways to join up services at a local level. In this context, shared accountability for delivery of outcomes will become the norm, against the backdrop of significantly raised political expectations. Skill sets to lead such fundamental change successfully need to evolve to meet the already high expectations around devolution.

2. More joined-up government

Local government has undergone radical reshaping and cost reduction in recent years. This intense focus is shifting to other sectors of government, including central government and the NHS. Areas of overlap and duplication are being targeted to further reduce public spending and improve outcomes for the customer. For example, considerable work is taking place to enable the integration of NHS health and social care services at a local level; also the provision of local economic growth and targeting unemployment, currently led at a national level. The resultant change will, at the least, involve much greater partnership working; however, it is likely also to lead to merger and integration of government organizations under devolution. Are leaders of change across the public sector ready for such fundamental change, bringing together organizational cultures from across different sectors to deliver services at a local level? This challenge is to fundamentally rethink the approach to delivery, adapting to the complexity of bringing together services at a local level. Such organizations have significantly different organization cultures. For example, will the culture of organizations within the NHS seamlessly blend with those across local government? Much work remains to be done on integration of cultures and ways of working.

3. Further cost pressures and rationalization

In the past five years, local government has undergone radical reshaping, with significant budget cuts and fewer staff at all levels. Much has been achieved and the sector is considerably leaner than it was ten years ago, albeit with significantly less money to spend on services. Going forward, one thing is clear: the number of councils will reduce with mergers, integration and the need to share services. It is likely that staff numbers will further reduce across the sector as budgets are targeted for further spending reduction. There is a limit to what the sector can endure across a sustained long-term period; however, devolution and the policy for councils to keep an element of business rates growth after 2020 will offer some relief. In addition, new models of capital funding, such as tax increment financing (TIF), will become more common. While external factors such as devolution will drive major change over the next few years, there will still be a continued focus on internal change to meet near-term cost pressures. The challenge for leaders is balancing the focus on immediate internal change against the major external agendas emerging through devolution and new radical cross-government ways of working. The skill set to manage both change agendas in parallel is different and one that the sector will need to adapt to quickly.

4. Greater reliance on partnership working and volunteering

With responsibility for delivery of services across local government ever more dependent on the private and voluntary sectors, jointly delivered change is as high a priority as ever. Outsourcing remains high on the agenda for local government, despite recent high-profile negative cases in the media. Overall, partnering is on the rise. It is no surprise that the US model of local government has a strong reliance on local volunteers and community champions; this is a well-embedded culture. In recent years, this concept has started to take hold within the UK, where volunteers undertake appropriate roles on behalf of local authorities, for example running libraries or formally befriending the vulnerable in the community. As cost pressures increase, councils will have to make difficult decisions either to stop services or bring in different operating models, potentially using volunteers to deliver appropriate services. Building successful delivery teams through partnering is always challenging; over the next few years, it will become more complex than ever to bring together teams from different organizations partnering to deliver common outcomes. This is at the same time as devolution and more joined-up government is taking hold. Are leaders of change across the public sector ready for such complex and inclusive change all in a similar timeframe?

5. Commercialization of assets

Every local authority has an asset base with significant commercial potential for income generation. Commercial potential is dependent on complex factors, such as location, size, economic density and nearness to major transport infrastructure. Government has made it clear that public sector organizations are expected to be self-sufficient where this is a realistic expectation and particularly where they operate in a competitive marketplace. Traditionally, public sector organizations have viewed their asset base as a resource and not necessarily as an important income stream to replace mainstream government funding. Change in income generation across local government has been slow, yet the opportunity remains significant; successfully delivering sustainable income can be complex and challenging. The challenges are lack of 'profit and loss' commercial experience, political acceptance and risk aversion to 'invest to earn'. Recognizing commercial opportunity is the easy step, delivering the success is the complex and challenging part. What does this mean for leaders of change? The imperative for income generation is no longer optional and the clock is ticking on windows of opportunity. Seizing the opportunity requires cultural change, commercially savvy governance and the ability to deliver commercial income projects at pace. This skill set has become an urgent priority as local authorities run out of options for cost reduction and difficult choices have to be made on delivery of services.

6. Making digital change sustainable: 'climbing the maturity curve'

Government is embracing digital as one of the silver bullets to drive efficiency, improve the customer experience and save cost. Digital change is being widely delivered across government; however, is it really taking hold on the ground? The initial focus has been on delivering digital technologies, showcasing quick wins and cross-watching what other peer organizations are doing across the sector and beyond.

Evidence suggests that some local authorities are struggling to embed 'sustainable' digital change at a front-line service level, despite best intentions. There are many great examples of technologies being deployed to drive specific solutions such as online customer accounts, mobile working and also high-volume web-form transactions. While this is sensible and admirable, is there too much focus on technology and not enough on designing and embedding the digital change at the front line? The issues are emotive and complex, requiring strong operational leadership within different digital ways of working. This is a maturity curve challenge and one that local government may be taking too long to travel vis-à-vis expectations.

The other key challenge facing the sector is how digital solutions will support cross-government working, planned as part of the national devolution agenda. Are digital solutions enabled to align with devolution and cross-government working, or is there risk of duplicate and redundant solutions as services and organizations join up? There is no easy answer to this; standardization and common architecture will surely go a long way to enabling a more joined-up digital government. The future challenge will be to avoid significant disinvestment in redundant technology.

Bringing it all together

Overall, the consequences are far-reaching as the landscape for government moves to new integrated ways of working and the breaking down of organization boundaries to achieve shared outcomes. These radical changes don't just impact local government or the wider public sector, they also impact private sector and third sector organizations that work with government. The challenge for leaders of change is to embrace cross-organizational delivery of change and the mixing of organizational cultures, and to work successfully within transitional governance structures. Not an easy ask of any sector or organization, particularly in the context of fundamentally new ways of working not seen before across government.

The critical question is: how ready are government organizations, their suppliers and partners for such fundamental change, when the past few years of cost reduction have seemed about as complex and intense as it could get? One thing is clear: those leaders who don't rise to the challenge will risk being overtaken and becoming irrelevant in the new world of government beyond 2020.

Opinion piece 6 22

The future and healthcare

ADI GASKELL

It's tempting to think of change in purely technological terms as news of these developments emerge on a daily basis. While this is undeniable, changes in healthcare are more significantly underpinned by the demographic changes in society.

The demographic boom of the post-war years has largely run its course, with falling fertility rates combining with greater life expectancy turning a demographic premium, whereby societies benefit from a large working-age population and a relatively small retired population, into a considerable burden for Western economies as the baby boomers move into retirement. Winter and Teitelbaum (2013) suggest that 60 per cent of the world's population are living in a country with fertility rates lower than the replacement rate, including the majority of Western countries. Indeed, Moody's (2014) revealed recently that by 2030 there will be 34 nations where over 20 per cent of the population will be 65 or older.

Health changes for an ageing population

Automation is one way that these challenges may be met, and recent experiments have tested the use of mobile service robots in elderly care environments. For instance, researchers from the University of Lincoln recently entered a collaboration with LACE Housing Association to provide care homes with mobile service robots to support residents. The aim is to help residents stay active and independent for longer. Within the trial the robots, which are known as ENRICHME (Enabling Robot and assisted living environment for Independent Care and Health Monitoring of the Elderly), will operate within a smart-home environment.

Mann *et al*'s (2015) research aimed to quantify the reaction to robot carers by patients. Participants in the study were given a robot carer in their home for a three-month trial period. Interestingly, while there were predictable benefits such as medication reminders for patients, the participants also appreciated the companionship provided by the robots. 'The results suggest the healthcare robots were feasible for use with a rural population and may have benefits for some patients in reducing the need for medical care, increasing quality of life, reminding patients to take medicine on time, and providing companionship', reported the authors.

Walden *et al* (2015) tested how elderly patients responded to robot support staff. The patients revealed that they usually found the robots extremely useful in a physical, informational and interactional sense; they were keen not just on the robots performing helpful tasks, but also providing entertainment and information. 'Even with concerns about control, we consistently heard that robots could be very useful to seniors', the authors say. 'As we age, our physical and interactional needs change. Robots in that human-command and robot-servient role have the potential to help seniors fill several of those needs.'

The findings from this experiment remind us that reality can often throw up unexpected outcomes, which underlines the importance of an experimental approach that tests the validity and practical use of ideas.

Smarter homes

Researchers are beginning to pull all of this together in a care home laden with smart technologies. A prime example is a model home created by researchers at the University of Texas, Arlington, who have built what they call the Smart Care Home (SCM). The SCM includes a range of technologies, including:

- sensors underneath tiles on the floor to allow researchers to measure and evaluate changes in walking gaits and weight that might suggest illness or injury;
- a special camera embedded in a bathroom mirror that will tell researchers about day-to-day heart rate, facial expression and skin colour: changes in expression and skin colour can reveal aspects of overall health status as well as about oxygen content of the blood;
- lift chair to help residents stand;
- smart appliances such as an LG microwave, range and refrigerator;
- connected exercise equipment, including a recumbent bike and interactive Kinect-based Tai Chi trainer;

- other systems that will detect whether medication is being properly managed or if the resident is not sleeping well or staying in bed too long.

Data from the home are fed into a mission-control-style laboratory where patients can be monitored, have their behavioural information interpreted and their remote capabilities evaluated.

Bringing the doctor to you

Central to this is the capability afforded by telehealth, which promises to bring medical support and diagnosis to patients, wherever their location, via existing telecommunication networks, such as the web and smartphones. A number of services have evolved in this space, including Babylon, Vida and even a virtual nurse called Molly, developed by Sense.ly. These services aim to take a preventative approach to medicine, allowing users to upload their data to the sites where AI engines monitor sleep patterns to dietary habits, medication routines to exercise levels. They also typically allow users to have a Skype-like consultation with a professional where the session is recorded so that it can be viewed back at a later time, either by the patients themselves or by their family.

Several studies have highlighted the benefits of such telehealth platforms, particularly for elderly patients. Yang *et al* (2015) revealed the considerable cost savings possible for healthcare providers by keeping patients out of emergency rooms. Their research shows that savings are particularly pronounced in rural areas that use telemedicine to connect up emergency departments with doctors at much larger hospitals. It suggests that even once the costs of installation and maintenance are considered, the savings work out at around $4,662 per use on average.

A similar study was conducted in the National Health Service at Airedale NHS trust. They installed a telehealth system in a care home for the elderly, thus affording patients 24/7 care. When the system was tested, it resulted in a 35 per cent reduction in emergency admissions and a 53 per cent drop in A&E attendance.

Mobile health

The rise of telehealth is a part of a much bigger trend for the provision of health support while we're on the move. Mobile health, or mhealth, is a market that began with a number of fitness applications but has since mushroomed into something much bigger. Devices such as LifeTip can be attached to clothing to provide a live ECG monitor. If the device detects an irregular rhythm, it activates your smartphone and calls for help. The SNIFFPHONE project aims to use your mobile phone to analyse your breath for signs of disease. This Israeli-led project works by using an array of micro- and nano-sensors that analyse the breath as it is exhaled and then communicate that information back to the smartphone for interpretation.

A project from Massachusetts General Hospital (Im *et al*, 2015) is using your smartphone to hunt for cancer by using holographic technology to collect microscopic images for analysis of cells and tissues for cancer. The technology provides a low-cost way of dealing with the rapidly growing volume of genomic and biologic cancer data.

Other current examples of mobile healthcare innovations are the Cupris device for conducting ear examinations via your phone, or Peek Vision for detecting the onset of blindness or other sight problems. These kinds of device are particularly helpful for elderly people, to provide them with a greater degree of independence while also allowing their support network access to the data produced by the devices.

Pulling this all together

Of course, as fantastic as many of these technologies seem, the challenge of integrating them into our modern healthcare systems is a significant one. Lehoux *et al* (2015) explored why valuable technologies fail to be adopted and found that commercial factors can often overwhelm health factors.

Aside from the commercial factors affecting decision making, the volume of innovations can make it incredibly difficult for large health organizations to adapt quickly enough to ensure that new technologies and approaches are integrated successfully into business as usual.

Driving change in the UK's National Health Service

The UK's National Health Service (NHS) has tried several approaches to overcome this issue. For instance, the Test Beds initiative was developed out of the Five Year Forward View (NHS, 2014). This was designed to provide a real-world setting to test out various promising technologies and approaches. The first seven test-bed sites were announced in early 2016 and looked at a number of areas, particularly in the management of long-term care in areas such as diabetes and ageing. As with some of the smart-home initiatives mentioned above, there are also attempts to better enable patients to receive care while remaining at home.

The seven sites work with a mixture of large and small companies, as well as universities, to bring cutting-edge thinking into the NHS and allow things to be tested in a live environment. The long-term aim is that this will provide a means not only to bring innovation into the system, but also to better support its dissemination throughout the NHS.

There have also been attempts to include many of the technologies mentioned above in smarter and healthier housing developments. The NHS's Healthy New Towns initiative works with 10 housing developments from across the UK to try to rethink how we live our lives. The project marks a concerted effort to take a bigger role in the lives of the population in general rather than waiting for sickness to emerge before taking an interest. The developments range from small <1,000 home developments up to larger 10,000+ projects. The aim is to ensure that healthy living is factored into home building from the very start.

Central to both of these projects is the willingness to look for innovations in a wide range of environments. This approach will see organizations working with both big and small companies, universities and the non-profit sector.

It's an approach that drug companies such as GlaxoSmithKline (GSK) has adopted with its OpenLabs concept, allowing GSK researchers to collaborate with researchers from a range of organizations in the hope of breakthrough innovations. This approach is also behind the cutting-edge Stevenage Bioscience Catalyst open innovation park, of which GSK is an anchor tenant.

Whether public or private, healthcare organizations are realizing that to survive in the modern world, they need to be open to external ideas and partnerships, and adaptable enough to test and integrate those ideas into their way of working. They are attempting to build what Stephan Haeckel (1993) famously referred to as a 'sense and respond' organization. He contrasted organizations as either 'make and sell', whereby certainty is assumed in terms of both customer expectation and market conditions, or 'sense and respond', where uncertainty is the dominant trait.

Conclusion

While the social and demographic drivers described above are naturally unfolding at a slower pace, the technological and organizational responses to them are changing on an almost daily basis. It will be increasingly important, therefore, not only that organizations in health and social care are responsive and adaptable enough to cope with this level and pace of upheaval, but that the supply chains to these types of organization are also.

References

Anguera, JA *et al* (2013) Video game training enhances cognitive control in older adults. *Nature*, 5 September

Haeckel, S (1993) [Accessed 29 March 2016] Managing by wire. *Harvard Business Review* [Online] http://hbr.org/product/managing-by-wire/an/93503-PDF-ENG

Im, H *et al* (2015) Digital diffraction analysis enables low-cost molecular diagnostics on a smartphone. *Proceedings of the National Academy of Sciences of the United States of America*, **112** (18), pp 5613–18

Lehoux, P *et al* (2015) How venture capitalists decide which new medical technologies come to exist. *Science and Public Policy*, **43** (3), pp. 375–85. First published online 27 August, doi: 10.1093/scipol/scv051

Mann, JA *et al* (2015) People respond better to robots than computer tablets delivering healthcare instructions. *Computers in Human Behavior*, **43** (February), pp 112–17

Moody's (2014) Aging will reduce economic growth worldwide in the next two decades, Global Credit Research, 6 August

NHS (2014) [Accessed 29 March 2016] *Five Year Forward Review* [Online] www.england.nhs.uk/ourwork/futurenhs/

Walden, J *et al* (2015) Mental models of robots among senior citizens: An interview study of interaction expectations and design implications. *Interaction Studies*, **16** (1), pp 68–88

Winter, J and Teitelbaum, M (2013) *Population, Fear, and Uncertainty: The global spread of fertility decline*, Yale University Press, New Haven, CT

Yang, NH *et al* (2015) [accessed 29 March 2016] Economic evaluation of pediatric telemedicine consultations to rural emergency departments' medical decision making [online]mdm.sagepub.com/content/early/2015/05/07/02729 89X15584916.abstract

INDEX